Above: Malcolm Norris and John Page-Phillips examining a brass together; opposite: Roger Greenwood in a Norfolk church. This book is dedicated to their memory.

MONUMENTAL BRASSES

AS ART AND HISTORY

EDITED BY FR JEROME BERTRAM

FOREWORD BY NIGEL SAUL

ALAN SUTTON PUBLISHING LIMITED

MONUMENTAL BRASS SOCIETY

First published in the United Kingdom in 1996
Alan Sutton Publishing Limited
Phoenix Mill · Far Thrupp · Stroud · Gloucestershire
in association with
The Monumental Brass Society

British Library Cataloguing in Publication Data

A catalogue record for this book is available from the British Library.

ISBN 0-7509-1051-8

Typeset in 11/13 Perpetua.
Typesetting and origination by
Alan Sutton Publishing Limited.
Printed in Great Britain by
Hartnolls, Bodmin, Cornwall.

Contents

List of Illustrations

95 Thomasina Tendryng, d. 1485, with seven children; Yoxford, Suffolk, M.S. IV. London style D, except children in ordinary dress, Norwich style 3. *Rubbing, Jerome Bertram.*

96 Civilian and two wives, made *c.* 1500, Newnham, Hertfordshire, M.S. I; London style D and G. *Rubbing, John Page-Phillips.*

97 Abbot William Albon, d. 1476; St Alban's Abbey, Hertfordshire, M.S. II. London F. *M.B.S. Portfolio.*

98 Sir Thomas Burton, d. 1381, and wife Margery, made *c.* 1420; Little Casterton, Rutland, M.S. I. London B. *M.B.S. Portfolio.*

99 Robert Whyte, esq., d. 1512, figure made (?) *c.* 1490; South Warnborough, Hampshire M.S. I. London D. *M.B.S. Portfolio.*

100 Palimpsest 'waster', *c.* 1440, Offard Darcy, Huntingdonshire, M.S. I. London B. *Rubbing, John Page-Phillips.*

101 Palimpsest 'waster', *c.* 1860, Thorncombe, Dorset, M.S. I. Waller Bros. *Rubbing, John Page-Phillips.*

102 Dame Alice, d. 1538, second wife of Sir Robert Clere, Great Ormesby, Norfolk M.S. I. Norwich adaptation of London work. *Rubbing, John Page-Phillips.*

103 Two groups of children, 1566, Westerham, Kent, M.S. VIII, and palimpsest reverses. *M.B.S. Transactions.*

104 Miracle of St Edmund, palimpsest reverse of Frenze, Norfolk, M.S. VII. *Rubbing, John Page-Phillips.*

105 Palimpsest weight, obverse and reverse, *c.* 1540. British Museum Ref.1988.10–5,1. *Photograph, British Museum.*

106 A mason's angle, cut from an inscription of *c.* 1580 from Brightwell Prior, Oxfordshire. Now in Society of Antiquaries. *Rubbing, John Page-Phillips.*

107 Indent of lady of *c.* 1590, Cople, Beds., M.S. X, once completely hiding the indent of an earlier sixteenth-century lady. *Rubbing, John Page-Phillips.*

108 Palimpsest reverse from Ashby St Ledgers, Northants., M.S. VI; the lower half of a Knight of St John, *c.* 1430. *Rubbing, John Page-Phillips.*

109 Fragments of Flemish brass to a civilian, fifteenth century, on backs of brasses at Goodnestone-next-Wingham, Kent, M.S. IV, 1558; Barrow, Suffolk, M.S. I, 1569; Boreham, Essex, M.S. I, 1573. *Rubbings, John Page-Phillips.*

110 Reconstruction of brass of Tristan van Hallewin, d. 1474, and wife Cornelie, d. 1489, Oudenburgh, Flanders, on reverse of brasses at Whichford, Warwickshire, M.S. I, 1582; Walkern, Hertfordshire, M.S. III, 1583; Marsworth, Buckinghamshire, M.S. II, 1583; Lee St Margaret, Kent, M.S. III, 1582. *Rubbings, John Page-Phillips.*

111 William Wryghsley, York Herald, 1509, probably from St Giles,

List of Contributors

The late John Page-Phillips MA, FSA, was President of the Monumental Brass Society from 1985 to 1992: he was a distinguished scholar who worked particularly on 'palimpsest' brasses, and the sixteenth-century English schools of engraving which most often conceal palimpsests. The Flemish connections of many of these led him to an interest in Flemish brasses, and his last achievement was to organise the Society's successful conference in Bruges in September 1992.

The late Dr Malcolm Norris MA, PhD, FSA, Head of Public Policy at Birmingham University, succeeded John Page-Phillips as President only a few hours before the latter's death in autumn 1992. He was the first to explore the brasses behind the then Iron Curtain in the 1950s, and in his extensive writings on brasses has always taken a European perspective. He worked particularly on the stylistic analysis which by revealing the connections between brasses has shed much light on their origins. At the time of his unexpected early death he was working on a major breakthrough in our understanding of the very earliest English brasses and incised slabs.

Claude Blair MA, FSA, OBE, one of the Society's Vice-Presidents, an international authority on armour, was for many years Keeper of Metalwork at the Victoria and Albert Museum. He has since been involved in several important public campaigns in the cause of scholarship, and is a member both of the Redundant Churches Fund and the Council for the Care of Churches.

The late J. Roger Greenwood BA, FSA, a probation officer and another Vice-President, worked especially in East Anglia, identifying local schools of engraving, and was diligent in compiling and publishing the revised lists of brasses. His documentary researches in Norfolk are most thorough and have unearthed much new information.

Martin Stuchfield, a printer, is the Society's Hon. Secretary and has embarked with others in a long-term project of publishing the complete brasses of England, county by county, illustrated with many of his expert rubbings.

Fr Jerome Bertram MA, FSA, a priest of the Oratory, is the Society's Editor: he has researched and written on a wide range of topics connected with brasses, particularly on the evidence for lost brasses.

Jon Bayliss BA worked closely with Roger Greenwood on East Anglian material, has greatly advanced knowledge on the Coventry workshop, and has also carried out research on the seventeenth-century brasses and their schools of engraving.

Paul Cockerham MA, Vet MB, MRCVS, a country vet, has written erudite articles on many brasses, tracing the family histories involved, particularly if they are connected with the Throckmorton family. He is the Society's Treasurer.

John Goodall MA, FSA, FRNS, a distinguished and widely-read antiquary, has contributed many studies to societies and journals, and given invaluable advice and information to other writers, heraldry being perhaps his greatest field of knowledge.

Peter Heseltine, a playground safety adviser, has collected copious information on brasses which has been published in several books dealing with the monuments of particular counties or churches.

Cecil Humphery-Smith FSA, is a leading genaealogist and active in the increasingly important field of family history.

Revd David Meara MA, STh, a Buckinghamshire rector, has made a special study of the brasses of the last two centuries which were formerly ignored: his latest work is on the elder Pugin.

Nicholas Rogers MA, MLitt, a Cambridge archivist, has worked in the area of art-history, particularly on illuminated manuscripts, and has published widely on aspects of mediaeval culture.

Kay Staniland AMA, CCHD, of the Museum of London, is well known as an authority on historical costume and its development.

Foreword

Brasses have long attracted attention by their beauty and historical interest. Since at least the seventeenth century people have been doing rubbings or impressions of them. A painting of a church interior by the Dutch master Louys Elsevier (1617–75) shows a little group on their hands and knees rubbing a brass or slab. In England, the scholarly study of brasses began in the eighteenth and nineteenth centuries in the wake of the Gothic Revival. The earliest surviving rubbing appears to have been made in about 1693 by one Henry Prescott at Macclesfield (Cheshire). By roughly the 1780s antiquaries were going around doing the rubbings that form the basis of our great national collections today. Doubtless the fact that brasses can be 'rubbed' will long assure them a vigorous popular following.

Different generations have brought different approaches to the study of brasses. In the late nineteenth and early twentieth centuries the study of the subject was largely costume-driven; in other words, brasses were classified and analysed according to the style of dress of the commemorated. In the widely used works by Macklin, Suffling and Druitt there were chapters on armour, civilian attire, academic and ecclesiastical dress and so on. In similar fashion, the chronological development of brasses was largely considered in terms of the transition from one style of dress or armour to another.

A great deal has changed since then. Nowadays, brasses are looked at from a variety of perspectives. A notable development in recent decades has been the classification of brasses by 'style' – in other words, by workshop origin. Identification of the main series (London series 'A', 'B', Suffolk 1 and 2, and so on) has opened perspectives on the organisation of the trade and has facilitated analysis of the growth of the market in different parts of Britain. A parallel development has been the investigation of the sources of design. To this, the art historians have made a major contribution. By looking at brasses and allied arts alongside each other, they have shown the extent to which brass engravers drew on patterns used by workers in other mediums; and this insight in turn has encouraged speculation about the engravers' dependence on other trades. A third line of enquiry has centred on looking at brasses as a source for the study of history. Growing interest has been shown in what heraldry, livery badges and inscriptions can tell about the self-image of the commemorated, while there is a new appreciation of the value of devotional imagery for the study of piety.

Members of the Monumental Brass Society have played a leading role in these advances in the study of brasses. It is highly appropriate, then, that the present volume should be the fruit of a co-operative endeavour by the Society. In the past, synoptic studies of brasses have mostly resulted from individual initiative: John Page-Phillips' edition of Macklin's *Monumental Brasses*, for example, was written by one past president of the Society and revised by another. This book is different. It brings together a pool of talents. The result is not only an attractive and richly illustrated study; it is also a particularly well informed one. *Monumental Brasses as Art and History* should be the standard work in its field for some time to come. I welcome its appearance warmly.

Nigel Saul
President, Monumental Brass Society

Editor's Note

This book has been long in preparation, so long that not all of those who have worked on it are still with us. My thanks are due not only to those who have actually written passages or contributed illustrations, but to many other members of the Society and its Council who have been involved in this book over the years. In particular, in the last stages, I am grateful to Nigel Saul and Sally Badham for encouraging help in revising the text and commending it for publication.

For illustrations I must thank all those whose names appear in the List of Illustrations for contributing rubbings or photographs. In particular many of the illustrations came from Malcolm Norris' great collection of photographs. Specific copyright holders are the National Museum of Ancient Art in Lisbon for fig. 17; Gloucester City Library for fig. 19; the Royal Commission on Ancient and Historical Monuments, Scotland for fig. 61; the Hardman Archives, Birmingham, for fig. 64; the Society of Antiquaries of London for figs 68–70, 73, 74, 106, 116 and 131; the British Museum for figs. 47, 105 and 115; the Royal Commission on Historical Monuments, England, for fig. 121; the Bodleian Library, Oxford, for fig. 129. If any copyrights have been inadvertantly infringed, I offer my apologies.

It should be noted that county boundaries are, at the time of writing, once again under revision. It is therefore our policy always to refer to traditional county boundaries as they were before 1974, and as used in the *Buildings of England* series.

Notes appear at the end of the book: where a note contains additional information, this is indicated with an asterisk* in the text; all other notes are simply references.

JB

CHAPTER 1

Introduction

It is with feelings of trepidation that I attempt to introduce this book, given that three of the major authors have died tragically before their time. In a few years most of the enthusiastic generation of post-war brass scholars have been lost, and their work was by no means complete. John Page-Phillips, Roger Greenwood and Malcolm Norris were the leading lights in a revolution in the study of monumental brasses, bringing the subject new insights and new methods which transformed our whole approach, giving us new ways of understanding these monuments, while opening up vistas which will provide material for future generations to study.

The book was primarily the idea of John Page-Phillips, warmly supported by Malcolm Norris, who was to succeed him as President of the Monumental Brass Society. The idea was to call on as wide as possible a range of the Society's members, each to contribute on different aspects of brasses, to show how the study has developed since 1945, adopting a very different approach from the traditional 'manual of monumental brasses' which as a framework may be said to have begun with Herbert Haines' youthful work under that title in 1849, and ended with Page-Phillips' and Norris' own earlier works in the 1960s. The list of authors and acknowledgments shows how many responded to the project, although there were others who were unable to contribute owing to pressure of work. It is therefore doubly sad that the book was in the event delayed following the deaths of John Page-Phillips and Roger Greenwood – in the time that has elapsed since the book was first compiled others might have been able to add their own expertise.

It was Malcolm Norris who was determined that the book should not be lost, and took the initiative in securing the co-operation of the present publishers. It was hoped he would write this introductory chapter, as well as providing revised versions of his own sections of the book. His sudden death left us determined to ensure the production of the work, even if it means that I have to write this chapter for him, so that it may serve in some little way as a memorial to those three scholars to whose memory it must now be dedicated.

Quorum animabus propicietur Deus.

Recent Work on Monumental Brasses

From the earliest days of English antiquarian studies, a special interest has been taken in monumental brasses often to the exclusion of other forms of church monument, and our libraries contain a large number of books on the subject, as well as comprehensive collections of brass rubbings. On the other hand, at least in this century, serious archaeologists and antiquaries have tended rather to ignore, or even despise, the study of brasses. I suspect this may be partly because brasses, like all things medieval, were for a time considered rather suspect – real archaeology ends with Anglo-Saxon grave goods. Brasses imply brass rubbing, the hobby of late Victorian young ladies and earnest cycling schoolboys in the 1960s. Brass rubbing implies a certain frivolity, an interest in pretty things from the past without scholarly credentials, without the academic respectability of robber trenches.

It is perhaps time to make the point that the study of brasses has moved on during this century, and the last fifty years in particular have seen several remarkable developments. Of these the most prominent has been the recent research in the field of stylistic analysis of medieval brasses, which has transformed our whole understanding of these monuments. The approach adopted, and the resulting publications, are described in detail in Dr Norris' chapter. The topic has fascinated several members of the Monumental Brass Society, although it must be admitted that many other members have been rather bored with the apparently endless refinements of styles and series. In fact for many years the establishment, if I may so call it, seems to have done its best to be unaware of the whole business. The dominant tendency, inherited from the nineteenth century, was to collect brasses not so much for their archaeological or art-historical interest, but as examples of costume and armour, for genealogy and family history. They do indeed have great value for such studies, and chapters in this volume by Miss Staniland and Messrs Blair, Humphery-Smith and Goodall show us that there is still much to learn. Yet Claude Blair's chapter sounds a warning that the representations of armour are not as accurate as one might expect, and even the heraldry and genealogy are not above suspicion in some places. In fact, not to put too fine a point on it, occasionally the information on brasses can be shown to be deliberately fraudulent, designed to back up dubious pedigrees, and spurious claims to gentility or property – the Rugeley brass (fig. 4) is a case in point.

Stylistic Analysis

For many years it was often assumed that brasses were a vernacular craft, and that the brasses of a particular county could be expected to show regional characteristics which distinguished them from those of neighbouring counties. This may be partly because so much material was published in county archaeological journals, which may be appropriate for domestic architecture and agricultural implements, or even Anglo-Saxon grave goods, but can be positively misleading when it comes to artefacts of a national distribution. We can tell a Kentish sixth-century brooch from an Oxfordshire one, and the occasional intruder is a welcome indicator of trade-routes, but brasses on the whole were made in national centres, and distributed over a wide area. Too often studies have concentrated on listing and illustrating the brasses of a particular county as if they formed a discrete and identifiable group, the brasses of Oxfordshire being totally unlike those of Berkshire, for instance. The popular image dies hard, of the village brass-engraver sitting in his shop under the spreading chestnut tree, ever willing to pop round to the manor house to make a quick sketch of the rapidly firming features of the dear departed to be transferred to the metal in a local traditional style.

Speaking for myself, it was actually while I was an earnest cycling schoolboy collecting brass rubbings in the 1960s that I first noticed the inadequacy of this assumption. I had rubbed the well-known brasses of 1441 at West Grinstead (fig. 1), two worthy Sussex figures, with features remarkably similar to those of their ancestor in the same church, and a good Sussex monk in the next village. A few weeks later I received rare permission to rub the academic brasses at Merton College, including Master John Kyllingworth, 1445 (fig. 2). Being a sagacious youth, it did not take me long to realise that these two brasses, as well as others that I had found in Surrey, Hertfordshire and Kent had too many characteristics in common for coincidence. What particularly struck me was the peculiar square chins of them all. It was several years before I discovered that the research had in fact already been done: the seminal work by J.P.C. Kent had been published in 1949.[1] My little group of square-chinned effigies was part of the major 'Series B', found all over England and clearly stemming from London.

Dr Kent's analysis, which was done almost entirely from rubbings, is still largely accepted as valid, and inspired a number of other members of the Society to expand and elaborate on his work, as Dr Norris explains. Brasses can be classified into distinct 'series' or groups, plausibly stemming from distinct workshops or schools. The pattern emerges that for most of the later Middle Ages there were two major traditions operating in London, which produced large numbers of

1 Sir Hugh and Joyce Hailsham, 1441, West Grinstead, Sussex: a typical large military brass of style 'B' (detail).

2 John Kyllingworth, M.A., 1445, Merton College, Oxford: a typical small academic brass of style 'B'.

brasses, often imitating each others' designs, while two short-lived minor workshops operated in competition. Further research began to reveal the names of some of the masons concerned, whose dates conveniently explain the ending of one series and the beginning of another within one or other of the two main traditions.

The task of continuing the analysis into the sixteenth century was taken up by our former President, John Page-Phillips. It appeared that a new situation had arisen. No longer were there discrete series of brasses which could be plausibly assigned to separate and rival workshops, but the mid-sixteenth-century engravers often worked together, sharing patterns and presumably co-operating in the actual production of brasses. Continuing the story into the seventeenth century we find once again distinct workshop traditions, this time with more documentary evidence, particularly for the consistent series of brasses coming from the workshop of Edward Marshall in Fetter Lane. Marshall was not only commissioned to make monuments for the recently departed, but was quite prepared to repair earlier brasses or even fabricate them completely. The fascinating series of Barttelot family brasses at Stopham were all repaired and improved in the Marshall workshop, adding heraldry and groups of children to prove beyond all shadow of doubt the descent which had been registered by the heralds (fig. 3). In the same way a totally spurious brass was engraved for Sir Richard Weston, the Earl of Portland, in about 1630, to back up his claim to respectable antiquity by presenting one John Weston who died at Rugeley in 1566, in fact no relation, as a gentleman with a coat of arms (fig. 4). The fraud was accompanied by a splendid but quite unscrupulous manuscript pedigree certified by the then Garter King of Arms.[2]

3 John and Joan Bartelot, at Stopham, Sussex; a brass 'improved' by later generations. A London brass of the 'sub-B' series, made in about 1470, and showing the same costume excesses as on fig. 22, was restored and added to in about 1630 by the Marshall workshop which repaired most of the Stopham brasses.

While the majority of brasses have been shown to be of London manufacture, there were also a number of provincial centres of manufacture, and it has been the work of our members Sally Badham, and the late Malcolm Norris and Roger Greenwood to analyse them in the same way. We are still a far cry from the village whitesmith: these were efficient and prolific workshops, though no centre operated continuously for as long a period as the London workshops. Roger Greenwood's chapter on wills shows the extent of documentary evidence that is available, and the detailed analysis that can be extracted from it about locally made brasses.

Nearly all surviving brasses later than the time of the Black Death having been classified, it was natural to turn our attention to the earlier ones. Here a different problem arose: very few brasses actually survive from that period, and even fewer could be accurately dated. The early brasses have always attracted notice, for they can be spectacular and are strikingly designed, but even such a well-known example as that in Higham Ferrers (fig. 6), now dated at 1337, was uncertainly dated, and

4 John Weston, d. 1566, at Rugeley, Staffs. This brass was made in about 1630, probably by the Marshall workshop, to support a spurious genealogy.

it was only in the last few years that someone spotted the maker's stamp in the lower right corner of the supercanopy. Little can be made of the surviving examples without incorporating information about lost brasses. Of the pre-Black Death brasses only a tiny fraction survive, but the indents of lost ones are very revealing.

An indent is basically what archaeologists call a 'robber trench'. The brass plates were set flush into the stone slab, and the outlines of missing plates are perfectly preserved as long as the surface of the stone remains. (We shall return to the subject of indents in more detail in a later chapter.) It is a fortunate characteristic of these early brasses that every letter of the inscription was separately inlaid, and often remains legible in the indent. By comparison of drawings and tracings of indents, as well as by original documentary research, John Blair, Paul Binski, Malcolm Norris and Nicholas Rogers were able to cooperate on a study[3] which not only classified the early brasses into series but even gave us the name of one of the principal pioneers, Adam of Corfe, who can be credited with some of the best-known early brasses, such as that of Margaret de Camoys which is typical of the great figures from the first quarter of the fourteenth century (fig. 5).

Documentary research by a number of scholars has enabled us to re-date the majority of the early brasses, usually putting them a generation later than they were formerly believed to be. There was a moment

5 Marguerite de Camoys, of Trotton, Sussex. A detail of one of the finest early brasses, made between 1310 and 1320. Lost parts are easily reconstructed from the indents in the stone.

when it seemed that virtually no brasses were being made before the turn of the fourteenth century, and Lady Camoys put in a bid to be the earliest surviving English brass at 1310–19. This, however, would leave the brass inscription around the Westminster Abbey pavement, securely dated at 1268, dangerously isolated, and also gave the surprising impression that the very earliest London-made brasses were full-grown and competently executed figures. Recent work by Malcolm Norris and Sally Badham has succeeded in putting brasses back into the thirteenth century, and showing that, as we might have expected, the earliest brasses were comparatively simple metal inlays in stone compositions. Of surviving brasses, our attention has been drawn to an obscure little fragment surviving at Ashford in Kent which now seems to bid fair to be the earliest surviving English brass (fig. 7). Still tantalisingly unidentified, the priest concerned was probably the predecessor of an incumbent who came to Ashford in 1282. It is obviously very similar in design to the incised slab of Richard de Gratton at Pyrton, Oxfordshire (who is believed to have died between 1280 and 1289), which had an inscription in brass letters.

This last reminds us that brasses and incised slabs were often produced by the same workshops for the same clients for the same purposes, and that treating them in isolation is often misleading. Badham and Norris were compiling information on slabs in Purbeck marble from the thirteenth and early fourteenth centuries, which should be published before too long. They have shown that the series of early brasses were also represented in stone, and that the same workshops produced monuments in both media at the same period and for the same sort of clients. This is also true of the late sixteenth and seventeenth centuries – it is less true in England of the intervening period, when the majority of incised slabs were executed in Midlands alabaster by workshops which had little interest in brasses.

6 A detail from the huge brass of Lawrence de St Maur, 1337, at Higham Ferrers, Northants. This little figure represents an unknown abbot saint from the array of saints in the canopy shafts.

The European Dimension

By now we can classify virtually all the brasses of English manufacture, and the phase of stylistic analysis is all but over. There are certainly still gaps, perhaps the most significant being the local workshops of the post-Reformation period, which produced enormous numbers of very boring inscription brasses, but for something more exciting we must turn to the continent. Within the last few years much of Europe has suddenly become much more accessible. Although the remaining chapters in this book deal mainly with English brasses, we should not forget that brasses originated overseas, and that despite fearful destruction in wars and revolutions a very large number of interesting brasses and incised slabs survive in every country of Latin Christendom.

7 Now believed to be the earliest surviving English brass, an unknown priest of about 1282, at Ashford, Kent.

Attention has traditionally been focused on the great fourteenth-century Flemish school of engraving, which was thoroughly investigated by our former president Dr Keith Cameron. Stemming from workshops in and around Tournai, these spectacular brasses were exported for prestigious clients all around the European seaboard. Well-known examples in England survive at Kings Lynn, St Albans, Newark, Topcliffe (fig. 8) and Newcastle, but the evidence of the Tournai slabs with indents for lost brasses of this school shows that there were very many more, particularly in Scotland (fig. 61).

English antiquaries explored the Low Countries thoroughly in the last century, but we may now raise our gaze to look further east, where there are enormous numbers of unknown brasses and incised slabs. The pioneer in this field, as in so many others, was Malcolm Norris, who penetrated the Iron Curtain in the 1950s and was the first to discover and publish the spectacular brasses of the fourteenth-century Silesian school. In the derelict Abbey of Lubiąż near Wrocław are the remains of four large brasses of this style, probably made in about 1305 for members of the ruling Przemyslid dynasty. When Norris discovered them, only fragments of the brass inlays remained in the slabs, which he found buried under piles of timber: the remaining plates were distributed among three museums in Wrocław. I rubbed them in 1970, by which time the loose parts were at least collected into the same museum, where I found also the fine tomb and effigy of Duke Henry IV of Silesia, 1321. Clearly there is a connection between brass and tomb, the same pose, with the sword-belt wrapped fetchingly around the scabbard, the same bold Lombardic lettering. The style is curiously reminiscent of the French royal tombs in St Denis, which raises interesting questions about the movement of craftsmen and pattern books in the thirteenth century.

In the city and neighbourhood of Wrocław are the remains of several more brasses in the early Silesian style, a couple of bishops in Sw. Krzyzy, a pair of nuns in Sw. Klara. The characteristic canopies, now entirely lost, were of cut and pierced plate, with the stone showing through a filigree of tracery; the lettering varying from simple bold forms to elaborate shapes adorned with foliage. Figures are boldly drawn, staring full-face at the beholder, and less conventional than the English or Flemish school in the way they hold their hands. The close similarity to carved and relief effigies is maintained, and some of the later slabs combine engraved and cast metal with carved stone in composite memorials that take us far beyond the possibilities of brass rubbing. Nor is this style confined to Silesia: a late thirteenth-century incised slab in the National Museum in Prague seems to be of the same school. We must remember that however tempted we may be to refer to Wrocław as Breslau, at the time these monuments were made it was called Vratislava and was part of the Kingdom of Bohemia. It is surely in

8 A small but typical product of the great fourteenth-century Flemish school at Topcliffe, Yorks., 1391. The figures stand beneath a very elaborate canopy with attendant angels, and their souls being taken up into heaven. At the corners are the four evangelists.

the towns and villages of Bohemia that we must search for more examples. I remember in 1974 seeing four fragments of an indent of lettering of the same Silesio-Bohemian style on the outside of the then closed cathedral of Bratislava in Slovakia. There is clearly a great deal to be done in this region, now at last freely accessible to the western antiquary.

Another region only recently opened up is the Baltic coast of Germany where I was recently able to make an exploratory expedition. Malcolm Norris had already suggested the existence of a Baltic school of brasses, probably based at Lübeck, but I suspect he was unaware of quite how widespread these brasses were. The finest and earliest in the series is the well-known memorial at Väster Åker near Uppsala, the only surviving brass of any consequence in the whole of Sweden. On the whole, Lutheran churches preserve their medieval works of art far better than either Catholic or Calvinist, but unfortunately for us the Thirty Years War saw the almost complete stripping of the metal from memorials all round the Baltic. As a result we have few complete brasses, but many indents, and a quite phenomenal number of incised slabs. Clearly these slabs derive from the same workshop traditions as brasses, and the same designs were used: indeed, Malcolm Norris has suggested that the relative clumsiness of line on most Baltic brasses may be due to the engravers being trained in incised slab work, and unaccustomed to the more delicate medium.

As an example, the Hanseatic port of Stralsund contains major architectural and historic monuments, and should certainly be on the antiquary's itinerary. The huge parish church of St Nicholas, still in course of restoration, is full of works of art in many media, though here as throughout the Swedish dominions the Thirty Years War has taken its toll. One well-known Flemish brass remains in remarkably good condition, but the indents tell of a great many more. There are actually thirteen indents of brasses in the church, five of the Flemish school, and the remainder of local Baltic manufacture. In other parts of Mecklenburg and Pomerania are similar slabs in very large numbers, all along the coast from Lübeck to Gdańsk and doubtless further. There are certainly many incised slabs in the Baltic styles in Elbląg and Frombork and around the corner on the coast of Latvia. During my brief trip I found 165 effigial incised slabs and 99 indents, hardly any of which had been recorded here before. With proper recording the whole tradition of Baltic engraving will lie before us.

Technical Aspects

In the church at Stralsund, the indents of Baltic origin were most easily distinguished from the Flemish by the type of stone used, which brings us to another area of modern research which cannot possibly be studied from brass rubbings, namely the petrology of the slabs in which brasses are laid. All the evidence is that the majority of medieval brasses were set into their stones in the workshop and these heavy stones were transported, often across vast distances, to their destinations. We find Tournai marble slabs, with or without their brasses, in Sussex and Fife, far up the Vistula into Poland and on the island of Madeira. Of the Stralsund indents five are in black Tournai limestone, in which the surviving Flemish brass is also set. The remainder are in a pale limestone from Gottland, which is the common material behind nearly all the Baltic brasses. The same limestone is used, and frequently re-used, for the incised slabs of the same tradition. There is no workable stone in north Germany, and after a courageous but ludicrous attempt on Rügen Island to incise granite, the Baltic engravers imported all their slabs from Gottland.

Similarly in England, London-made brasses were nearly always set into slabs of Purbeck marble in the workshop, and transported with their slabs even into districts which had perfectly good workable stone of their own. Purbeck marble, from Dorset, was widely used as a decorative stone. In the thirteenth and fourteenth centuries blocks thick enough to carve effigies were still available, but as the quarries were exploited with the increasing demand for monumental brasses only thin slabs were available, and the supply virtually ceased in the mid-sixteenth century. As a substitute, the similar but more friable Wealden marbles were often used for post-Reformation brasses, even in regions far from their native Sussex or Kent.

The true Purbeck marble is found in two varieties, with or without the white paraboloid streaks of 'Unio' shells – these shells are visible for instance in fig. 128. The two types of stone may come from the same quarry, but there is a certain correlation between the London engraving series and the choice of plain or streaky Purbeck, which suggests that the workshops instructed their buyers to look out for the appropriate slabs. In other words even if a brass is totally lost, the type of stone may serve to indicate not only the place of origin but even from which workshop it came. Regional workshops in areas where good stone was available used the local material. Some West-Country brasses were laid in blue lias, the Yorkshire and north-western workshops used a variety of stones, such as Ashford Black and 'Bird's Eye' marble from Derbyshire, or the pretty Frosterly marble from County Durham. Some Lincolnshire and Norfolk brasses used Ancaster stone, while in Suffolk a compacted sandstone is found.

In a few cases we do find fourteenth- or fifteenth-century London brasses set in local stones, which implies that they could sometimes take the obviously more sensible expedient of sending out the brass plates loose from London to be fixed by a local mason (see chapter 10 for an example). After the mid-sixteenth century this seems to have become a more common practice. Prestigious brasses were still professionally fixed in quality stones like the Ashford Black limestone used by the Marshall workshop, but many smaller brasses are roughly fixed into local stones, or even into the available paving or wall masonry. Following the turmoil of the Dissolution of the Monasteries a large number of second-hand Purbeck marble slabs came on to the market, and these were frequently recycled for brasses in the 1540s and 1550s. John Page-Phillips' chapter on palimpsests tells of how the metal too was re-used, but it is not often realised how many of these palimpsest brasses are set in previously used Purbeck marble slabs, in which only the planed-down lead plugs which once held the rivets can still be seen.

It must of course be remembered that many brasses have been relaid over the years, and may not be in their original settings. Usually this will be obvious, but occasionally there can be real doubt over whether we have the original stone or not. The stone was in fact the most important item in the eyes of the person commemorated, as is shown in Roger Greenwood's chapter on wills, which so often request the purchase of a tombstone, and mention the brass embellishments as a secondary consideration. The will may ask for a large stone covering the whole grave, sometimes called a 'through-stone' in English wills, or if money is short they may ask for a small 'heartstone' just covering the heart. It is worth remarking that a brass derives much of its meaning from the slab and the church in which it is set, just as an archaeological artefact makes sense only in its excavation context. Detached brasses are like unprovenanced handaxes, of comparatively little value. It is unfortunate that the habit of pulling brasses out of their stones and displaying them out of context is still very much with us – one hears disturbing reports of architects still proposing to rip up brasses like this and clear them out of the way of a new floor.

Another field for research, which has really only just begun, is the technical analysis of the metal used in these brasses. Dr Cameron pioneered the investigation, publishing a major article on the subject, but only had a limited number of samples to work from. Since then one of our principal conservators, William Lack, has been accumulating a very large bank of information on the composition of every metal plate that passes through his workshop, information which only awaits a researcher to co-ordinate. Medieval copper alloys are still an area of exploration, and terminology does seem to be exceptionally fluid.

Received wisdom is that at least the pre-Reformation brasses are made of a deliberate alloy of copper, zinc, tin and lead, produced exclusively in the Maastricht–Aachen–Liège area. This is usually called 'latten' (spelt in an interesting variety of ways) and was certainly imported into England in sheet form. English and Flemish brasses at least were engraved on plates of this alloy, usually measuring not much more than 60 cm across. The plates were used as cast, about 4 mm thick, and the wrinkly effect of the cooling metal can often be seen on the reverse. In contrast, the only Baltic brass analysed by Cameron turned out to be plain copper and tin, or what we would call bronze, and is a single huge sheet. If this is general in the Baltic region it may be another explanation for the clumsy engraving, bronze being much less ductile than latten. Superficially one can see that pre-Reformation brasses can vary between red, brown and even green in colour, and the analysed English brasses seem to vary in metal content considerably even within a single memorial. This may be a clue to trade routes and the importation of metal from Maastricht, but we must bear in mind the possibility of using recycled metal, including Roman bronze or brass artefacts, which could have been recast in England.

After the Reformation 'brass' began to be made in England, and it appears that the deliberate ingredients in the metal were simply copper and zinc, producing a yellowish-coloured metal. The plates were cast at a considerable thickness and were subseqently hammered to a thickness of approximately 2 mm. This proved to be too thin for brasses on the floor, and the resulting plates too brittle, so in the seventeenth century thicker metal was again used, at least by the prestigious London workshops. Again, many post-Reformation brasses are made of recycled metal. This is very obvious in the case of the 'palimpsests' where existing plates were simply turned over, cut to shape, smoothed down and re-engraved, but presumably the scrap metal left over from this process must have been melted down and recast, producing an unpredictable alloy.

Some 'brasses' are not of copper alloy at all, but of pure copper: the little inscription of 1241 at Ashbourne in Derbyshire, often cited as the earliest English brass (though it is not a funeral monument), is actually of gilded copper. It is possible, though difficult, to gild the alloys; it is virtually impossible to enamel them, and the truly enamelled brasses such as those at Stoke d'Abernon or Carshalton (front cover) have always turned out to be made of copper or to have copper plates let into them. There is still a great deal of research to do in this field, and eventually it may be possible to allocate brasses to specific workshops by the composition of the alloy, and to settle the question of the origin of the plates.

The Meaning of the Design

Another major area of modern study is that of the iconography of brasses, the meaning of the designs themselves, an area which is only now receiving attention. Art historians like Paul Binski, Nicholas Rogers and Lynda Dennison have begun to show us that brasses do not exist in isolation from the conventions of European art, but express the same ideas and the same forms as stone and wood carving, glass painting and manuscript illumination. In Nicholas Rogers' chapter we shall see how useful it can be to compare works of art in different media, and how in particular local traditions may show themselves in the monuments as well as the windows and service-books of a church.

In considering the iconography of brasses it seems to me – and here I am going ahead on my own – that there are four major themes. Their origins and original meanings are very different, but they each overlap and influence the other. The first is the simple inscription, either across the slab or around the margin, a label designed to lay claim to the stone which protects the body beneath. The message is to the churchwardens and sextons, that this area of church floor is taken, and they are not to try to bury anybody else here. A marginal inscription marks out the full area of the stone; like the milling on a coin it shows up any tampering with the grave area. The heartstone with its straight inscription is a poor second best. In fact on southern English slabs it is rare to find a marginal inscription on its own, or with no more than a coat-of-arms in the middle, whereas in Germany it is by far the most common type: my recent expedition turned up over 300 of them. The London workshops, and even more so those in Norwich, turned out enormous numbers of brasses consisting simply of a small rectangular inscription plate laid across the middle of the stone.

The second theme, a peculiarly English type, is the cross-brass, which derives its sometimes bizarre forms from the simple coffin-lid embellished with a cross either incised or in relief. This sort of cross-slab is very commonly found in churches and ruins all over Britain, but is curiously rare in Europe. Early examples are literally the lids of stone coffins, hence the tapering form, designed for a niche in the wall, to stand on the floor, or to be sunk into it.[4] In the thirteenth century carvers began to play around with the design, producing an interesting range of variations in which part of the human body can be seen through or behind the cross, as if the upper part of the coffin lid had been removed, revealing the head and shoulders of the body within. Other slabs show an opening in the centre of the cross through which you can glimpse the face alone, or perhaps the hands holding a heart. Some also open at the feet. More confusingly, the relationship may be reversed, as on the earliest Merton College brass of 1322 (fig. 9), where the deceased has as it were elbowed his way out through the hole in the centre of the cross, and appears to be superimposed on the cross-head. An almost identical half-effigy occurs without the cross at all, incised in stone at Barking, Essex (fig. 10). The next stage in the development of the type is seen on the East Wickham brass (fig. 11), where the cross-

9 Richard de Hakeborne, 1322, Merton College, Oxford. This striking half-effigy was superimposed on the head of a leafy cross, most of which is now lost

head opens up to enclose two half-effigies. The final form, in which a full-length standing figure is enclosed by the cross-head (e.g. fig. 118), is at first sight inexplicable; we feel that if anyone is to be displayed on the cross it should be Our Lord, not the deceased, yet by tracing its development we can understand what this sort of brass means. It remained a popular type for the rest of the fourteenth century, after which it is rare, revived occasionally at the whim of an antiquary, who might commission a brass of an obsolete type to match one already in his church. A fine example of this antiquarianism is at Buxted in Sussex, where an early fourteenth-century cross-brass inspired derivative brasses in about 1420 and again in 1877. A rather bizarre variation of the cross-brass is the 'bracket' (e.g. fig. 16) where the upper half of the cross disappears altogether and we see the figures standing on a pedestal or bracket, often in turn surmounted by a canopy.

10 Martin, vicar of Barking, Essex; an incised slab clearly made from the same design as the Hakeborne brass (fig. 9).

When we look at these cross-head or bracket figures, we see immediately that they take the form of miniature versions of the full-length effigies, which constitute our third main theme. This type, which we instinctively think of as the normal sort of brass or incised slab, is found all over Europe, and has given rise to considerable speculation over its meaning (to which we return in chapter 3,V). The earliest full-length figures in brass are simply vertical views of three-dimensional effigies of a familiar type, complete with crossed legs, a beast at the feet, ailettes at the shoulders (e.g. figs 12 and 117). Many of these effigial brasses of the 1320s and '30s, have their heads pillowed on a helmet or cushion, or they may have angels on either side of the head; everything in fact that we see on the stone effigy is paralleled in brass.

11 A rare survival of what was once a common type of brass, the miniature half-effigies of John and Maud de Bladigdone, seen through the centre of a cross, of about 1325, at East Wickham, Kent.

It is not however quite as simple as that. Both carved recumbent effigies and flat horizontal brasses frequently have canopies above the heads. The figures are clearly designed to lie on the horizontal slab, but may be surmounted by triple-gabled canopies the architecture of which equally clearly demands a vertical stance. The gables are there to keep the rain off, the side-shafts to support the gables. The canopy of a typical brass or incised slab, like the carved canopies over the heads of many stone effigies, is obviously an attempt to represent something like the canopied niche over the head of a saint or hero on the façade of a church. The explanation is presumably that two contradictory concepts are jostling within the mind of the sculptor. On the one hand he wants to portray the deceased as a dead body, laid out on a slab prior to burial, dressed indeed in all his finery, but definitely dead. On the other hand he is trying to portray the deceased as a hero, or a potential saint, to be shown alive, dignified by a canopy and other accessories such as a supporting console beneath the feet. Certainly English, Flemish, French and German brasses nearly always show the deceased as alive and awake, with eyes open, even if the limbs are usually in more repose than the

12 A large brass, now rather worn and lacking its canopy and inscription, shows a knight of the Bacon family, about 1330–40, at Gorleston near Lowestoft.

early cross-legged effigies. It is worth noting in passing that Italian incised slabs and effigies usually show the deceased with the eyes closed, apparently laid out for burial without ambiguity.

Whatever the original idea in the mind of thirteenth- or fourteenth-century designers, there can be no doubt that succeeding generations simply continued to make brasses and effigies in well-established conventions, without fretting over the ambiguity of horizontal or vertical depiction. It is not uncommon to find a figure on a brass standing with both feet planted firmly on a tiled floor or grass patch, yet with the head still resting on a helmet or cushion (e.g. fig. 79). We should not be dismayed: exactly this ambiguity appears on the earliest incised slab illustrated by Panovsky, on a Carthaginian sarcophagus of several centuries BC, where a standing priest holding a bowl full of wine contrives to rest his head on a pillow.[5]

A fourth type of brass, in which there is no ambiguity at all, is the mural composition, usually called an 'epitaph' by continental writers. The distinction between brasses designed to lie on the floor, and those intended for a mural position has not, I think, been clearly enough made. It is not a question of the sexton simply running out of floor space and ordering the brass to be set on the wall; there is a fundamentally different design concept. The source is probably the continental practice in the fourteenth or fifteenth centuries of placing carved wall tablets above a grave, showing the deceased kneeling in a scene of the Virgin and Child enthroned among the saints, or as a witness to a scene from the life of Christ, exactly like the donor figure in an *ex voto* panel painting or altarpiece. These slabs are not *ex votos*, they are sepulchral monuments, as the inscriptions make clear, but they are intended to be set on the walls of a church near, rather than precisely over, the burial.

This sort of scene can be exactly paralleled on brasses. As far as I know the earliest mural brass in England is that to Judge Cottusmore and his wife Amice in Brightwell Baldwin (fig. 13). The mural epitaph shows them kneeling, with prayer-scrolls, before a representation of the Holy Trinity on a bracket, and with a long inscription below. This is clearly meant to complement, rather than replace, a floor brass, for the same couple have one of these as well. There is no inscription to the floor brass, which shows full-length recumbent figures under a canopy in the conventional way, but with two groups of children shown kneeling, thus adding to the confusion. Malcolm Norris dates the floor brass to *c.* 1439, the date of death of the judge, whereas the mural brass must be about fifteen years later, and the inscription mentions the death of his widow.

Mural brasses became very popular from the last quarter of the fifteenth century, possibly as churches began to be pewed, but keeping

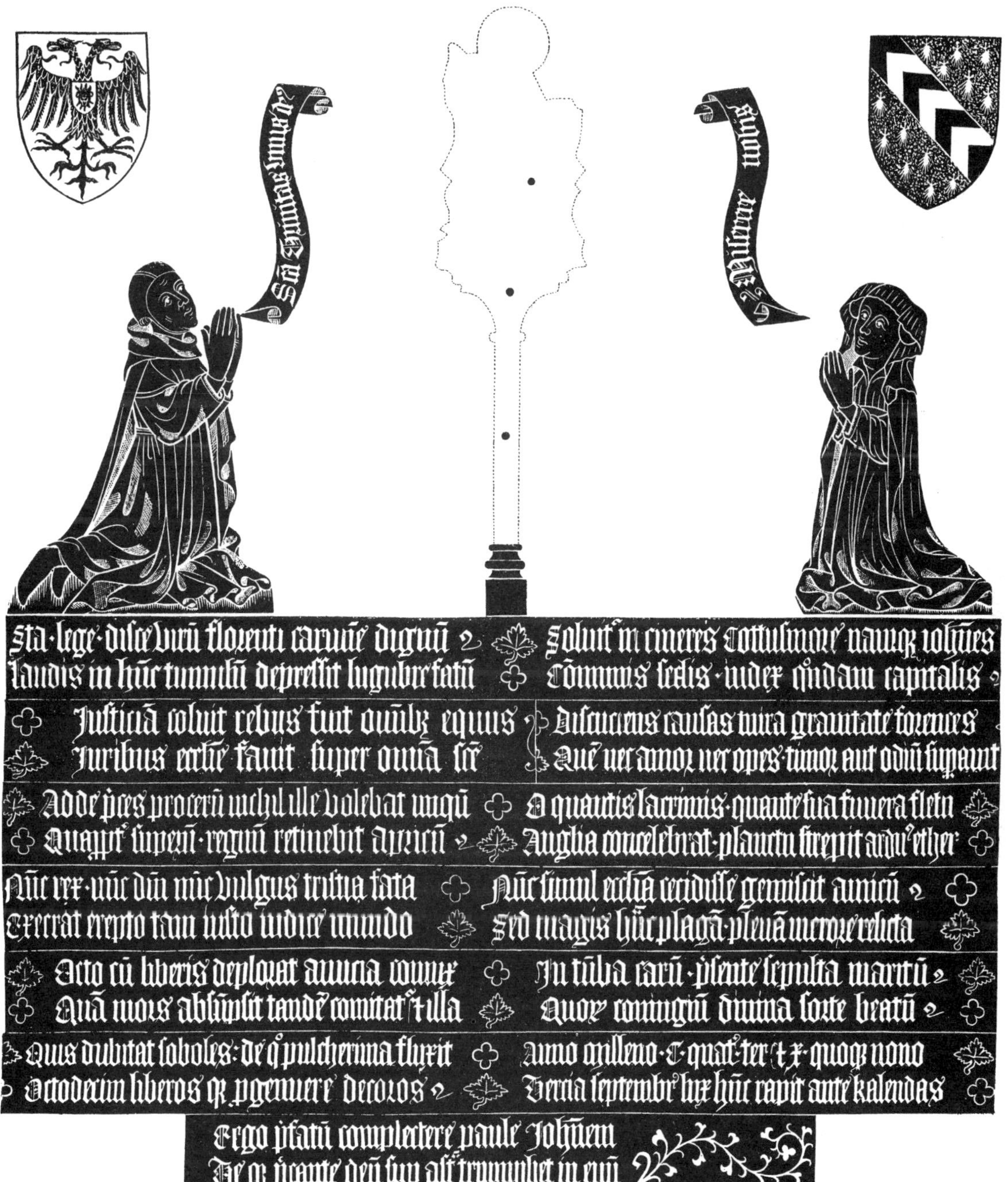

13 Judge John Cottusmore (d. 1439) and his wife Amice, Brightwell Baldwin, Oxon. Probably engraved about 1455, this is the earliest known English mural brass, showing kneeling figures in prayer before a lost representation of the Holy Trinity.

14 *An early Tudor family group: John Haryson, alderman of Hull, with his wives and children, 1525, at St Mary's, Kingston-upon-Hull. The emblem of the Holy Trinity between them has been chiselled away by Protestants.*

consistent with the established type of kneeling figures addressing an object of worship. A typical example is that at Hull (fig. 14) where the whole family kneels in prayer. The Holy Trinity (now defaced) was enthroned in the centre; there is no ambiguity whatsoever about the mural position. Inevitably there are occasional brasses in the later period that do confuse the vertical and the horizontal type; but with very few exceptions, a full-length standing figure is only found on a floor brass. Kneeling figures do sometimes occur on brasses on the floor or on top of table tombs, and indeed on some of the earliest, but the scene showing the deceased and his family engaged in worship is always a mural type. (We must of course remember that ignorant church restorers have frequently reared up floor brasses against the wall, and occasionally set mural epitaphs into the floor.)

A drastic change in English brass design came naturally with the Reformation. Graphic representations of the Deity or the saints, literally 'graven images', were prohibited, thus forcing the designers of brasses to

15 An Elizabethan family group: Edward Gage and his wife Mary Shelley, 1595, at Framfield, Sussex. Although they were Catholics, the design shows no religious imagery. The Shelley coat of arms is incorrectly shown.

think again. The solution was not far to seek – they simply substituted the family coat of arms, and hundreds of late sixteenth- and early seventeenth-century English brasses show the deceased devoutly worshipping their ancestors in heraldic display, even in the case of recusant Catholic families like the Gages and Shelleys of Sussex (fig. 15). Their co-religionists on the continent were not so restricted, and late sixteenth-century brasses in Belgium show us the sort of mural epitaph that would still be produced in Catholic, and for that matter Lutheran, countries, for some time to come.

Production and Documentation

The subject of iconography is one I am hoping to pursue further, but there remain several other areas in the field of brasses which are now under consideration. A considerable amount of documentary work has been done recently by many scholars, such as John Blair, Malcolm Norris, Jon Bayliss and especially by Roger Greenwood among wills in the late Norwich city library. The whole story of the making of brasses, their positioning, and their eventual fate can be pieced together from records of many different types scattered through libraries and record offices throughout the country.

16 The heraldic 'bracket' brass of Sir John Foxle, 1378, and his wives, depicted as he requested in his will, at Bray, Berks., with a fox at the base.

The first stage in the production of a brass was normally in the will of the deceased, requesting burial in a specific place, and stipulating that the grave should be covered with a stone, small or large, embellished with brass. A famous example is that of Sir John Foxle[6] who requested burial at All Saints church, Bray, with a 'marble stone sufficient for my grave . . . and that the said stone be adorned with writings and images of metal' of himself and his two wives depicted in their coats of arms. The brass was duly made and most of it survives in Bray church (fig. 16). Many examples of wills are given by Roger Greenwood in chapter 4, and more are known from all dates, though naturally becoming more accessible in the later period. A common alternative was to arrange for the tombstone and brass to be prepared in advance (often on the death of a spouse) in which case the date of death was left blank to be filled in later. Many brasses survive where this date was never in fact filled in, or can be seen to have been added in a later hand (e.g. figs 30, 73 and 80).

For the making of the brass a contract would be necessary with a firm of monumental masons. An example of how such a contract worked in practice is given in the case of the Atherington brass in chapter 10: several actual examples of contracts are known, again mostly from the later period. The most detailed are those of the nineteenth century studied by the Revd David Meara, from which we have to extrapolate backwards to what must have been the earlier practice. The mason, although taking primary responsibility, would need to subcontract to a number of other craftsmen. The actual design would be provided by a draftsman, usually deriving the basic components from existing pattern books. In the famous case of the Gage brasses at Firle in Sussex the first draft survives, with the client's comments written in the borders.[7]

The metal needed to be acquired, imported in most cases from the Low Country ports. The design would then be transferred to the metal by one or more engravers: sometimes it is possible to see how the more important parts of a brass were evidently cut by the more experienced craftsmen, whereas less interesting pieces would be entrusted to the juniors in the workshop. It is not uncommon to find a piece of trial engraving of a detail on the back of the finished plate, and in some cases quite substantial reject work is found recycled as what Page-Phillips calls a 'workshop waster'.

Meanwhile the stone slab needed to be acquired and prepared. This was, as we have seen, the major consideration, and the responsibility of the mason himself. Slabs would be bought in the quarries at Purbeck or elsewhere, transported to the workshop, presumably by water, and then cut and polished to the appropriate dimensions. The indent would be cut to the exact size of the brass plates – although errors are not unknown as at Norbury, Derbyshire, where the indent for the bottom fillet of the marginal inscription was first outlined much too high on the slab.

The actual fixing of the brass into the slab was a highly complicated matter. In the case of the earliest brasses the plates were simply stuck down with pitch, aided a little by the bands of solder or strips of brass which joined the different plates at the back and were sunk into deeper grooves in the stone. This proved inadequate, so a system of riveting was evolved. The plates were pierced with 4 mm holes, corresponding to which sockets were cut into the bottom of the indents. Channels ran from these sockets to the edge of the indents, so that molten lead could be run into them from the edges under the positioned brass plates, to secure the brass rivets which were passed through the holes in the plates. This must have meant tilting the slabs this way and that to allow the lead to flow downwards in the right direction, and given the size of some of these slabs this postulates supporting the stones on some very sturdy pivoted framework.

Once the lead had set it seems that the brasses were usually lifted off their rivets again, and the lead in the sockets consolidated with a punch. The bed of the indent was then covered with pitch, the brass plates repositioned, the rivets cut off level with the surface, and hammered to swell them and so secure the brass. The whole process must have been messy and noisy, and it was clearly unsuitable to do it in the church, though it evidently could be if necessary. Some brasses were certainly fixed into slabs already in the church, in which case it seems that wooden plugs were often used instead of the lead filling of the sockets, particularly for mural brasses.

Once the brass was securely fixed, it was ready for finishing. Probably a large proportion of medieval brasses were gilded in some way, although in most cases all trace of this has long since been lost. The engraved lines might be filled with mastic, usually black, but with other colours for contrast. Some of the large continental brasses, such as that of 1607 in the Byloke Museum at Ghent, still retain quite a lot of this colouring matter. Certain areas, particularly heraldry, would be coloured, again usually with mastic, although lead could be run over a hatched area to represent silver or fur. True enamel on plates of copper could be inserted into recesses in a brass, as was probably the case at Trotton where coloured shields must have been set into the figure (fig. 5).

Having finished the brass it remained to transport it to the place of burial, which might be a long and expensive process, particularly if there was no adequate waterway to the site. It was presumably the responsibility of local workmen to excavate the church floor and position the slab bearing the brass, although in some cases there is evidence that a representative of the workshop would come along to supervise. The documents for the Wyndham brasses at Felbrigg, Norfolk, specify this supervision.[8]

It appears from Roger Greenwood's researches that most often the aim was to have the brass in position for the anniversary of the death of the commemorated, when we can imagine the family and friends would assemble for the anniversary Mass and to admire the new brass, resplendent with its colour and gilding. After that it was as often as not left to its fate.

What that fate was can also be reconstructed from documentary research, at least in the case of deliberate destruction or alienation. Brasses on the floor must have decayed naturally even in the best-cared-for churches, the gilding and colouring trodden away almost at once, plates working loose as the pitch dried up and the rivets became detached, slabs cracking as the floor was disturbed for nearby interments. There is evidence that even in the Middle Ages brasses were becoming damaged, and were sometimes repaired. The huge early fourteenth-century indent in Durham shows that most of the brass was only held by its weight and some pitch, but a few parts were riveted, presumably in some late medieval restoration. There are occasional references in family or church records to such repair work.

The deliberate destruction of brasses in England is now known to have occurred not so much in the seventeenth-century Civil War as in the sixteenth-century attack on traditional religion chronicled in the recent landmark book *The Stripping of the Altars*, by Eamonn Duffy. During the brief but destructive reign of Edward VI the religious innovators expelled virtually every item of ecclesiastical art from our churches, and brasses were torn up and sold in large numbers. Most of the cathedrals lost nearly all their brasses at this period; those from the monastic houses had of course gone in the 1530s when the houses were dissolved. Over and over again we find churchwardens' accounts recording the sale of brasses from the tombstones, often in staggering quantities. The evidence is also to be seen on the ground, for many church floors still consist of slabs bearing indents of brasses destroyed in this period. Tantalising glimpses of what has been lost are afforded by the earliest of the heralds' visitations (see p. 27).

Comparatively few brasses have been lost from English churches, as far as we can tell, since the accession of Queen Mary when the destruction was stopped, although in a few cases it is true that they were requisitioned for the metal in the Civil War – by Cavalier as well as Roundhead. Subsequent losses have been mostly through petty theft, negligent restorers, fire or enemy action. But of the brasses lost since the end of the sixteenth century I suspect the great majority have been recorded for us in the multitudinous church notes collected by antiquaries and amateurs and preserved in a wide range of libraries and institutions. Through such documentary research we have been able to recover a great deal of lost information about brasses and incised slabs, enough sometimes to make significant differences to our understanding of them.

The tale on the continent has been more depressing, as the great majority of brasses were destroyed, not for ideological reasons, but simply for the metal value, during the Thirty Years War in Scandinavia and along the Baltic coasts, and during the Great Revolution in France, which unfortunately at the time included the Low Countries. French brasses have been virtually wiped out, but the best were preserved for us in a series of drawings made for Roger de Gaignières in the late seventeenth century.[9] From these alone we can tell what styles of engraving, what iconography, what types of costume and armour were represented on the products of what was, in fact, the earliest and probably the most artistic of brass-producing countries.

Preserving the record for the future is still important, as with the increasing number of churches becoming redundant brasses are becoming lost, or are being separated from their slabs and centralised in museums. While rubbings must now exist of every English brass, adequate records of the type of stone, the accompanying carved or painted work, and any associated features in the churches still need to be compiled, and these records properly filed and made accessible. It is one of the stated aims of the Monumental Brass Society to preserve such records, and at the time of writing an exciting possibility is being opened for a centre, to be named after Dr Malcolm Norris, where rubbings, notes and photographs will be made available for scholars of the future.

This book is to a large extent a record of the work that has been done on monumental brasses during the last fifty years, but there is just as much remaining to be done in the next half-century. It is to be hoped that new enthusiasts will be inspired to come forward and fill the gap so sadly left by Roger Greenwood, Malcolm Norris and John Page Phillips.

CHAPTER 2

Past Writers on Brasses

JEROME BERTRAM

The earliest literary reference to incised memorials must be in Dante's *Purgatorio* where the poet feigns that the floor of Purgatory is paved with incised slabs:

> Just as the gravestones lying on the floor
> Bear effigies of those who lie beneath
> In order that their memory survive
> And prompt the piteous eye to many a tear
> So saw I sculptured there . . .[1]

But this, like the oft-quoted passing references to brasses or incised slabs in Langland or Shakespeare, tells us no more than that medieval and renaissance writers were aware that these monuments existed: they tell us nothing about the monuments themselves. It was left for an age later, for the most part, than the period of the creation of the monuments, to record, study and reproduce them.

Why are brasses in particular so widely studied and cherished? It must be admitted, right from the start, that the popularity of brasses over other relics of antiquity lies purely and simply in the fact that they are fun to rub. Surely all the sober antiquarians who have contributed to the study of these memorials began their career like the children who are shown on so many seventeenth-century Dutch paintings happily rubbing brasses on the floor of grim Calvinist churches (fig. 17). Indeed your present author at the age of eleven earned the rebuke of a learned Jesuit for spending so much of his time on his knees in Protestant churches! But brass rubbing soon leads to an interest in the brasses themselves, their costumes, inscriptions, heraldry and history. Some progress to the incised slabs, so much more difficult to rub, while others eventually abandon the heelball in favour of the learned tome, the antiquarian manuscript and, increasingly, the photograph. These discover in turn that brasses are only part of a wider world of medieval and renaissance art, and can be studied in conjunction with

17 *A painting of 1653 showing the interior of a Dutch church with children rubbing brasses or incised slabs.*

sculptured stone and wood, panel painting, architecture and stained glass.

The history of the study of brasses and incised slabs shows how different ages saw different meanings in the past, the anxious concerns of one century being no more than a footnote for the next. The literature on brasses is now very extensive, and new writers appear still, bringing new insights to the subject. In an important study Richard Busby has compiled a bibliography, with biographical notes of writers on brasses to which regular additions are made in the pages of the Monumental Brass Society's *Bulletin*.[2] Some idea of the range and field can be outlined here, and the bibliography at the end of this volume will include most of what has been significant in the study, but more remains to be found, hidden in learned journals or local histories. Access to the library at the Society of Antiquaries or one of the major copyright libraries is essential for any profound study of brasses, but no serious student should have any difficulty getting a reader's ticket, and with it the entrée to the huge world of brass literature.

Medieval and Renaissance Man

It can be difficult for us to understand that pre-modern man had scant artistic appreciation of the works of his predecessors, each age being remarkably indifferent to the works of art of the age before; 'art' for its own sake was not a concept familiar before the eighteenth century. The artists and craftsmen that created the great treasures of the past seem to have been oblivious to the value of what they replaced and destroyed. English brass-engravers in the late sixteenth century happily cut up the exquisite creations of the Flemish school to make palimpsests, and church builders saw no difficulty in sweeping away previous buildings, their carvings, windows, woodwork and monuments as so much builder's rubbish.

In the period during which brasses were actually being made, no one seems to have considered that an old monument was worth preserving or recording simply because it was old, or an attractive work of art. The only motive was the much more practical and down-to-earth one of property rights. A brass inscription, a series of shields on a monument, or even the number of children shown on a brass, could be crucial evidence for establishing a family pedigree, and in an age when the hereditary principle was unchallenged, pedigree meant property. To prove descent from an ancient landowner would prove a right to the rents and revenues of his land. Hence care was taken by legitimate heirs to preserve at least the memory of family monuments – and one wonders whether rival claimants might have been responsible for the destruction of shields and inscriptions which preserved embarrassing evidence. Brasses were salvaged from suppressed monasteries and moved to parish churches to preserve the family inheritance, and damaged brasses were repaired, and sometimes equipped with extra shields and children (fig. 3). On occasion brasses could even be forged to support dubious claims, as happened in the 1630s at Rugeley, Staffordshire (fig. 4), and Pluckley, Kent.

The literary evidence of the pre-antiquarian age is almost entirely composed of the writings of genealogists, either professional or amateur. The heralds were commissioned to draw up family pedigrees, and conducted regular 'visitations', in the course of which they investigated heraldry displayed in public places, notably churches. The College of Arms preserves their findings: rough notes taken in the field, or beautifully written and illustrated records for the counties covered in the visitations. Tantalisingly, nearly always they only record the salient facts: names, dates of death, family connections and coats of arms. After the mid-seventeenth century visitations give abstracts of inscriptions, more often in the rough notes than in the final drafts, and may tell us that such-and-such a monument was of brass, or stone. Occasionally they give a brief description; for instance at St James, Garlickhythe, London, we are told *jacet ibi in vetusto monumento mulier quaedam honorabilis, cum infante en les swathing-clothes advaient: mulier induta est paludamb. aub. quart. 1 q. lion surgens entre + 2 france sans differentia. . . .* This extraordinary jumble of three languages indicates an old monument with a noblewoman holding an infant in swaddling-clothes; she is dressed in an armorial mantle bearing a lion rampant between crosslets quartering France, undifferentiated. But who she was is not recorded.[3]

It was the heralds who first began to get interested in recording church monuments over and above the call of duty. William Camden (1551–1623), Clarenceux King of Arms, published an historical survey of the whole country in which brasses are occasionally mentioned.[4] John Philipot (1588/9–1645), Somerset Herald, collected much material for the history of Kent with notes of tombs and brasses, including rough sketches, many of which have been reproduced.[5] Elias Ashmole (1617–92), Windsor Herald, collected large numbers of inscriptions and church notes particularly in Berkshire.[6] Sir William Dugdale (1605–86), Garter King of Arms, was the first to publish an illustrated county history in which many Warwickshire monuments are featured.[7] Much of the manuscript material in the College of Arms or the British Museum still remains to be examined, and much information on lost or damaged brasses can be recovered from a diligent search. Occasionally real gems are found – a manuscript pedigree for the Quarles family includes a beautifully drawn large-scale reproduction of a brass from the Southwark workshop once in the church of St Peter-le-Poor, London, showing John Quarles, d. 1577, and his three wives.[8]

Besides the heralds a few other topographers gathered and published information on brasses and slabs. An exceptionally early one was John Leland, who toured the country in the 1530s and '40s, though he is most tantalising in that he records so little about monuments, despite having visited most of the abbeys before their dissolution, and the cathedrals and parish churches before the Edwardian destruction. A generation later, John Stow (1525–1605) surveyed London for genealogical purposes, and recorded huge numbers of names of those buried in the innumerable city churches, mostly copied from monumental inscriptions of which nearly all perished in the Fire of 1666 or subsequent rebuildings.[9] More often than not he gives no more than a name, though on occasion he spreads himself, as in this description of a tomb at St James, Garlickhythe:

> *Richard Lions*, a famous Merchant of Wines, and a Lapidary, some time one of the Sheriffs, beheaded in *Cheape* by *Wat Tyler*, and other Rebels, in the Year 1381; his Picture on his Gravestone is very fair and large; his Hair is rounded by his Ears, and curled; a little Beard forked; a Gown girt to him down to his Feet, of branched Damask, wrought with the likeness of Flowers; a large Purse on his right Side, hanging in a Belt from his left Shoulder: a plain Hood about his Neck, covering his Shoulders, and hanging back behind him.[10]

It is clear from this that we had here a brass or incised slab, most likely from the Flemish school, though possibly of London work similar to the brass of Walter Pescod, 1398, at Boston; in either case undoubtedly a monument of major importance. Better known in brass circles is John Weever (1576–1632), who published a vast quantity of material relating to the dioceses of Canterbury, Rochester, London and Norwich in 1631 which, although not particularly accurate, is an invaluable source for lost brasses.[11] Yet he too only illustrates a handful of brasses, and in the majority of cases gives only the inscription with no indication of whether there were figures, canopies or the other accessories that later ages found so much more attractive.

Gathering information for local history became popular, and particularly after the Civil War, many gentlemen occupied their leisure with transcribing epitaphs, tricking coats of arms, and compiling material for historical treatises, some of which were actually published. Most famous is Richard Gough's *History of Myddle*, compiled in 1700–09, in which a meticulous account is given of the doings and deaths of the inhabitants of one small Shropshire village.[12] Like his later namesake, he took an interest in the inscriptions of brasses in his parish church. His manuscript was not published until long after his death: there must be many other village Camdens still lying unknown awaiting an editor.

The Society of Antiquaries

A change of attitude comes in the eighteenth century, when for the first time people valued the relics of the past because of their age. It was a period of exploration. Barrows were emptied before breakfast at country house parties to bring back burial urns or green bronze axes to grace the squire's collection. Hoards of ancient coins were carefully catalogued and published, antique sculpture was gathered from southern Europe and worked into garden architecture. To begin with, only classical antiquity was truly valued: relics of more primitive times were collected as curiosities, those of post-antique ages were spurned as 'Gothic'.

The Society of Antiquaries was founded in 1707 to concentrate the efforts of those who delighted in antiquity for its own sake. From the beginning their scope was wide: not only the classical remains of Greece and Rome, but also prehistoric and medieval antiquities were the subject of their study. In the pages of the society's publications much information was gathered and the study of church monuments began in earnest. More material is to be found scattered throughout the copious pages of the *Gentleman's Magazine* and the systematic process of recording and publishing brasses and other church monuments was set in train.

The greatest name of the eighteenth-century society was Richard Gough (1735–1809), apparently no relation to the historian of Myddle. He seems to have been the first to use rubbings on a large scale as a means to the study of brasses. Among the manuscripts left by him to the Bodleian Library in Oxford are the materials used for his *magnum opus*, the vast folio volumes of *Sepulchral Monuments*, or gathered for a proposed second edition.[13] Gough illustrated his books with engravings by James Basire or Jacob Schnebbelie, who worked either from drawings done on the spot by young art students like William Blake, or graphite rubbings, many of which survive. Some, for instance that of the huge Coney brass at King's Lynn, provide unique records of brasses since destroyed. There are also a number of direct prints, using the process described in chapter 9 as practised by Craven Ord (fig. 130). There are sketches and finished drawings as well, not all of which found a place in the finished work, showing carved monuments and tombs. But it was the possibility of reproduction by rubbing that made Gough's study of brasses in particular so thorough.

Gough was scathing in his criticism of the genealogists who saw brasses as no more than evidence for pedigrees. Writing of one of the great fourteenth-century Flemish brasses at King's Lynn he uses the language of art criticism for the first time:

> . . . a brass plate so highly finished, and so exquisitely embellished, that one knows not what censure to pass on those tasteless Topographers who content themselves with a hasty transcript of its epitaph . . . this admirable brass, the exertion of some Cellini of the 14th century, is the monument of a burgess of one of our most commercial and opulent boroughs.[14]

Other early antiquaries were men like Roger Dodsworth (1585–1654), James Torre (1649–99), another Roger Dodsworth (d. 1723), William Stukeley (1687–1765), Sir John Cullum (1733–85), John Nichols (1745–1826), John Carter (1784–1817) and Craven Ord (1756–1832), all of whom collected notes on brasses, and some of whom published them. The scourge of the antiquary throughout the ages has been unpublished research. Some of the eighteenth-century antiquaries served posterity by editing and publishing the manuscripts of their predecessors, as for instance John Gutch (1746–1831) who gave the world the antiquarian collections of the seventeenth-century Anthony Wood.[15]*

18 John Browne and his sister Winifred, 1597, from St John Sepulchre, Norwich. This engraving by John Sell Cotman shows a brass of Southwark design.

Reproductions of brasses improved in accuracy and beauty at the hands of artists among the next generation of antiquaries, such as Thomas Fisher (1781–1836) and John Sell Cotman (1782–1842). The latter produced what is probably the first work devoted exclusively to brasses, his series of engravings of the brasses of Norfolk and Suffolk.[16] Our fig. 18 is taken from Cotman, and shows the calibre of his work. More accurate engravings were issued by the Waller brothers, a specimen of whose work can be seen in fig. 40. The Wallers accompanied each plate with a page or so of text, describing the brass and setting it in its historical context.[17]

Description and recording remained the priority for the Victorian antiquaries. Conscious of the loss of so many brasses, they were eager to make as complete a record as possible of those that remained. Whereas the first brass rubbings had been valued only as patterns for engraving, later antiquaries carefully amassed them as records in their own right, and the great collection at the Society of Antiquaries was well established by the middle of the nineteenth century. In the work of collecting brass-rubbings and publishing complete lists of brasses, the older antiquaries were superseded by the young men from the Universities.

The Oxford Manual

It was, naturally, the senior university that first applied itself to the scientific study of brasses, although some undergraduates from Cambridge had published a series of illustrations of brasses of varying quality.[18] The first really important monograph on brasses was the anonymous *Oxford Manual*, produced by the Oxford Architectural Society in 1848.[19] In this brasses are compared, deductions made about costume and armour, and the development of the art of brass-engraving followed chronologically. The bulk of the book consists however in a descriptive catalogue of the rubbings in the Architectural Society's possession, giving the inscriptions of each, and thus providing a comprehensive guide to the variety and types of monumental brasses, if not a complete list.

19 The first scientific writer on brasses: Revd Herbert Haines, 1826–72.

The first actual 'list' of brasses in England had in fact appeared slightly earlier, compiled by Charles Robertson Manning in 1846.[20] Although superseded by later more complete lists, it was a pioneering work. Brasses were remarkably popular in the 1840s, brass rubbing became a popular pastime, and several writers moved to meet the demand of a reading public. The Revd Charles Boutell (1812–77) produced a monograph on brasses in 1847, a wider work on Christian monuments in 1849, and a prestigious publication of huge folio plates of brasses in the same year.[21] His work was illustrated with woodcuts mostly by Robert Brooke Utting, (1817–86), many of which reappeared in Cutts' *Sepulcral Slabs and Crosses* also in 1849.[22]

The anonymity of the *Oxford Manual* was unveiled when it reappeared in a revised and expanded form under its author's name, Herbert Haines (1826–72, fig. 19).[23] Many of Utting's engravings were recycled for this work, which is on an altogether larger scale than any of its predecessors. Haines not only recorded brasses but made serious efforts to place them in their artistic context, examining styles of engraving and speculating on workshops.[24] Moreover the new *Manual* contained a vastly expanded and all-but complete list of brasses in the British Isles, including many works of contemporary engravers, and much information on known lost brasses. Haines' book, unlike most of the mid-Victorian ones, remains of serious value today.

As the nineteenth century wore on, brass rubbing dwindled in popularity as it periodically does, but a steady stream of articles on brasses appeared in the journals of the many local archaeological societies which were formed at this period. The emphasis was still on recording and listing, and brasses were by and large studied in isolation from the other arts. People like Sir A.W. Franks (1826–97) and Albert Way (1805–74) wrote scholarly articles, while others produced cheap hack-work with poor quality illustrations which are perhaps best forgotten.

It was surprisingly long before brass rubbers turned their attention to the continent of Europe, which contained brasses fewer in number but often larger and far more spectacular than anything in England. The pioneers in foreign brass study were James Weale (1832–1917), who lived long in Bruges and collected material for a definitive work on the brasses of Flanders which never appeared,[25] and the Revd William Frederick Creeny (1825–97), who was not such a scholar but travelled energetically, rubbing and publishing brasses from Poland and Sweden as well as the more commonly visited countries.[26]

Brass rubbing came back into fashion in the 1890s, when societies were founded in both universities and the first journals devoted exclusively to the study of brasses were issued.

The Cambridge Association

20 The founder of the Monumental Brass Society: Revd Herbert Macklin, 1866–1917.

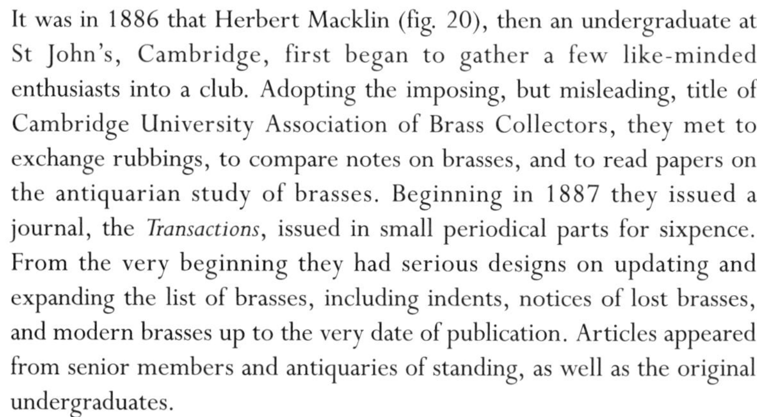

It was in 1886 that Herbert Macklin (fig. 20), then an undergraduate at St John's, Cambridge, first began to gather a few like-minded enthusiasts into a club. Adopting the imposing, but misleading, title of Cambridge University Association of Brass Collectors, they met to exchange rubbings, to compare notes on brasses, and to read papers on the antiquarian study of brasses. Beginning in 1887 they issued a journal, the *Transactions*, issued in small periodical parts for sixpence. From the very beginning they had serious designs on updating and expanding the list of brasses, including indents, notices of lost brasses, and modern brasses up to the very date of publication. Articles appeared from senior members and antiquaries of standing, as well as the original undergraduates.

By the mid-1890s the *Transactions* had become a respected learned journal, and the association adopted the more sensible name of Monumental Brass Society (MBS), making it clear that the scope of its membership and activities was to be not only national but international if possible. In 1893 the *Transactions* were joined by a second publication, the *Portfolio*, issued as loose plates of large-scale reproductions of brasses, usually six to an issue. The aim was to reproduce all the major brasses of Europe, and to accompany the illustrations by articles in the *Transactions*. These two publications continued without a break until the First World War.

In the meantime Oxford had not been dormant. Interest continued to be taken in brasses, and in 1893 the Oxford University Brass Rubbing Society was founded by Herbert Haines' son Harry. It was slower to publish, producing its first Journal in 1897: a work of considerable weight. An *Oxford Portfolio* duly followed, but the two publications did not thrive, and ceased in 1901, except for an annoying late outrider to the Journal which appeared in 1912 and is usually missing from collected sets. The two societies indeed published much the same sort of material, and there really was little need for separate publications.

During the first decade of this century popular interest in brasses continued to grow, and several books were published, including two by

Macklin, who became President of the MBS in 1903. None of these Edwardian books is of particular importance, and as outlined by Malcolm Norris in chapter 5 and Nicholas Rogers in chapter 8 they failed to take seriously the art-historical context of brasses, ignored the pioneer work of Haines on style, and concentrated on costume and armour as if brasses were the only sources of information.

The Oxford Society continued without a break, changing its name and expanding its scope into the Oxford University Archaeological Society in 1919. The Monumental Brass Society however suspended activities in 1914, and did not revive for twenty years. During the interregnum the main work that continued was that of listing. One of the Cambridge men, Mill Stephenson (1857–1937; fig. 21) devoted his life to cataloguing the great collection of rubbings at the Society of Antiquaries. With the indefatigable help of John Hopkins, then assistant librarian, rubbings were unfolded across the library, brasses identified, dated and set in order. If rubbings were missing Stephenson persuaded his friends to supply them, often sending them on long journeys to rub dubious brasses in poor condition. One of the most long-suffering of these rubbers was Ralph Griffin (1854–1941), who took the opportunity to build a second major collection at the Cambridge

21 The indefatigable cataloguer of brasses: Mill Stephenson, 1857–1937.

University Museum of Archaeology and Ethnology. He was secretary of the Society of Antiquaries, and travelled in a large car whose chauffeur frequently did the actual rubbing. Griffin's own rubbings can be identified not only by their quality but by the caustic comments often written in the margins. The following is written on a rubbing made at Stone, Staffordshire, in 1920: 'Dabbing an inscription on an altar tomb in the open on a damp morning with the wind blowing gives rise to language unfit even for a churchyard.'

The result of this inter-war work was two superb collections of rubbings, both virtually complete for the British Isles, and the publication of Stephenson's famous *List*,[27] which immediately became the standard work of reference. In the meantime F.A.Greenhill (1896–1983) turned his attention to the largely unexplored territory of incised slabs, compiling huge amounts of information on slabs of all dates from all countries, taking in China and the then Soviet Union as well as Leicestershire and Rutland. It was these two last that formed the subject of his first monograph on the subject. Much of his material and the full lists he compiled still remain to be edited: the momentous *Incised Effigial Slabs* of 1975 records only those slabs with figures, and great areas of Europe remain largely unexplored. Work on Greenhill's collections continues under the auspices of the Francis Coales Trust, already responsible for the publication of the Lincolnshire volume.[28]

The Monumental Brass Society was revived in 1934 through the energy and enthusiasm of Reginald Pearson (1878–1961), and resumed the publication of both *Transactions* and *Portfolio*. Stephenson died soon after, commemorated by an appendix to his *List*, but the other lonely pioneers came into the society and continued to contribute to the study of brasses and slabs. The Second World War failed to daunt the enthusiasm of its members, and in the post-war period an important change occurred in the whole approach to the study of brasses. J.P.C. Kent, apparently unaware of the society's existence, published his epoch-making article on the styles of brasses in the *Journal of the British Archaeological Association*,[29] but other young enthusiasts joined the society and, after initial discouragement by some older members, succeeded in transforming the nature of its work.

It was Oxford that provided the first stimulus, with Malcolm Norris, Roger Greenwood, Nancy Briggs, David Rutter, Hector Catling and others: they revived the *Oxford Portfolio* for another five numbers, and began to work seriously on stylistic analysis, joined by John Page-Phillips from Cambridge. Malcolm Norris' *Brass Rubbing* of 1965 and John Page-Phillips' revision of Macklin's *Monumental Brasses* in 1969 brought these new ideas to a wider public. A second wave of Oxford enthusiasts, notably Robin Emmerson, John Blair and your editor, appeared in the early 1970s, at a time when brasses and brass rubbing were becoming embarrassingly popular. The nature of this work, on stylistic analysis, is described in Malcolm Norris' chapter 5.

The Monumental Brass Society increased enormously in numbers during the 1970s, and supplemented its publications with a thrice-yearly *Bulletin* which contained notes and articles of more immediate interest than the scholarly work expected in the *Transactions*. In 1971 began a concerted effort to revise and expand Mill Stephenson's *List*, under the direction of Walter Mendelsson. The original idea was to produce a single new volume, like the 1926 one but updated: it rapidly became clear that this would be impossible, and after the pilot publication of the Mill Stephenson Revision (MSR) for Warwickshire, it seemed that even individual parts for separate counties were unrealistic: not only was the amount of material found to be far greater than anticipated, but the rate of change, with churches becoming redundant, meant that publication could only be provisional. Later production of MSR material, under the enthusiastic direction of Roger Greenwood, was done in duplicated sheets distributed to members, the actual List being held on computer. The eventual outcome is a series of county books produced by three members of the society, which is intended to list every known brass, county by county in alphabetical order, and to illustrate at least all the figure-brasses.[30]

In the meantime H.K. Cameron (1907–85), another Cambridge man, was working on continental brasses, publishing several important studies of the great products of the Flemish school (e.g. fig. 8). His list of continental brasses[31] could only be provisional, but remains the sole pocket guide to foreign brasses. These, outside the scope of the present book, are systematically covered and comprehensively illustrated in Norris' *Memorials*.

Major publishing events of recent decades have been Greenhill's *Incised Effigial Slabs*, Norris' three-volume epic *Monumental Brasses The Craft* and *The Memorials*, Page-Phillips' *Palimpsests* and the society's centenary volume, *The Earliest English Brasses*. The *Transactions* and *Bulletin* continue to appear, but the *Portfolio* has been suspended, the occasion marked by the reissue of the complete series of plates, on a smaller scale, as the *Portfolio Plates*. Important work has continued, as already indicated.[32]

A change of emphasis which has yet to come to fruition is the increasing trend to see brasses once more in the context of other forms of art, not only sepulchral monuments. The great 'Age of Chivalry' exhibition at the Royal Academy in 1987 showed brasses for the first time in their medieval context. A new society was formed in 1979 to study all types of funerary monuments, beginning, like the MBS, with an unsuitably cumbrous title, the 'International Society for the Study of Church Monuments', but soon becoming the Church Monuments

Society, publishing a journal entitled *Church Monuments*. It has become clear from members' work that it is no longer sensible to study, for instance, the brasses engraved by Edward Marshall or the Southwark school, without taking into account the carved marble and alabaster monuments made in the same workshops by the same artists. Moving away from a narrow interest only in things that can be rubbed, one becomes aware of a whole new field of material to gather and compare: an obvious example being the low relief brass and stone slabs which use the same designs as flat engraved brasses. A few, as at Watchet, Somerset, are in Britain: many thousands more are overseas, like the splendid series of metal monuments in Würzburg Cathedral, Bavaria. There is still plenty of scope for future writers.

CHAPTER 3

How to Interpret Brasses

I) Armour and the Study of Brasses

CLAUDE BLAIR

It cannot be stressed too strongly that the armour on brasses – as also the costume – is no more than a two-dimensional representation of something that had an independent, three-dimensional existence. To attempt to treat it as a subject separate from the study of actual armour, and so ignore the latter's specialist literature,[1] is absurd, though, astonishingly, some past writers on brasses have attempted to do so.[2] For this reason, it must be said quite plainly that the technical information given about armour and arms in every general work on brasses published before Malcolm Norris' *Brass Rubbing* (1965) should be ignored; as should that in any later work that uses such nineteenth-century collectors' jargon as *genouillère, solleret, cyclas, tuille*, or any version of the outmoded classification according to named periods: 'Camail and Jupon', 'Lancastrian', 'Yorkist', 'Early Tudor or Mail Skirt', and so forth.

Armour had a low survival rate, and very little, apart from headpieces, remains from the period between the fall of the Roman Empire and the middle of the fifteenth century. In Britain, the survival rate has been particularly low, and only a handful of helms, helmets and gauntlets with historical associations with this country going back to before the sixteenth century is known, mostly forming part of funerary achievements in churches. Furthermore, apart from the rather special products of the royal 'Almain Armoury' at Greenwich, founded in 1516 by Henry VIII, not a single piece of English-made armour dating from before the seventeenth century can be identified with certainty. For much of our knowledge of medieval armour in England, therefore, we have to rely on documentary, graphic and sculptured sources, of which brasses, though very important, are only one. Like all such sources their reliability as evidence varies according to a number of factors, of which the most significant are the skill, knowledge and accuracy of the artists, and the extent to which these were affected by the conventions of their time about the form to be taken by funerary effigies.

22 Richard Willoughby, 1471, and his wife Anne appear on this style 'D' brass at Wollaton, Notts., with exaggerated head-dress and elbow-pieces like those on fig. 3. The whelk shells are the family badge.

Monumental effigies (including brasses) were always produced to formalised designs during the Middle Ages – and frequently also later – but the extent to which this affected accuracy of representation, or caused it to be old-fashioned in relation to the latest styles in use, is often very difficult to assess in individual cases. For example, the representation of armour on the earliest military brasses (figs 12 and 117) has every appearance of being very accurate, but none before *c.* 1330 shows any plate armour, other than knee-defences, although documents establish that complete defences for body, arm and leg, and gauntlets of plate were in use by the 1290s,[3]* and they are shown in illustrations of other kinds soon afterwards. On the other hand, the London 'D' knights like Richard Fox (d. 1439) at Arkesden, Essex, derive from a cartoon that must have been made directly from a recently imported north Italian field-armour of the very latest style.[4] The variety of types of armour shown on brasses and stone effigies is also much more limited than that depicted in illustrations of other kinds, for example on the sleeping guards carved on Easter Sepulchres like those at Heckington, Lincs. (*c.* 1340) and Northwold, Norfolk (*c.* 1380). This lack of variety becomes more marked in England from the 1370s onwards with the introduction, under the influence of the alabasterers, of an almost standard basic form of military figure (e.g. figs 16, 25, 77 and 98). Continental monuments were much less standardised, and the distinctive and naturalistically represented armour on the Knevynton brass of 1370 at Aveley, Essex (fig. 23), provides strong support for the generally accepted view that it is of foreign origin.

Some of the finest continental brasses, for example that to Duke Albrecht of Saxony (d. 1500) at Meissen, clearly depict actual armours with great fidelity. Nothing comparable can be identified in England – not even the magnificent figure of Sir Thomas Bullen (d. 1538) at Hever, Kent – though the armour on the best products of the London workshops down to the end of the fifteenth century, such as the London 'D' knights already mentioned, can be regarded as accurate in general form: however they often omit such details as straps, buckles and other fastenings, and even, sometimes, the articulating plates on which the free movement of an armour depends. Even with these, however, one can rarely be quite sure about the amount of formalisation, distortion or simplification introduced by the artist. The immense and impractical cowters on London 'D' knights like Robert Staunton (d. 1458) at Castle Donington, Leics., and Richard Wylloughby (d. 1467) at Wollaton, Notts. (fig. 22; see also fig. 3), provide a case in point: they are quite unparalleled elsewhere, and it is very difficult to believe that they could actually have existed, but the armours they accompany are otherwise rendered convincingly. In England in the late fifteenth century the obvious deterioration in accuracy that has been remarked on many times

23 *The canopied figure of Ralph de Knevynton, 1370, is clearly of foreign workmanship, probably Flemish, but it was equipped with a London-made inscription before laying at Aveley, Essex. The armour differs considerably from that on contemporary London brasses such as fig. 82.*

begins, and brasses increasingly depict armours that could not possibly have been worn. Some of these, like that of Sir John Bassett (d. 1528; fig. 132, discussed in Chapter 10), show only modest inaccuracies, but others are absurdly grotesque, as, for example, the London 'H' plate to George Stonnard (d. 1558) at Loughton, Essex, and the north-eastern workshop figures of Sir Robert Demoke (d. 1545) at Scrivelsby, Lincs.

During the last quarter of the sixteenth century there was a return in England to a more accurate portrayal of armour, which continued until the mid-seventeenth century. It can almost certainly be attributed to the immigrant Netherlandish tomb-makers, and especially Gerard Johnson's workshop in Southwark, which used cartoons, both for stone effigies[5] and brasses, that were based on armours produced in the royal 'Almain Armoury' at Greenwich. Characteristic examples are the figures of Sir Edward and John Gage (both engraved *c.* 1590) at West Firle, Sussex, for which Johnson's sketch-designs survive.[6] These last show Greenwich-type armours of earlier form than those depicted on the brasses themselves, both of which seem, in fact, to be based on cartoons derived from the same armour. Sir Edward's is the more accurately represented, but a comparison with a real Greenwich armour of the period, for example No. A 62 in the Wallace Collection, London, reveals many inaccuracies and omissions of detail. A later comparable brass from the Johnson tradition is that from St John Sepulcre, Norwich (fig. 18).

II) Civil Costume on Brasses

KAY STANILAND

Monumental brasses are an attractive and useful source for popular attire from the fourteenth to the seventeenth centuries. They are particularly helpful in the period from 1310 to 1400 when illustrations in European manuscripts are, for the most part, stylised and lacking in detail. However it needs to be remembered that the figures depicted on brasses are similarly stylised, though they may show more details, so that they too can provide only an incomplete record of contemporary clothing. Like the sculpted stone tomb effigies, monumental brasses usually present full-length figures which are compelling and realistic memorials of the dead, despite the conventions which governed their depiction. As time progressed, the increasing realism of panel painting gradually influenced the portraits on brasses so that in the later period (1400–1660) they are more lifelike and detailed. The realism of the oil paintings and portraits, however, means that those interested in dress are more likely to refer to them for information about contemporary clothing since the meticulous skills of the painters mean that much more detail is incorporated in their work. The presence of colour adds to the allure of this very valuable visual source for the dress historian.

Literary and documentary sources need to be used in conjunction with any visual source like monumental brasses to help give a clearer overall picture. Despite the confusing difficulties of terminology, written sources can provide a great deal of additional information about clothing – types of materials, range of colours, furs and accessories – which will extend understanding of the clothing worn by figures on brasses. Examples of clothing also survive, though they are rare, but more textiles and embroideries are available for examination. The persistent enthusiast will find tracking these down a very rewarding occupation.

At all times the student of brasses needs to bear in mind the specific problems which brasses themselves present. Brasses may be appropriated; brasses from provincial workshops may be affected by a time lag; continental imports may present elements foreign to English taste. Any problem of this kind inevitably will affect the nature of the information a brass, or a group of brasses, may provide. This is why reference should always be made to as much other source material as possible, and theories or observations supported soundly.

In their depiction of ladies of rank, and later wives of rich merchants, monumental brasses demonstrate the great changes that were beginning to overtake clothing in the later Middle Ages. The earlier brasses show women wearing long loose-fitting gowns, often revealing the buttoned close-fitting sleeves of an undergown (fig. 16). Buttons were a relatively recent innovation and were to be used in great excess in dress, as is admirably demonstrated in a number of brasses from the fourteenth century (fig. 25). They also show the gradual elaboration of women's head-dresses. From simple veils draped over hair dressed in coiled plaits at the ears or side of the face (figs 11, 16 or 24), there evolved layered and frilled head-dresses, the stiffness of the linen eventually being supported by metal frames in the fifteenth century; the excesses of this period are well demonstrated on brasses (figs 3, 22, 25, 37, 96, 98), as is their subsequent collapse and the rise of the gable-like hood of the sixteenth century (figs 14 or 26). By the mid- to late fourteenth century women's fashionable gowns had become very close-fitting, while the slits of the sleeveless overgown had become deep and broad (fig. 22). A loose all-enveloping gown was sometimes worn as an alternative fashion, eventually being constrained by a deep belt to emphasise the waist (fig. 77). Next, close-fitting bodices, first with deep V-necks with collars and cuffs to the sleeves (fig. 3), and later with wide square necks (fig. 132), were attached to increasingly full skirts (fig. 87). Often these skirts were open to reveal a richly patterned underskirt or petticoat, one of the few occasions when brasses indicate patterned textiles.

24 Robert de Haitfeld holding hands with his wife Ada, at Owston, Yorks., 1409; slightly unusual examples of lay dress.

25 Four members of the Felbrigg family are commemorated together on this brass of about 1380 at Felbrigg, Norf.; we see typical examples of the dress of a male civilian, a widow, a man-at-arms and a lady. It is of the 'B' style.

26 *A little rectangular plate from a West Country workshop depicts an attorney-general, William Huddesfeld, and his wife in heraldic display, at Shillingford, Devon, dated 1516.*

27 A typical small civilian-and-wife brass from the first Norwich workshop, John Puttok, d. 1442, and his wife Alice, d. 1469, at Thwaite, Norfolk.

28 Archbishop Walter Greenefeld, 1315, at York Minster. He is shown in the flowing vestments of the early fourteenth century; the canopy, inscription and feet of the figure have been destroyed.

Throughout the lifetime of brasses women's outerwear usually takes the form of the graceful circular or semi-circular mantle, held by cords across the chest (e.g. figs 25, 98).

Fewer brasses of men in civilian dress survive, particularly for the earlier period when knightly status was of supreme importance. Like women they normally wore layered clothing, the buttoned wrist of the tunic sleeve often being all that was visible apart from the supertunic (figs 8, 11). As on women's dress, buttons came to predominate in the fourteenth century, extending beyond the elbow (fig. 25) and often from neck to hem; they offered a simpler way of holding together the increasingly fitted and tailored tunics than lacing, and also afforded an opportunity for display in changing sets of buttons of gold or silver, enamelwork or semi-precious stones. The extensive changes in armour in the fourteenth century, and in particular the greater use of plate,

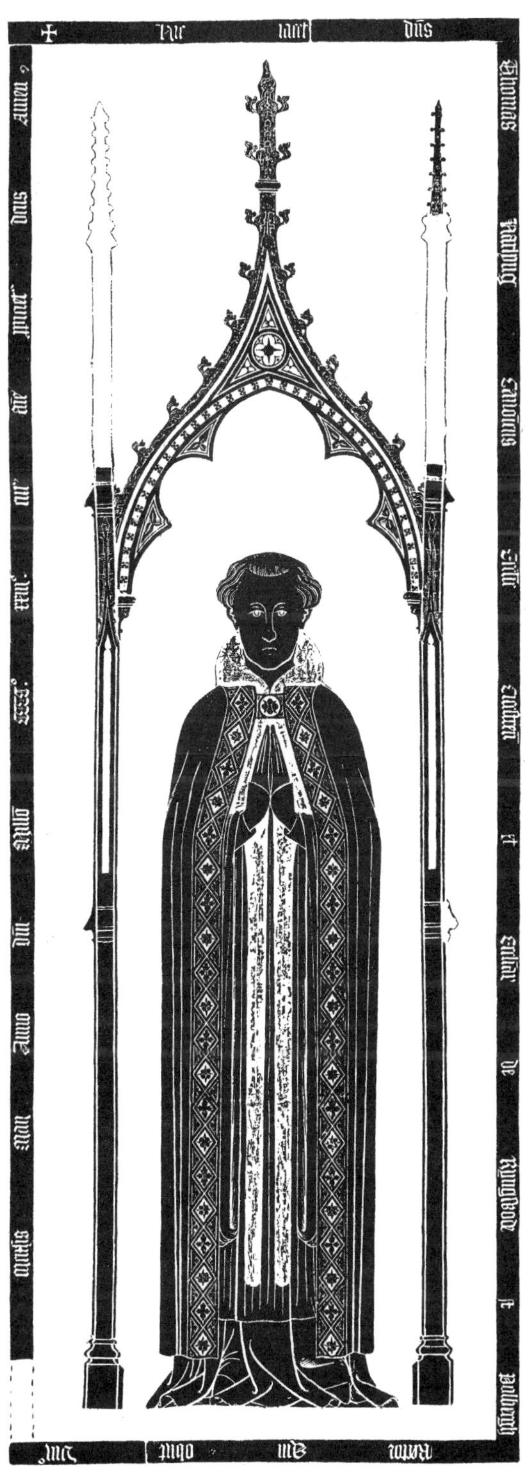

29 A typical brass of 1423 from the 'B' London workshop shows a canon of Chichester in his fur almuce and cope under a canopy; it is at Pulborough, Sussex (now virtually indecipherable after a disastrous 'restoration').

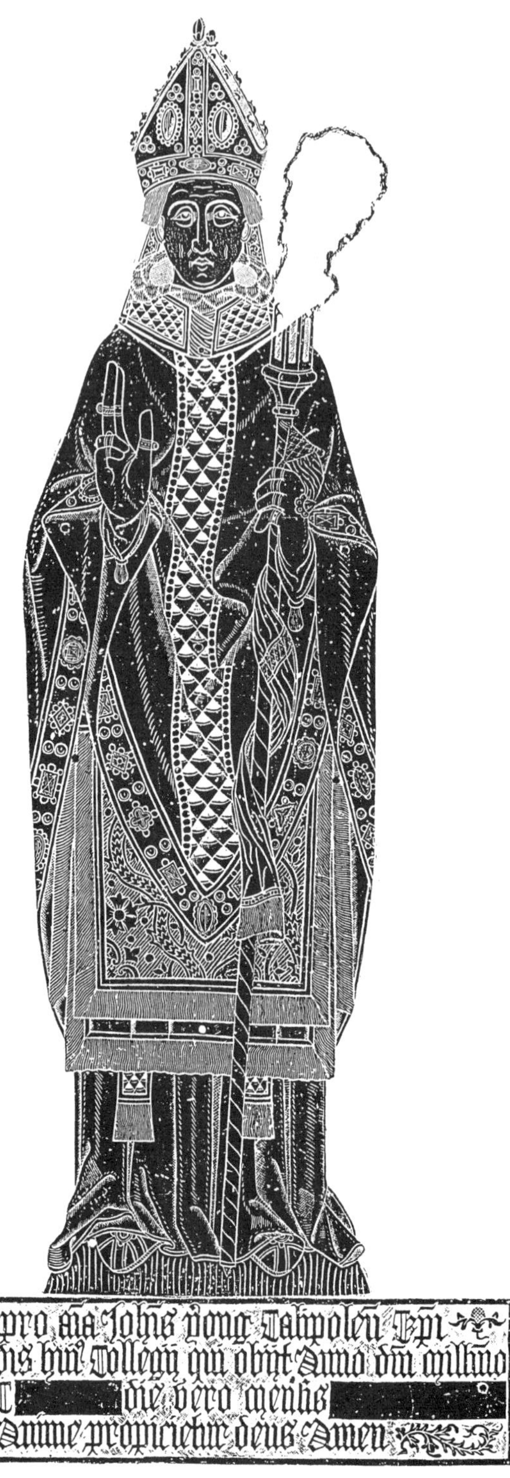

30 Bishop John Yong had this brass made not long before his death in 1526 at New College, Oxford. He is dressed in particularly sumptuous vestments, and the hood of his Augustinian habit is seen inside the amice at his neck. (The head is now lost but is illustrated from an old rubbing.)

were considerably to affect civilian dress. Changes were wrought in the fitted and padded doublet worn under mail and plate, and these were reflected in civilian wear. Towards the end of the fourteenth century men's tunics were short and close-fitting, often with extra padding in the chest. Very often a long loose-fitting robe was worn over this, eventually becoming the usual civilian dress for men in the fifteenth century. Long cloaks fastening on the right shoulder were usual male outerwear (fig. 25). Brasses of the fifteenth and early sixteenth century tend only to show the long, often loose-falling, full gown worn by men, typical wear for men of standing (figs 24, 27 or 78). By about 1500 men wore their hair longer, clubbed at the shoulders, and their gowns well endowed with rich imported furs, like sables, indicative of status (figs 14, 93 or 96).

Ecclesiastical, legal and academic dress are all represented on brasses throughout the period. The engraving technique used for brasses offers a most suitable vehicle for recording the rich decoration of ecclesiastical vestments. The series of brasses depicting the senior ranks of the clergy provide a very clear picture of the various vestments of the time, and the changes which gradually took place (figs 28, 29, 30, 94, 123). Fewer brasses survive showing legal robes (figs 13, 46) and academic dress (figs 92, 120) which, in the fifteenth century, were just coalescing into forms distinctive from civilian dress, although ultimately derived from earlier conventional fashions. These depictions are some of the most important in the monumental brass repertoire.

III) Heraldry Depicted on Brasses
JOHN A. GOODALL

Strictly speaking, the science of heraldry comprises all the duties of a herald but in common parlance has come to be understood as referring to armory – the art and science of coats of arms, and it is in this sense that it is used here. All the components of an achievement can be found on brasses: the shield and crest, badges and supporters, livery collars and devices with the Order of the Garter. Along with carved tombs, brasses are, with seals and rolls of arms, one of the most important classes of evidence for the arms borne by individuals in the Middle Ages. It is also from them, together with carvings on buildings, paintings on walls or ceilings and in books, and painted glass windows, that it has been possible to trace the rise and development of the art and science of armory during its formative period from the twelfth to sixteenth centuries.

As with all historical evidence, that of the heraldry on a brass needs to be examined with a critical eye. Only rarely does the enamel or

31 A crested helm behind the head of Sir Nicholas Dagworth, d. 1401; Blickling, Norf.

coloured wax infilling survive to give the true tinctures of the arms, so essential for their identification (see jacket illustration). The same coats may be found in church windows, or in old collections of church notes made in the sixteenth and seventeenth centuries, and should always be looked for. In some instances the arms can be wrongly drawn, as with the shield of the Salters' Company on the Flemish brass to Andrew Evyngar at All Hallows by the Tower, London (d. 1533, M.S. IV), where the *per chevron* division of the field has been inverted.[7] Similarly on the brasses at Clapham and Framfield made by Johnson for the Shelley family in 1595 the arms of Shelley are seriously garbled (fig. 15).

The use of hereditary devices borne on a flag or shield to identify the user in battle appears in many European countries during the first half of the twelfth century on seals, and on the famous enamel plaque from his *châsse* (like a reliquary) tomb at Le Mans for Geoffrey, Count of Anjou and ancestor of the Plantagenets.[8] In England the earliest armorial tombs were carved, but inlaid metal shields were once on the slab for John de Valence set in the floor to the east of the shrine of St Edward the Confessor in Westminster Abbey.[9] His father William de Valence (d. 1296) had many small enamelled shields, mostly lost, for his wide circle of relatives; a display far outnumbered by that of their kinsman Edmund Crouchback, Earl of Lancaster, whose tomb beside the high altar of the Abbey was adorned with more than seventy coats of arms for his relatives, the English earls and barons. Such displays were rare, most being content with their own shield and that of their wife, singly or in combination. The brass of Marguerite de Camoys at Trotton (fig. 5) depicts her wearing a gown formerly strewn with small shields and standing between six larger ones, also lost, two above the canopy.[10] The design was clearly influenced by French tombs like that for Robert of Brittany (d. 1259) or Oudart Havard (d. 1261) and his wife Richilde Durboise (d. 1259), the latter powdered with shields of her husband's arms.[11] In the Middle Ages influences and new developments spread rapidly and, with hardly any exceptions, no country's heraldry can be studied in isolation.

32 Crested helm and slanted shield for Sir John Harsick, d. 1384; Southacre, Norf.

The crest, a device worn for greater conspicuousness on the helmet, first appeared in the twelfth century but spread slowly outside the European mainland. Often specified in English wills as 'my helme',[12] no doubt because it was not in general use, it was often placed under the head (fig. 31). Others preferred to have it above a canted shield, like the designs used on seals and the Garter stallplates (fig. 32).[13] Sometimes the base of the helm and the crest could be added on separate plates. An indent of a late fourteenth-century knight at the entrance to Bishop Alcock's chantry at Ely shows that the main outline of the bascinet had been cut and then shallower indents added for the crest.

While devices, some hereditary, had been used on coins and seals from the eleventh century at the latest, the heraldic badge only came into widespread use during the later fourteenth century. The abuse of the system by retainers, often only loosely linked with the lord whose protection they used, flourished, despite legislation, until the Tudors finally brought it under control and limited the wearing of badges to the actual members of a household. About the same time the use of beasts to hold (perhaps guard) the achievement began. Such supporters were often identical with one of the badges. Isabel, Countess of Warwick (d. 1439), asked to have 'at my fete a Skochen of myn Armes departed with my lordys, and ij Greffons to bere hit uppe'.[14] Regrettably this brass with many unique details does not survive, and supporters are rare on brasses to peers and knights of the Garter. As late as 1687 no supporters appear on the brass at York on the vault of the earls of Strafford: we see the earl's arms surrounded by the Garter, with the coronet of his rank and the crests of his own and his wife's family at the sides.[15] In the Middle Ages the rules about who was entitled to supporters had not been formulated. The shield for Anthony Hansart (d. 1517) and his wife Katherine Southwell at March, Cambs., is supported by the crests of their families on wreaths, an unusual choice and a late example of the quasi-supporters of medieval seals (fig. 34).

Heraldic beasts at the feet of effigies can be found on several brasses. William, Viscount Beaumont at Wivenhoe, Essex (d. 1507, M.S. I), stands on an elephant and castle, repeated as a divider in the inscription (fig. 33), while Thomas (Bullen), Earl of Wiltshire and Ormunde, KG, at Hever, Kent (d. 1538, M.S. IV), wears the robes and insignia of his order and stands on a male gryphon, a rare heraldic monster.[16] Not all beasts placed under the feet of effigies, or used as inscription dividers, were heraldic (cf. fig. 46); likewise neither did the stars and other devices strewn on the background of some early brasses have a heraldic significance. Badges given by lords were seldom recorded at the time of their greatest use in the later fourteenth and fifteenth centuries, which makes the identification and history of these objects less certain. Confusingly the badge can be depicted on a shield of the livery colours, the chain and lock of Sir Symon Felbrigge being a good example (fig. 35). The couped feet on the brass for Thomas de Crewe and his wife at Wixford, War., illustrate a badge known only from this brass, while the beacons strewn on the background of the Compton brass in the Surrey Archaeological Society's collection at Guildford demonstrates the way in which the badge was used as a device on textile hangings.[17] A badge of a shell appears in the background of the brass at Wollaton, Notts. (fig. 22).

33 Elephants from inscription and at feet of William, Viscount Beaumont, d. 1507; Wivenhoe, Essex.

Strictly speaking a woman could not bear a crest since she did not bear arms in war or tournament. Nevertheless crested shields are found for women on both paintings and monuments as late as the seventeenth

34 Crests used as supporters for an impaled shield, for Anthony Hansart, d. 1517; March, Cambs.

35 Shields, crested helmet, badges and a banner, for Sir Symon Felbrigge, KG, and wife Margaret, 1416; Felbrigg, Norf.

century. Some of the earliest examples come from Austria: they clearly originate in a desire for a symmetrical design where the presence of figures interfered with having a single helm centrally above two canted shields, as would be more correct.[18] The reason for the English use of crests for both husband and wife is less clear, since marital arms were normally impaled and not displayed on shields placed side by side. The central achievement on the brass to Sir Edward Filmer (d. 1629) and his wife (fig. 36) may be compared with that on the Society of Antiquaries' portrait of William Burton, author of *The Anatomy of Melancholy*.

36 Achievement of arms, showing two crests, for Sir Edward Filmer, d. 1629, and wife Elizabeth; East Sutton, Kent.

During the fourteenth and fifteenth centuries the use of devices for tournament societies, and as tokens of allegiance to king or private lord, became widespread. The royal liveries of the houses of Lancaster and York, the collars of esses or suns-and-roses, are commonly found on brasses and other tombs, some as far afield as Austria.[19] Less common is the swan device, used by Henry IV in the right of his first wife Mary Bohun, coheiress of the earls of Hereford and a descendant of the Swan Knight. It is worn on the turned-down collar of her houppelande by Joan Peryent, *c.* 1415, at Digswell, Herts (M.S. I, fig. 37). Joan had served the queens of both Richard II and Henry IV and the engraving is identical in design and size with the Dunstable Swan jewel, enamelled *en ronde bosse* on gold, now in the British Museum.[20] Ignored by earlier writers on the subject as an independent device of the Lancastrian court, the swan appears to have been awarded to ladies at the court only during the reign of Henry IV, and no examples have been noted in the royal inventories of the period. Equally rare are the private collars of lords. The Markenfield effigy at Ripon wears a collar of palings with a stag couched, which has sometimes been assumed to be a Ricardian device, but it appears in a miniature of the Neville family added to the Neville hours at Paris *c.* 1425 and must be an unrecorded Neville livery collar; the only other example known to me is the collar of mermaids worn by Thomas Lord Berkeley (d. 1392, M.S. I) at Wotton-under-Edge, Glos.[21] Several brasses commemorate Garter knights, but only the Earl of Wiltshire and Ormunde at Hever has the full robes and insignia. Reference to liveries and order insignia are rare in wills specifying the design of a brass.[22]

37 Detail of figure of Joan Peryent, d. 1415, with swan badge; Digswell, Herts.

Arms could be combined to indicate marriages, the holding of an office, or the inheritance of lands and titles from an heiress ancestor. One of the earliest brasses (lost, but known from rubbings) showed the arms of Harcourt halved or dimidiated with those of Beke. Set in a round stone at Stanton Harcourt, Oxfordshire, it commemorated Sir Richard de Harcourt (d. 1293) who had married Margery, one of the daughters and coheirs of John Beke (d. 1301). The palar line was omitted because both coats had the same coloured field (fig. 38).[23] The bizarre results of such combinations (some Silesian shields halved lions

38 Dimidiated arms of Harcourt and Beke, 1293; Stanton Harcourt, Oxon., now lost.

39 An unusually late example of dimidiated arms flanking an incised figure at East Horndon, Essex.

with eagles[24]) led to the general abandoning of the method in favour of the clearer juxtaposition of the whole coats, either by impalement or by placing shields side by side. Dimidiation was however long continued in France, and a late example from England is to be found on the incised slab of French design for Alice Tyrell from East Horndon, now at Layer Marney, Essex (d. 1422, fig. 39).

Reference has already been made to the will of Sir John Foxle in 1379 prescribing the armorial dresses for his two wives (p. 20 and fig. 16). Later wills furnish other examples of ways to display the arms of husband and wife. In 1420 Sir Arnold Savage ordered a brass for his parents with: *una ymagine ad similitudinem matris mei iacentis in forma unius kertell de armis domini Willelmi de Echingham patris prefate domine et in uno mantello de armis patris mei* – 'one image in the likeness of my mother lying in the fashion of a kirtel of the arms of Sir William de Etchingham, father of the aforesaid lady, and in one mantle of my father's arms'.[25] Later Dame Katherine Gray asked for a shrouded effigy between 'the piktures of my two husbandes after their honour' and for 'ij scocheons of their armys and myn joyntly togeder at every ende of the same stone'.[26]

Such schemes could extend back over several generations, but the reasons for the inclusion of some coats can be hard to determine. The design could be specified in general terms, as John Langton in 1466: 'and with all my fedir, graunsir, ande auncestrez in small skochonz at my hede'; or, like Margaret Paston in 1482, naming the marriages to be commemorated.[27] The former of these monuments survives at Leeds, though badly damaged. Another severely damaged brass of interesting design is that to Sir Brian Roucliff (d. 1454) at Cowthorpe, Yorkshire. Originally the double canopy contained two sets of shields to commemorate his and his wife's ancestry for four generations (fig. 40). Not all such schemes were so equally divided and, like Margaret Paston's order, could favour one side of the family more than the other. In the Tudor period the multiplication of quarterings, genuine and false, became the rule. Old families wished to demonstrate their illustrious forebears, and the new men faked pedigrees and appropriated ancestors to rival them. By the end of the century such grandiose schemes were being justly criticised as being impractical for the primary purpose of arms – to be readily identifiable on the field of battle.[28] The popular small mural brasses often had three shields: the principal achievement flanked by impaled shields for wives (e.g. fig. 41). Such shields could be supplied with labels identifying them.

Armorial flags although arguably the oldest vehicle for displaying arms, are rare. The elder Sir John D'Abernon (d. 1327) has a pennon at his lance head, recalling the descriptions of knights in epics like the *Song of Roland* who 'penons to lances had corded'.[29] Almost as rare was the

40 *A canopy full of shields giving the family descent, Cowthorpe, Yorks.*

banner. An indent at Tewkesbury *c.* 1320 had four, two flanking the effigy and two on the canopy with six shields, an unusually rich display for the time.[30] Others are known in Kent, Sussex and Warwickshire. Although engraved long after his deposition the personal banner that Richard II adopted towards the end of his reign, with the arms attributed to Edward the Confessor impaling those of the king, is proudly borne by Sir Symon Felbrigge, Richard's banner-bearer (fig. 35). The curious brass at Sefton, Lancs., to Sir William Molyneux (d.

41 A typical mural brass with achievement and two shields, John and Jane Corbet, 1559, at Sprowston, Norf.

1548) who had fought at Flodden, has an achievement flanked by the standards taken from the Scots (fig. 87). In the same way standards captured at Antwerp in 1583 are displayed on the heart brass to Thomas Hodges at Wedmore (fig. 42).

Bereft of their gilding and bright colours medieval armorial brasses are but a shadow of their former glory. Enamel was too costly, and the technical problems of firing large plates perhaps too great for most craftsmen to contemplate. Wax mixed with mineral pigments was normally used, sometimes in conjunction with lead for silver shields or charges, but must have soon been damaged if trodden underfoot. With the rise of printing, woodcuts or copperplate engravings of heraldry were made as book illustrations, and as bookplates to mark ownership. Not surprisingly the techniques used

42 *Two ensigns captured in war displayed on an unusual heart brass at Wedmore, Som.*

for these prints were adopted by the brass-engravers. At first the hachurings added merely served to provide a contrast between the parts of the design and to make it easier to read.[31] In the seventeenth century the idea that these dots and lines could be used to denote the heraldic tinctures grew up, and the present system was first published in Rome by Father Silvestro Pietra Sancta in 1638. It was gradually adopted for bookplates, silver and brasses during the late seventeenth and eighteenth centuries.[32]

IV) Genealogy from Brasses
CECIL HUMPHERY-SMITH

Family history is a subject which fascinates many people, and brasses can shed much valuable light on it, taking lines of ancestry back often long before any written pedigrees. Where better to begin to illustrate the point than with one's own family?

Family legends name Rettendon in Essex as the place of origin of one line of ancestry. Following this up, I made a rubbing of the brass of Richard Humphrie senior (d. 1607) with his three sons and an inscription giving a curious note on the devolution of the estates.[33] On that day the parson kindly pointed out 'a document to do with the family – sorry but my Latin is rusty', hanging framed on a nearby wall. A quick glance at the large exchequer seal, the incept and closing lines told me it was a free pardon. Through the good offices of the county archivist I arranged for the original to be placed in the Essex Record Office, a splendid replica to hang in the church at Rettendon, and a photograph to come to me for study. The Heralds' Visitations for Essex[34] showed that our family was unlikely to have had a direct descent from Richard, but this provided pedigree work and inspiring history, for Richard Humphrie junior had accidentally shot his father with 'a birding piece'; Richard senior had died; the document was the pardon from a charge of manslaughter.

The ideal genealogical brass must surely be the rectangular plate with the family tree of the Lyndley and Palmes families placed in Otley church, Yorkshire, by Francis Palmes in 1593, now on the north transept wall (fig. 43). The four shields and the quarterly-of-six coat of arms in the centre of the monument would themselves provide genealogical data, but the tree gives in addition fifteen generations of descent from the thirteenth century, no doubt reasonably reliably, especially on dates of death. The wife of Francis Palmes was the eldest daughter and coheiress of Stephen Hadnoll; she had eleven children, and finally died in childbirth aged thirty-three in 1594. Her own brass is on the north wall of the church at Sherfield on Loddon, Hants, illustrating the extent of migration in the late sixteenth century.

One of the most outstanding pieces of family history on a monumental brass is constituted by the finely engraved portrait of Sir Edward Filmer (d. 1629) and his family at East Sutton, Kent, signed by Edward Marshall. Not only does the inscription identify his wife as Elizabeth, daughter of Richard Argall, but their nine sons and nine daughters are portrayed with the name of each inscribed above the figures. Without this, and in the absence of Heralds' Visitation pedigrees or parochial register entries, such information might barely

43 A long genealogical tree with heraldry traces the descent of the Palmes family of Otley, Yorks., from the thirteenth century. It was placed by Francis Palmes in 1593.

have been built up from the study of wills of the wider family, and even so the children that died young would probably escape notice in any documentation other than the brass. This monument, which in giving the arms of husband and wife is an early example of the use of two crests (fig. 36), has been extensively noticed.[35] A much earlier brass, that to Philippa Carreu (d. 1414), at Beddington, Surrey, gives the names of seven boys and six girls, not her children but her siblings (fig. 44).

Not all brasses were so helpful with the names of children. The little brass set into the incised slab of Francis Bluet (d. 1572) at Colan, Corn., with thirteen sons and nine daughters, and the mural brass at St Peter's in the East, Oxford, of Simon Parret (d. 1584) and his wife Elizabeth, with nine sons and ten daughters, show the polyphiloprogenitiveness of the age, but neither names the children.[36] Simon Parret is described as Master of Arts and Fellow of Magdalen College, twice Proctor of the University; his wife Elizabeth as daughter of Edward Love of Aynho, Northants. She 'departed in childbed' on 24 December 1572. Cadency marks on the impaled arms suggest that Simon was a third son of his father, and that Elizabeth's father was a second son.

No more helpful with regard to the names of children is the monument of William Notte (d. 1576) and his wife Elizabeth (d. 1587) at Thames Ditton, Surrey, which shows fourteen sons and five daughters (fig. 45). Above this on the wall is another, to Robert Smyth with kneeling figures of himself and four sons, his wife and three daughters. Robert Smyth (d. 1539) is described as a 'gentleman', his wife identified as Katheryn (d. 1549), the daughter of Sir Thomas Blounte of Kinlett, Knight. Elizabeth the wife of William Notte is described as the daughter of Robert and Katheryn Smyth. Parish registers are unlikely to have survived for this period, and in any case would not give as much information as these monuments. Wills of Robert, William, Sir Thomas and other relatives should be traceable through probate court records, and might help to identify those children who lived to maturity, for many would have died young.

The knowledge that children may have had of their parents' ancestry was often incomplete, as indeed it often is today. A brass placed around 1600 in Sawbridgeworth church, Herts, shows the armed figure of Edward Leventhorp Esquire, who died 'in December 1551 (being the eldest sonne of Thomas Leventhorp Esquire and Elizabeth his wife the daughter of —— Barlee of Aldbury Esquire)'.[37] Edward's grandfather can be identified from the heralds' records as Henry Barlee. The inscription goes on to state that the eldest son, also Edward, married Mary Parker, the second daughter of Sir Harry Parker, Knight, the eldest son of Harry Lord Morlie. The brasses of Sawbridgeworth provide information for a whole genealogical portrait of the

44 *An unusual brass at Beddington, Surrey, showing Philippa Carreu, d. 1414, and her brothers and sisters, all named.*

45 Two generations are shown on this brass at Thames Ditton, Surrey; the costume of the elder couple is deliberately shown in a fashion outmoded by the date of the brass, 1587.

Leventhorpe family from the thirteenth century, which can be supplemented by the heraldic detail of cadency marks on shields in the Great Cloister at Canterbury.

Many other examples could be cited of brass inscriptions giving family information. Often these tie in with wills, title deeds, feet of fines and parochial charity records to add to our knowledge of the family. Coats of arms with extensive quarterings provide much useful genealogical material, though not every quartering may have been legitimately brought in by a genuine heiress! Nevertheless, with an ability to blazon and use ordinaries, identification of arms leads to pedigree data from funeral certificates and records of the Heralds' Visitations. Wills, cartularies, licences and patent rolls refer to brasses, but seldom provide more than the name of the deceased. Relationships such as nephew, kinsman and cousin should be interpreted with care. They will often be identified from the wills and property deeds of local landowners. The hatch and match of genealogy is difficult to determine before the advent of general registration, but dates and time-scales may be deduced from context.

V) The Iconography of Brasses

JEROME BERTRAM

What does a brass *mean*? What does it represent? Is the figure alive or dead, standing or lying? Is the animal at its feet a pet or an enemy? These are the sort of questions asked by casual observers more than by scholars, yet they are important questions, and it is surely inadequate to study brasses and similar monuments without enquiring into what their makers and purchasers intended them to be and do.

The purpose of a medieval brass is more than just to mark a grave or glorify a dead person: it is, in common with every branch of church art, a visual lesson in the meaning of life, seen always in the context of faith. It is there to show us 'how shall all dead be': to give us an insight into the destiny of the human person beyond death, to encourage us to live worthily of such a destiny, and to pray for the dead that they might be swiftly purified in fulfilment of that destiny.

Having said that, we must begin by admitting that there were mixed motives and confused ideas, even at the very beginning of the manufacture of brasses. To understand the English brass, in fact, we have to begin by returning to the French originals, and seeing what they meant, so that we can follow their progressive misinterpretation at the hands of later designers.

To begin with, a brass or incised slab is an imitation of a three-

46 Judge de Lodyngton, 1419, at Gunby, Lincs. A typical effigial brass, trampling a beast (in this case a spotted pard or cat-a-mountain) and enshrined in a canopy.

47 The soul being received into the bosom of Abraham from a Flemish brass to a bishop, late fourteenth century, British Museum.

dimensional monument, and its meaning is to be sought in the classic effigy-tombs of thirteenth-century Europe. The effigy is not a dead body: rather it is an icon of the risen glorified body of the redeemed Christian. He is alive, never a portrait but an idealised figure at the prime of life, canopied like a saint in a niche, trampling underfoot the lion and the dragon which represent sin and Satan, and censed by admiring angels. 'He does nothing but contemplate, hands joined, a light which we do not yet see'.[38] The Gunby brass (fig. 46) is a typical example.

The main effigy represents the risen body, not the soul. The latter may also be represented, as a naked figure held protectively in the bosom of Abraham (fig. 47), awaiting the general resurrection in a forest of roofs and pinnacles representing the heavenly Jerusalem. Angels swing censers (fig. 48), and in the canopy shafts we may see attendant figures of 'those who say the *subvenite* with the priest' (fig. 131). Hooded figures at the sides are not monks: they are the family in mourning attire, gathered to pray at the funeral. Around may stand the twelve apostles, each holding his contribution to the Creed, and the four evangelists; signs of a faith rooted in the Scriptures and the Creed by which the deceased hopes to be saved. The huge Flemish brasses like that at Topcliffe, Yorkshire, show all these features (fig. 8).

On continental brasses the same motifs often persist until the Renaissance, but by the fourteenth century, at the hands of English workmen, the glorious French icon was misunderstood. The English effigies are alive, yes, but too much so: they roll over, cross their legs (fig. 117), draw their swords, hold hands with their wives (fig. 24).[39] At the same time the lion of sin has become a cuddly footrest, and is soon replaced by the favourite staghound or the lady's pet (fig. 83). As we saw in the introduction, there was confusion from the very beginning, in monuments of all types, over whether the figure is horizontal or vertical, and the canopy architecture is confused to match. This confusion was never in fact resolved, and until the end of their production both brasses and effigies betray this tension between live and dead, vertical and horizontal.[40]*

In fourteenth-century hands the canopy becomes merely an architectural frame; the mourners disappear to be replaced by angels, who leave their incense-swinging worship to act as shield bearers (fig. 49). Instead of the array of apostles proclaiming their faith we have a random selection of saints, chosen for local or personal reasons. Only the evangelistic symbols remain unchanged (fig. 97). Oddest of all, the figure of Abraham holding the soul in his bosom (fig. 47) developed first into the image of God the Father holding the soul, and then to that of the Father holding the dead body of Christ, to which was soon added a dove for the Holy Ghost, rendering it the Western icon of the Trinity (fig. 50), which continued to occupy the place in the canopy used for Abraham on continental brasses.

In place of the fourteenth-century cross-brass, derived from the carved coffin-lid with 'apertures', the idea of looking through the stone into the coffin might be taken to its logical conclusion in the fifteenth century, to show the rotting corpse within (fig. 51). Yet most of the 'shroud' brasses of the later medieval period show cheerful living faces (figs 67 and 95) – are they too showing us the moment of joyful resurrection? On mural compositions the figures are indisputably alive, risen to their knees, in a prayerful family group (fig. 14). It appears that few English brasses really intend to show the deceased person as an inanimate corpse, but that the emphasis right to the end is on eternal life. The intention is not so much to show the people as they were on this earth, nor, in most cases, as they are now beneath it, but as they shall be hereafter in the day of resurrection.[41]

The end of the old Christian idea comes in the mid-sixteenth century, as the old religion was broken up. The model becomes the pagan tomb of classical Rome or Etruria: made to glorify the dead person and their family, not to inspire us to wonder or to the worship of God. Although conventions died hard, and late seventeenth-century tombs may copy much earlier postures, the glory has departed. Seventeenth-century brasses might be exquisite works of art, beautifully drawn and composed, but they are simply pictures: the best are rectangular plates on the wall showing us the deceased as they were in life, often a real portrait, surrounded by real possessions (fig. 52): they are for memory only, not hope.

48 A worshipping angel with censor: fragment in private possession.

49 An angel holding a shield from a canopy, Long Melford, Suff.

50 *The Crucifix held in the Father's arms on a typical English Holy Trinity; Staveley, Derbys.*

VI) The Inscriptions of Brasses
JEROME BERTRAM

51 Thomas Childes, 1452, from St Lawrence, Norwich; a bare skeleton.

A brass is all but meaningless without the inscription that tells us who are commemorated, what sort of people they were, and when they lived. Yet the inscription may be difficult to read and more difficult to translate, and as a result is too often neglected by students of brasses.

The lettering used for inscriptions on brasses and slabs, with few exceptions, falls into one of three main styles. The earliest use rounded Uncial letters, usually called 'Lombardic' (figs 53, 54). Each letter is clear and distinct, and the inscriptions are easy to read, although the use of Norman French may make them obscure.

To increase the length of inscriptions engravers turned to the Gothic book hands, usually called 'black letter' (figs 55, 56). These use tightly packed vertical lines ('minims') with sharply angular flourishes which are intended, but usually fail, to distinguish the letters. Some inscriptions remain unreadable, even to the expert, and the immensely long sixteenth-century ones can be terribly daunting. The language is Latin or Middle English, often with bizarre and original spelling. Prose inscriptions are often predictable, but an obscure set of verses can defeat the most dedicated antiquary.

Towards the end of the sixteenth century the engravers turned to Roman lettering, at first usually only the capitals (fig. 57). These are much easier to read, but the even height of all the letters still makes long inscriptions tiring. It was only as the seventeenth century wore on that the engravers really began to care about legibility, and realised that the easiest of scripts to read is composed of small, lower case letters, reserving capitals for beginnings and proper names – the style, in fact, used for this book (fig. 58). At the end of the seventeenth century appears a flowing cursive script, frequently called 'copperplate', which can be quite beautiful, so that the later inscriptions, unlike those from the great days of figure brasses, can be objects of art in their own right.

The content and style of inscriptions varies enormously; oddly some of the finest figure brasses are associated with execrably poor wording, while some very plain inscription plates may be beautifully phrased. Many are in verse, which ranges from the absurd to the inspiring.

The early marginal inscriptions in separate letters are usually very simple, an undated statement of the deceased's name, and a prayer for the soul. Typical is that at Poynings, Sussex:

ISSI : GIST : DAMETTE : DE : BISKELEE :/ LABON : LASAGE : ELABENVRCE :/ DEV : DESA : AAME : ENAIT : PITEE

(Here lies dear Lady Bexley, who was good, wise and fortunate;
may God have mercy on her soul)

52 A late Flemish brass to an Aberdeen doctor, Duncan Liddel, 1613, shown in his surgery with the books and instruments of his profession.

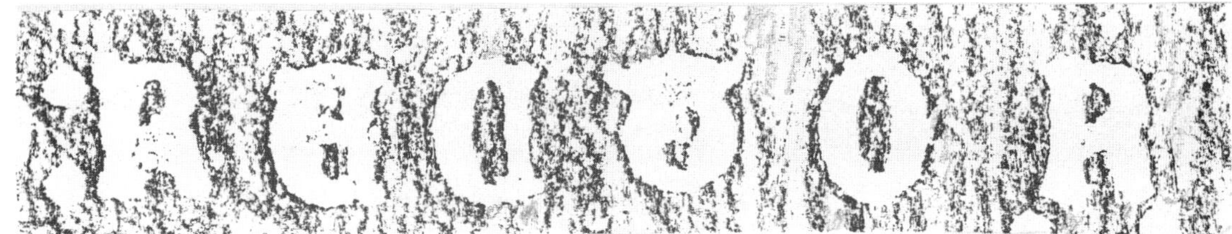

53 Indents for 'main group' Lombardic separate letters, early fourteenth century, Christ Church, Oxford.

54 Lombardic letters engraved on a marginal strip, early fourteenth century, found at Bury St Edmunds Abbey.

55 Decorative Gothic lettering in relief on a marginal strip; Burford, Oxon., about 1500.

56 Late Gothic lettering incised on a marginal strip, 1592, New College, Oxford.

57 Roman capitals incised on a marginal strip, 1619, New College, Oxford.

58 Decorative Roman lettering incised on a scroll, 1632, Christ Church, Oxford.

Some are in rhyme, with lines of uneven length. Most peculiar is the lost inscription to Sir Hugh Hastings at Elsing, Norfolk, which seems very poor quality for such a splendid brass:

> Hic jacet humatus Hastynges Hugo veneratus
> Ymodum fari potuit, petijt tumulari
> Luce ter x mense Julij mors hinc terit ense
> Anno fertur in M ter C quater x quoque septem.
> Vos qui transitis Christum rogitare velitis
> Hunc ut saluet a ve Finis sit cum pater Ave.[42]

This wretched doggerel, the exertion of some McGonagall of the fourteenth century, can only be rendered in kind:

> Here lies interred Hugh Hastings the revered,
> In the style in which he said he wanted to be buried.
> On the thirtieth day of July his time came to die,
> Aspiring to heaven in 1347.
> You who are here today be so good as to pray
> For him to be free from worry say an 'Our Father' and 'Hail Mary'.

Inscriptions tend to be simpler and more predictable in the late fourteenth and early fifteenth centuries, often no more than the name and date of death with the stock introduction 'Here lie(s)' and the stock ending 'on whose soul(s) may God have mercy'. More flamboyant inscriptions appear in the later fifteenth century, with the revival of classical learning. Attempts were made to write verse in the ancient metres, the hexameter or elegiac couplet, in which the rhythm is provided not by stress (as in English verse) but by length of syllable. To complicate matters they often inserted rhymes (which the ancient Romans *never* did) and made excruciating attempts to put the date into the verse. Here is part of a typical example, found on the back of a brass at Lullingstone in Kent:

> Quisquis es, O Frater, mu[n]do ne fide Cadenti
> Infernae mortis c[a]edimur arbitrio
> Interceptus obit Rupi de forte benignus
> Wilelmus vera religione pater
> Qui fuit insigni doctorum fretus honore
> Dogmatis et sum[m]i gloria prima dei

(Whoever you are, O brother, trust not the passing world; we are cut down at the will of infernal Death. The benign William of the Strong Rock (Rochfort) is snatched away and dead; a true father in religion, he was supported by the distinguished honour of a doctorate in divinity and by the primal glory of the highest God...)

Rochfort was an interesting character, having been condemned to death for treason in 1494 for his involvement with Lambert Simnel; he was subsequently pardoned and remained Provincial of the English Blackfriars.

In the sixteenth century a dramatic change of character comes over brasses and inscriptions with the change of religion – or indeed, to judge by many inscriptions, the virtual abolition of religion. Some are immensely long verses in ballad metre describing everything one could desire to know about the deceased's merits and achievements, but of course without any suggestion that one could pray for their souls. Here is a brief specimen of 1559 from Brundish in Suffolk:

Within this grave entombed lieth a man of noble fame
A souldier to the Prince was he, John Colby hight his name.
He lived Forty yeares and nyne, in Credit with the best,
And died such as here yow see his soule in heven doth rest.

These fourteen-syllable lines can get very tedious in quantity, and some of them do go on for twenty lines or more.

A few inscriptions appeal more by their quaintness than quality, and although facetious verses are mercifully rare, some human touches are worth recording: one at Edwardstone, Suffolk, 1636.

To the precious memory of Benjamin Brand, of Edwardstone Hal Esq; and Elizabeth his wife; whom, when Providence, after 35 yeares conjunction divided, Death, after 12 dayes divorcement reunited: Who leaving their rare examples to 6 sonnes and 6 daughters (all nurs'd with her unborrowed Milk). Blest with pooremens prayrers, Embaulmd with numerous teares, lye here Reposed.

By the middle of the seventeenth century literary standards had risen, and a few brasses display poetry of some quality. The 'metaphysical' style of Herbert and Donne is called on at Lowestoft to the memory of John Wylde, 1644:

The Cropp full ripe appears
To stoope to'th earth
And from its fruitfull eares
A numerous birth
Unto the reapers reares.
Thus weare his labours prosperously shed
Which weare to some a being, to many bread.
And heere his living stocke is; thoughe's dead.

T'is true! hee's sowed agen,
But not for men
His soule is gone,
And to her rest is flowne:
But when they meet,
And that the Knotted sheete
Shall be untyed
By his Tryumphant bryde
His dust shall Curdle into flesh and bone
And sleight the Toombe-stone.
Thus mett, thus joyn'd, thus both, with innocence drest
They'le passe to th'ever-living, ever blest.
Till when his ashes heere must rest.

VII) Information from Indents
JEROME BERTRAM

Once we have appreciated that the stone slab was the primary consideration in the mind of those who made brasses, we can move beyond the rather narrow custom of noticing only the brass parts of a monument and ignoring the rest. Many brass inscriptions listed by Mill Stephenson will be found to be attached to altar-tombs, often richly carved, sometimes with recumbent effigies in alabaster or elaborately painted heraldic canopies (e.g. figs 41, 59, 72 and 133). At Brading on the Isle of Wight, for example, a series of remarkable seventeenth-century wooden effigies have small brass inscriptions attached to the tomb-chests: only the inscription plates are listed as 'brasses'. Better known is the great Percy tomb at Beverley Minster, an exquisitely carved stone canopy over a slab, on which were the indents for a brass: we can hardly call this monument simply a 'lost brass'![43] There are many fine tombs all over Britain of which the brass plates are lost but the carved stone chests, canopies, effigies and heraldry remain. These are well worth our study, and should be recorded integrally. Far too often only the brass indents have been noted, and the remainder of the tomb ignored.

59 *A canopied altar-tomb of 1500, probably intended for an Easter Sepulchre, at Fairford, Glos.*

To record a brass properly we have to take account of its stone setting, and to record an indent of a lost brass it is not enough merely to outline the lost plates, although these will usually provide the most informative evidence. Ideally we should have a photograph as well as a rubbing and a drawing, since each method of recording adds something to the others. Carved stonework should be photographed, preferably in colour, as there may be painted parts. A rubbing, if the indent is in good condition, can be invaluable for comparing sizes and outlines. A drawing can pick up the faintest of evidence and can be easily stored and reproduced. As well as the outlines we should be noticing the rivets for fixing the brass, if any: are they set in lead or, as on many late mural brasses, in wooden plugs? Are there channels for pouring the lead, or deepenings for backing plates or bands of solder which held parts of the brass together? Such deepenings, especially if there are no rivets, indicate a very early brass. Even on the great rectangular Flemish indents it is worth noting the pattern of rivets which outline the different plates used to build up the composition.

Indents on simple flat slabs (probably the majority) can usually be adequately recorded by scale drawing, though we should remember that some were decorated with incising or even paint, often virtually destroyed and therefore easy to miss. Conventions have been established whereby normally a well-preserved outline is indicated with a solid line, a conjectural one with a broken line: surviving rivets are marked as an encircled dot, lead plugs with a solid dot, and empty plug-holes with a simple circle. A one-metre scale should be attached. Since indents are rapidly disappearing as they become worn away, broken up during church reflooring, or covered with concrete as coffee rooms are constructed inside churches, it is urgent to record as many indents as possible while we still can. It is hoped that the projected national repository for rubbings will also house scale drawings of indents, accompanied by photographs or rubbings if appropriate.

60 Indent at Rickling, Essex, of a cross with kneeling donor, possibly for Humphrey Walden, c. 1340.

Indents and records of lost brasses tell us about rather fewer brasses than the numbers actually surviving. That might lead us to think that there would be little that the lost ones could add to our knowledge of brasses. However the pattern of destruction of brasses was not uniform: monastic and cathedral churches were plundered on a scale that parish churches were not, and the earlier frailer brasses were destroyed even without deliberate iconoclasm. As a result, whereas we still have the vast majority of post-Reformation brasses, virtually all the pre-Black Death, and at least half the later medieval brasses have gone. Certain categories of brass are known to us now only from indents. Most obviously these include the indents for the earliest English brasses, an example of which is that now mouldering in the churchyard at Rickling in Essex (fig. 60). It shows a cross of a very common form, surrounded by a fillet for an inscription. The unique feature is the kneeling figure at the head of the cross, holding what must be a model church. There were no rivets: the slab is of Purbeck marble. It is evidently the founder or benefactor of the church, and is probably that recorded by Weever:[44] + *Humfrey Waldene le premer gist icy, Dieu de salme eit mercy* ('Humphrey Walden the first lies here: may God have mercy on his soul'). It must date from about 1340.

A category that appears to have suffered more than most is that of the Flemish brasses imported into England and Scotland, possibly because the large rectangular plates contained a greater quantity of saleable metal. Good specimens of despoiled slabs of Flemish origin are to be seen in St Andrews, Dunblane, Aberdeen, Dunkeld, Elgin, Whithorn, Iona (fig. 61) and Seton Chapel. Most of these slabs contained vast rectangular brasses, made up of many plates joined together, while others had cut-out compositions, with figures, canopies, shields and inscriptions outlined in the stone. On some the faces and hands of the figures were inlaid not in brass but in white marble, for which deeper indents were cut. In England also many indents survive in Tournai marble, both for rectangular compositions and cut-out figures, for instance at Newark, Ipswich, Chichester, Winchelsea, Salisbury, St Albans and Boston.

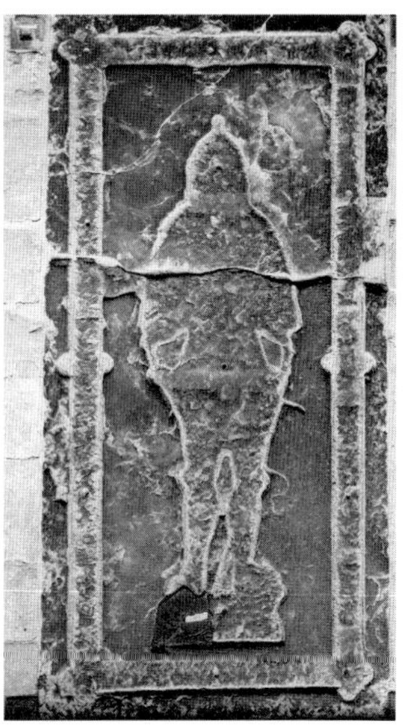

61 The indent of a Flemish brass, formerly showing a man in armour (a tiny fragment remains), surrounded by an inscription, c. 1410, Iona Cathedral.

A most remarkable indent that has not previously been adequately noticed is at Chichester Cathedral (fig. 62). It is very large indeed, the slab of Purbeck marble nearly four metres long. Clear indents remain for the figure of a bishop, over two metres tall. He is surmounted by a canopy with six subsidiary figures in canopied niches up the sides, using the marginal fillet to serve as outer side-shafts. (A tiny scrap of brass survives in one of these niches.) On the inner pinnacles are two angels. At the top are two figures on little brackets inclining towards each other, and a number of rivets indicating some complication in the middle for which the indents are completely effaced. There are four shields: otherwise the slab is filled with stars and crescents. These last made Victorian antiquaries attribute the slab to Bishop William Rede (1368–85), on the grounds that he was said to be an amateur astrologer. For many decades the slab was covered and has only recently become available to study: it is clear at first glance that a date of 1385 is impossibly late, and the slab must come from the middle of the century. The figure has the slight sway characteristic of the 1340s and '50s, but the clumsy arrangement of canopy and marginal fillet implies a date near the beginning of that range. The stars and crescents are paralleled on a slab at Hanslope in Bucks,[45] dated in the 1340s. However the brass was fully riveted, and there were no joining strips behind plates, so we are dealing with a progressive workshop, as the very fine quality of the brass indicates.

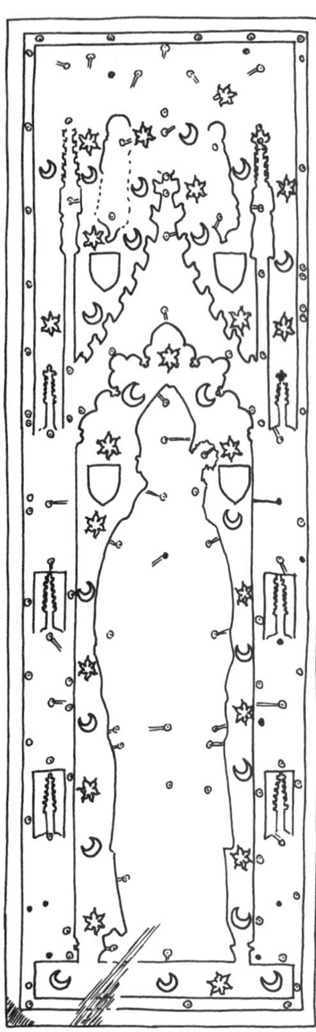

62 *Elaborate indent at Chichester Cathedral, Sussex, possibly made in 1353 for St Richard Wych, d. 1253.*

Of the fourteenth-century bishops of Chichester there was none who died at the right date. The two who ruled from 1305–62 have stone effigies recently confirmed as belonging to them.[46] The puzzle is resolved when we realise that the slab lies by the column in the nave nearest to the Chapel of St Edmund, precisely where St Richard of Chichester had been buried in 1253. After his canonisation in 1276 the body was removed to a shrine behind the high altar, but the site of the original burial remained a cult centre, and eventually a chapel was screened off there.[47]* It seems therefore that this stupendous brass was commissioned to mark the original resting place of St Richard (perhaps for his centenary in 1353). At the desecration of the cathedral in the 1530s the shrine was destroyed, and the little chapel at the original burial place dismantled, but the slab remained, though stripped of its brasses. (We know that all the Chichester brasses had gone by 1630, most probably during the reign of Edward VI.[48]) It is just possible that the saint's body was reburied under the slab.

If this is so, we have at Chichester the indent for one of the small number of brasses to saints. The only brass laid immediately on the death of a saint was that to St Thomas of Hereford, who died in 1282: here the indent survives on the original site of the saint's burial, on a tomb-shrine of 1287 (the surviving fragment of the brass is a figure of St Ethelbert, fig. 63). Other saints commemorated by brasses long after their time are St Ina of Wessex, in Wells Cathedral, made in the early fourteenth century; St Ethelred of Wessex, in Wimborne Minster, made about 1440 (and surviving); and St Beornewald of Bampton, Oxon., where an indent and traces of a shrine of the early fifteenth century remain. It is noticeable that on none of these brasses is the figure shown with a halo or nimbus, unlike the famous brass of St Ulrich in Augsburg.[49] The discovery of this category of brasses to saints made long after their death warns us that an unidentified brass or indent may not represent someone of the period of manufacture at all, but could be for some semi-legendary character of centuries earlier.

VIII) Modern Brasses

DAVID MEARA

At first sight the nineteenth-century revival of the art of brass design and manufacture may seem a very different phenomenon from what is described in other chapters of this book. However, on closer inspection what began as a consciously antiquarian gesture can be seen to share many of the same features as medieval brass production.

During the early years of the nineteenth century there was a renewed interest in scientific archaeology, and a fascination with the past which expressed itself in the founding of a number of antiquarian societies. This combined with the romantic appeal of the novels of Walter Scott to produce an intense passion for the art and life of the Middle Ages. For the churches too it was a time of change. The Roman Catholic Church was beginning to emerge from years of persecution and secrecy, while the Oxford Movement, which began in the common rooms of the University of Oxford, was beginning to make an impact on the parishes of the Church of England. New churches were being built, the ancient rituals were being restored, and there was renewed interest in 'correct' church furnishings.

63 The figure of St Ethelbert from the brass of St Thomas Cantilupe, 1282, at Hereford.

These forces were dramatically harnessed by Augustus Welby Northmore Pugin (1812–52), the son of a French refugee and architect, who was developing as an influential church architect himself, and a powerful polemicist through his writings.[50] Pugin shared the desire to recreate the glories of the Middle Ages, and he harnessed his considerable skills to design churches, chapels, convents, cathedrals and every conceivable item of church furniture, including memorial brasses, in the Gothic style. He had a genius for ornament and design which in 1838 found its counterpart in the manufacturing ability and business sense of John Hardman Junior, a button manufacturer of Birmingham. Between them they set up a 'medieval manufactory' and produced many memorial brasses, the earliest of which is the splendid figure of Bishop John Milner, engraved in 1842, in the chapel of Oscott College, Birmingham.[51]*

Pugin's own designs are distinguished by the use of small kneeling figures, geometric patterns which include fleurs-de-lys, initials, symbols of Mary, and scrolls. They are bold, confident and self-consciously historicist, often repeating features and figures from medieval examples and previous commissions. The Hardman archives in the Birmingham Museum and Library show how Hardman subcontracted the metal engraving and stonework to outside firms such as John Heath of Great Charles Street, because he did not have the necessary skilled craftsmen within his own works. Typical Pugin designs are Mrs Catherine Chadwick, 1846, at St Gregory's Roman Catholic church, Weld Bank, Chorley, Lancs. (fig. 64), and the Hon. Lady Gertrude Fitzpatrick, 1842, at Grafton Underwood, Northants.

On Pugin's death in 1852 Hardmans continued to manufacture brasses from his designs, adding to their stock of patterns and turning out hundreds of compositions, often with figures, until the end of the First World War. The series in St Edmund's College, Ware, Herts., is a good example of their work.

There were other firms in the field, the earliest of which were the Waller brothers of London, who designed and restored brasses. John Green Waller (1813–1905) was trained at the Royal Academy Schools,

64 Mrs Catherine Chadwick, died 1846, brass engraved 1847, Chorley, Lancs. A typical Pugin design showing the kneeling figure of Mrs Chadwick at prayer with St Catherine standing behind her. The brass was set in a black marble slab and cost £37 according to the Hardman Archives.

and with his brother Lionel (1816–99) became a specialist in designing stained glass and memorial brasses.[52] An interesting note from them in the *Gentleman's Magazine*[53] states that although frequently asked to imitate ancient brasses, they do not simply make 'servile copies'. 'Copy or Creation' could well sum up the Victorian revival, and in truth both apply to brass production. The Wallers' designs are always bold, with wide deep lines and usually signed with their distinctive engraver's mark, a capital W pierced by a cross. Good examples can be seen at Ely Cathedral, Cambs., to George Basevi, 1845; Gresford, Denbighshire, to the Revd Christopher Parkins, 1843, and at Lichfield Cathedral, Staffs., to Lieutenant-Colonel Peter Petit, 1852.

Most of the nineteenth-century ecclesiastical metalworking firms also produced brasses, and good examples can be found by Hart, Son Peard & Co, Heaton Butler & Bayne, and Cox, Sons & Buckley. Two later firms in the field were Singer & Sons of Frome, and Barkentin & Krall of London, who specialised in large ornate compositions and produced some of the finest figure brasses of the late nineteenth century. (See Dr West, 1893, St Mary Magdalene, Paddington, London, and the Saunders brass in St Nicholas, Guildford, Surrey.)

One interesting feature is the large number of architects who also designed brasses, showing their close link with the world of architectural design. As well as Pugin, the architects William Butterfield, William Burges, G.E. Street, George Gilbert Scott, George Frederick Bodley, W.D. Caroe, Alfred Waterhouse and John Ninian Comper all designed brasses, many of extremely high quality, as the splendid series in Westminster Abbey and St Barnabas, Pimlico, London, testify. They show that although Victorian brasses are unmistakably modern the traditions of later medieval design and manufacture still lingered. Stock patterns were sometimes used, individual firms had their own house style, and the finest architects of the day were often used to supply the designs. What had vanished was the anonymity of the medieval craftsman.

Towards the end of the century the popularity of brasses declined. Writers such as J.S.M. Ward and Lawrence Weaver made disparaging remarks about the use of modern costume and the poor quality of design. But there was an increasing interest in sculptured and semi-relief work, which could be of high quality, as the tombs in the crypt of St Paul's Cathedral testify. Of particular merit are the ledger slabs to Sir Lawrence Alma-Tadema, d. 1912; Frederick Leighton, d. 1896; Sir John Millais, d. 1896; Sir Arthur Sullivan, d. 1900; Sir George Grey, d. 1898, and Sir George Williams, d. 1905. All are sumptuous combinations of brass with engraved and semi-relief features, set in black marble slabs. They are reflections of a late Victorian and Edwardian movement called 'the New Sculpture', characterised by sensuous detail, naturalism and vitality, and associated with artists such as George Frampton, Onslow Ford, Hamo Thornycroft and Richard Norman Shaw.

This memorial sculpture betrays an ambiguity in form and design. Were such memorials primarily architectural or sculptural? Lawrence Weaver[54] discussed the interrelationships of the two disciplines, and shows that by this period the sculptural tradition had decisively won. However, the flame of Gothic art and architecture was kept alight by architects like Bodley (1827–1907) and Comper (1864–1960). Bodley went into partnership with Thomas Garner and designed a number of brasses (G.E. Street, d. 1881, in Westminster Abbey, and Revd E.B. Penfold, d. 1907, in St Michael's, Camden Town, London), which are large and elaborately rich compositions. Their pupil Comper was the last great exponent of the Gothic tradition, producing work which openly drew on Pugin. Examples of his work can be found at Kemsing, Kent; Stockcross, Berks., and St Barnabas, Pimlico, London.

Meanwhile one development which was to influence brass design was a renewed interest in fine lettering stimulated by the writings of the calligrapher Edward Johnson and the work of Eric Gill. Both had been influenced by the Arts and Crafts Movement and the desire to return to hand craftsmanship, to simple things well made. A generation of artists and craftsmen were to follow this tradition, including a number who designed brasses, such as Gilbert Ledward, Julian Allan and George Friend, a teacher at the Central School of Arts and Crafts, whom Eric Gill got interested in metal engraving. In 1912 Friend took over a small nineteenth-century engraving firm and set up his workshop in Holborn. He produced many inscription plates, and some figure work, including the Higgins-Bernard brass at Nether Winchendon, Bucks., 1935, designed by the printer Lloyd Haberly, and that to Susan Harcourt, 1894 (fig. 65), provenance unknown.

Another contemporary of Gill's was Allan Gairdner Wyon (1882–1962), a member of a family of medallists and engravers, many of whom had been chief engravers at the Royal Mint. He became a sculptor and medallist, was ordained priest in 1933, and designed brasses to Bishop Walter Frere (d. 1935), Truro Cathedral, Cornwall (fig. 66); and Bishop Timothy Rees (d. 1939) at Llandaff Cathedral, Glamorgan. Both are full of detail and show a 'family likeness'.

During this century craftsmen of many kinds have engraved brasses – including silversmiths (George Friend, Francis Cooper, Omar Ramsden), sculptors (Sir Robert Lorimer, Eric Gill, Julian Allan), medallists (A.G. Wyon, Christopher Ironside), architects (W.D. Caroe, R.N. Shaw) and painters (Byam Shaw, Aymer Vallance). The few remaining firms such as T.J. Gawthorp & Son and Osborne & Co Ltd produced good memorials. Osborne's in particular produced some fine

65 Susan Harriet Harcourt, d. 1894. A delightful figure brass with fine lettering, made by George Friend in his Holborn workshop. Present location unknown.

66 *Bishop Walter Howard Frere, died 1938, Truro Cathedral, Cornwall. A figure brass showing the bishop in full pontifical vestments and designed by Allan Gairdner Wyon.*

baroque and classical designs for ecclesiastical brasses, as at All Saints, Boyn Hill, Maidenhead, 1925; St Barnabas, Jericho, Oxford, 1929; Shrine of Our Lady, Walsingham, Norfolk, 1935. To Gawthorp's must go the distinction of producing one of the most extraordinary brasses of this century, the figures filling the panels of the village cross at Sledmere in Yorkshire in memory of Colonel Sir Mark Sykes and men of the West Yorkshire Regiment.

Sadly since the Second World War the old traditions of engraving have died out and the price of hand-engraved work has become prohibitive. There continue to be individual artists who turn their hand to brass design, such as John Skelton (Etchingham, Sussex), Ralph Beyer (Coventry Cathedral) and Douglas Lincoln (Petersfield, Hants.), and most recently the late Christopher Ironside. He brought new life to the craft with his innovative use of stainless steel and pierced marble, which can be seen in the brasses to the late Duke of Norfolk, in the Fitzalan Chapel, Arundel (engraved in 1979) and to Lord and Lady Mountbatten (engraved 1985) in Westminster Abbey. Both of these have been etched rather than hand engraved.

Today the assumption of Pugin that brasses and other memorials were the natural means by which to commemorate the deceased has gradually vanished. If a memorial is erected it is most likely to be a plain lettered tablet or plate with no elaboration or figure work. Pugin wrote in 1838: 'Most fervently is it to be hoped that the brass effigy and the *orate pro anima* will again distinguish the graves of the faithful.' For a while they did, but times have changed, and engraving by hammer and hand is once again almost a lost craft. Christopher Ironside has shown that new avenues of design and technique are possible, but are there patrons who will foster and encourage the continued use of memorial brasses into the twenty-first century? It will be sad if the craft does not survive.

CHAPTER 4

Wills and Brasses: Some Conclusions from a Norfolk Study

J. ROGER GREENWOOD

(Note: Most places referred to in this chapter are in Norfolk. Only those outside Norfolk will have their county indicated.)

Introduction

Medieval wills were not written for the historian, but for a particular purpose, to convey the testator's wishes about the disposal of his soul, body and property after death. There was no uniformity of content. Frequently the executor would have known these wishes well and would have been trusted to carry them out without instructions in the will. Wills were often written on the deathbed, for example when Roger Pall 'by occasion of grete age disease and feeblenesse' wrote his will in 1504 (1),[1] but they may have been written years before. Wills are unreliable about family members: eight children are shown on Thomas Pownder's brass, 1525, formerly of St Mary le Quay, Ipswich, Suffolk, but only five are mentioned in his will (2). Some may have predeceased him, or received their portion previously.

The great mass of wills are copied into the registers of the various ecclesiastical courts where they were proved. This chapter is based on the wills of the Norwich Consistory Court, or bishop's court, which have been read from *c.* 1495 to *c.* 1555, with a smattering of items from the archdeacons' courts and Norfolk items from the Prerogative Court of Canterbury, or archbishop's court. The higher court registered the wills of the wealthier testator and of those whose property lay in more than one lower administration. The testator died between the date of the will and the date of its proving. This has provided dating for many undated brasses.

When we consider different categories of brasses in relation to the lifestyle or income of the deceased, we can see how the brasses themselves reflect those they commemorate. For example, what can wills tell of the choice of workshop? The Symonds family of Cley (fig. 67) were shipowners, had a relative in London, and chose a London workshop (3, 4, 5). However, here I want to consider how wills can contribute to the study of brasses.

Wills only very occasionally reveal who made brasses. John Ayleward, parson of East Harling, requested in 1503, 'I Will ther be bought a marbill ston of William heyward of Norwiche, price of it w[t] y[e] werke of laten y[t] shalbe uppon it xl[s]. Item I Will ther be acrosse upon y[e] ston W[t] a Roll Wyndyng a baught y[e] Crosse aft[r] y[e] Warkemans ordinaunce'(6). The indent remains at the east end of the nave of East Harling church, just where John Ayleward requested burial. Such incidental evidence is very important, and in this case started a whole line of enquiry. William Heyward is known as a Norwich glazier, which may explain why many Norfolk brasses share features with local glass.

What at first sight appears to be insignificant can take on a much greater importance when collated with other evidence from a large scale survey of wills. The rest of this chapter will concentrate on this important aspect.

Understanding Gravestones

The majority of known brasses have no matching will at all. Many wills of people commemorated by brasses do not refer to the brass but merely to the stone.[2]* At Letheringham, Suffolk (7)[3]* a brass, originally with three armed effigies, a foot inscription and six shields, was described in William Wyngfeld's will as a 'stoone' (fig. 130). In all the wills requesting a brass the stone is mentioned first.

Many wills requested paving, especially near the grave. William Fak of the Chapel of the Fields in 1485 requested burial in the college: 'And yf I be beryed befor y[e] crucifix for y[e] brekyng of y[e] grownde for y[e] grave shalbe pathed w[t] xxj of di yerd[4] ston of marbyll & xl[ti] of foot ston leyde on both sydys of y[e] grave to yeve an example to other men for to pathe forthe in y[e] church w[t] marbyll' (8). Paving was an important part of marblers' work.

Remains of early sixteenth-century paving at Castle Acre is tucked around the edges of pews and pillar bases, and was part of the generous bequest of William Fuller, whose modest Suffolk-style brass, dated 1523, is laid in the same type of stone. He requested 'that the Alye in the body of the said church of saint James that is to say from the Chancel door to the Steeple and also the alys both North and South of the said church to be beryd with marble stone at my costs and charges except I

67 *John Symondis, 1505, and wives Agnes and Margaret, at Cley; a London-made brass in a Norfolk church, showing shrouded figures.*

will that the said Township of Castleacre shall carry the said stone from the water to Castleacre at their costs and charges and to find 2 men to serve the mason while the said stone is in laying' (9).

At Bedingham there are foot marbles with indents for brass inscriptions. These are so much smaller than the usual stones bearing brasses that they require some explanation, such as may be afforded by the will of William Lamyn, parson of Thorpe Morieux, Suffolk. He requested, 'I will have over me a stone of marble with my name written and the stone over my heart and c.' (10) This suggests a small stone placed over the heart, where the inscription is usually placed in most inscription-only brasses set in normal sized slabs.

Such small stones may be the remains of graves originally covered by several small stones. In 1507 Elizabeth Swardeston requested burial in the churchyard of Ilketshall St Margaret, Suffolk, and 'I will have 6 small stones of marble to cover my grave with' (11). There are five examples of 'heart stones', which clearly do not refer to heart burials. In 1512 Robert Burnham, chaplain, requested burial in the Chapel of the Field in Norwich, and that 'my executors shall buy a heart stone of marble to lie upon me with some remembrance of scripture' (12). The other four examples incorporate the heart stone into the overall paving of the grave. John Sandwich in 1500 requested burial in the Austin Friars at Norwich and that 'my grave be paved with an hart stone of marble and broad tile' (13). John Ston of Trowse in 1507 requested churchyard burial and 'my grave to be covered with an heart stone of marble and all the other part of my grave with flint stones' (14). Henry Larke in 1528 requested burial in the pathway of the churchyard of All Saints, Norwich, and 'that the said my grave be pathed with stone and a hart stone in the myddes with a superscription of my name therin' (15). Agnes Chamberlayn in 1539 requested burial in the churchyard of St Peter Mancroft, Norwich, in the alleyway leading to the north porch, and 'I will have my grave covered with paving stone, brick round about, with an heart stone in the myddys with my name' (16). This evidence about small stones and heart stones helps towards a new understanding of church floors.

Wills help little with the type of stone to be used. In East Anglia from about 1470 to about 1540 there was a choice of stone: that which came from Purbeck via the London workshops, and that other stone, frequently pinkish, and probably from the limestone quarries of Northamptonshire or Lincolnshire, via the East Anglian workshops. Two wills from 1524 and 1531 (17, 18) request grey marble. John Foxe of Wethersdale, Suffolk, requests a coverstone for his churchyard tomb-chest, 'well chosen of the best that will well last' (19). John Rushburghe of Aylsham in 1518 was specific about the coverstone for his churchyard tomb-chest, that it should be of 'marble stone of corve [i.e. Corfe, and hence Purbeck marble]' (20). In 1519 Thomas Sharrington of Cranworth requested a coverstone 'of marble or ffreston'(21). Thomas Gausell in 1500 requested burial in Dereham Abbey and 'a Burwell stone to lay upon me' (22). Clunch was quarried at Burwell, Cambs., but seems a curious stone to use. It is possible that 'Burwell' is a corruption of 'burial', but I have not met such usage elsewhere. The vast majority of those requesting marble gravestones were apparently indifferent to the type of stone to be used. As it was the workshop that decided which stone was used, the choice of workshop was probably of greater importance to most testators than the choice of stone.

The Size and Price of Gravestones and Brasses

Slabs in Norfolk churches vary in size from the foot marbles up to the 13 × 5 feet, 2½ inches (396 × 149.5 cm) in the North Porch of St Andrew's, Norwich. Traditionally the length of a grave is 6 feet. A stone for a single grave might thus be 6 × 2½–3 feet (183 × 76 to 91.5 cm), which was requested by Thomas Chyld of St Edmund Fishergate, Norwich, in 1509/10 (35), by Thomas Smyth, parson of South Elmham St Peter, Suffolk, in 1524 (17) and by Thomas Abbys of Buxton in 1532/3 (36), for they all specified 6 × 3 feet. Edmund Wethyr requested 6 × 4 feet with an effigy of a priest 'to the leynght of a large foote' in 1524/5 for his grave in Norwich Cathedral (37). In 1504 Thomas Gerard, parson of Stokesby, mentioned the length of 7 feet, but not the width. His brass effigy was to have been a yard long (38). Regrettably the original stone is lost or covered, for the London-made half-effigy is now fixed to a Norwich-made inscription (fig. 68). John Smyth, parson of Brisley, in 1536 requested 'a graveston vij foote in lenght and iij fote of brede w^{t} a pyctor thereupon and writing of the daie and yere of my departing' (39). Elizabeth Thompson in 1514 requested burial in St James, Lynn, and to 'Cover the grave of Thomas Coldwedder layt my husbond and myn with a marble stone of ij Ellys long & one brede or ther a bowght' (40). Seven feet six by three feet nine (228.5 × 114.5 cm) seems a reasonable size for a double grave.

These few complete my references to gravestone sizes. There are many more giving prices, but none a size and a price.[5]* This coincidence must be significant. Price probably indicated size. Whether prices were for the stone alone or included the brass is a complication. Transport costs were doubtless extra. I will consider the prices mentioned in the wills, starting with the cheapest.

Henry Bothom of East Tuddenham in 1512 requested a 4*s* gravestone (41). Katheryne Toddenham of Breckles in 1510 gave 13*s* 4*d* to buy two stones (42).

Eight stones cost 10*s* (43–50) of which four request that a name be

68 Thomas Gerard, rector, a London style 'G' figure associated with a 'Norwich 5' inscription of 1506, Stokesby, Norf.

recorded (44, 46, 47, 48). Two (47, 48) of this four exclude the brass from the price, for example Sir Juan Carre, vicar of Bures St Mary, Suffolk, in 1530 requested, 'that my executors shall by a stone of Marbill price x[s] to lie over me and my name to be graved in the same' (47). The other two (44, 46), however, seem to include the brass in the price, as requested by William Alexander in 1524/5 for his burial in St Clement, Norwich: 'I wull have a grave stone & a scrow uppon yt the price x[s]' (46). Only one of these eight has an extant brass; John Felde, parson of Belaugh in 1508 sought a 10*s* gravestone (43). His unrequested chalice and inscription remain (fig. 69), but they have been relaid with no sign of the original stone. There are many gravestones in Norfolk that fall well short of the 'normal' size. The evidence is inconclusive but 10*s* would probably have bought an inscription on a stone about 4 feet 6 inches by 1 foot 10 inches (107 × 56 cm).

All the prices but 4*s*, 11*s* or 12*s* are 'round figures'. One of the 11*s*

69 *John Felde, 1508, Belaugh, Norf.; a 'Norwich 6' style chalice and inscription.*

items (51) and that at 12*s* (52) were for stones without mentioning an inscription. The other 11*s* item (53) apparently includes the inscription in the price. It is difficult to distinguish these stones from those at 10*s*.

There are nine examples at one mark or 13*s* 4*d*. Seven do not mention any brass (26, 54–59), but a brass remains for one of them, an undated inscription for John Isbellys now in the care of the Norwich Museums. The original stone has gone. His will dates the brass 1521 (26). Of the other two at this price, Thomas Lynsted, probably buried in the 'churche of our lady in the marrisshe' requested 'a marble stoone with a scripture to ye value of xiij^s iiij^d' (60). William Nellson, curate of St Peter's, Felixstowe, Suffolk, asked in 1531/2, 'that my Syster Esabell do bye or cause to be boughte a grave stone of graye marbylle the pryce of A Marke of Sterlinge monye currante in Englande wyth a pictor of a preste In gravyde wyth a Challesse in his hande and a hoste wythin ytte' (18). It seems fitting that the brass work is excluded from this price. Thirteen shillings and fourpence would also be for less than the 'normal' size, say about 5 feet by 1 foot 10 inches(152.5 × 56 cm).

Seventeen shillings, nine and one-third pence requested by Marion Belaws in 1501 (61) represents a unit price out of a total of four marks for three stones.

Six of the nine examples priced at 20*s* (62–67) merely request a stone. One was a coverstone: William Hagges in 1537 requests burial in Reydon churchyard, Suffolk, and to 'have a gravestone the pryce of xxs to be layed upon my grave after my disceace. Item I wyll that my grave shall be heynded above the grownde with masoncrafte iij quarters of a yarde and pynned upp with stone' (67). Of the other three, Edmund Wright in 1505 requested burial in the churchyard of St Andrew, Norwich, beside his wife, and to 'have a gravestone w^t an ymage of me and my wiff w^t a scripture ther upon for the wiche stone I geve 20^s and I will y[t] my grave stone be heyned hallf a yerd heye w[t] stone and lyme or tyle' (68). He clearly separates the price of the stone from the rest of the memorial. Another in 1496 also asks for a stone to cover two people and the inscription is excluded from the price (69). The last 20*s* example is from 1535: 'I will have a stone of marble the price thereof xx[s] to be layde upon me for a Remembrance' (70). This well demonstrates how the stone outclasses the brass, for there could be no 'Remembrance' without an inscription, whether in brass or incised in the stone.

Twenty-two shillings and two and two-thirds pence requested by Nicholas Gegebald in 1460 (71) represents the individual price of six stones, of which the total price was ten marks.

The sum of 25*s* and 8*d* requested by John Revis in 1518 (72) is a clerical error for 26*s* and 8*d*, or two marks. Including this, there are seventeen examples at 26*s* 8*d* (24, 73–84, and 3 × 59). This is by far the most popular price, and possibly therefore can be matched with the 'normal' size of 6 feet by 2 feet 6 inches to 3 feet. This appears to be contradicted by two examples. In 1505 William Wynne of Upton requested a stone priced 26*s* 8*d*, but the extant brass inscription for him is set in a slab 7 feet 11 inches by 3 feet 11 inches (75). John Bukton in 1511/12 requested burial at Wilton and a gravestone valued at 26s 8*d* (76). His brass inscription remains for him in a large slab (fig. 70). Both inscriptions include their wives, who were among the executors. The will of Ellen Dorand, widow, dated 1514 (78), requests burial at Barnham Broom, and 'I will have a graveston of xxvj[s] viij[d] and in the same a pictur in brasse ther upon w[t] my arms blasid in the same yf hit may be borne'. The price is for the stone, not the brass. There are two effigies, a foot inscription with a depending shield of arms, and the slab measures 6 feet 4 inches by 3 feet and half an inch (193 by 92.5 cm) (fig. 71).

Of the seventeen examples at 26*s* 8*d*, eleven request merely a stone (72–4, 76, 82–4, and 3 × 59). Of those requesting more, two mention the stone and inscription valued together (77, 81), and another two (78, 80) separate the price of the stone from that of the brass composition. A fifth example is that of John Thurston, who in 1519 requested burial,

70 John Bukton, 1511/12, Wilton, Norf.; a 'Suffolk 2' style inscription strayed across the border.

71 *John and Ellen Dorant, 1514, Barnham Broom, Norf. A badly worn brass of the 'Norwich 6' style.*

possibly in Ormesby, and, 'I will have upon my grave a fineral ston callid a grave stone with a scripture ther upon sone after my departing price of the same *by estimacion* xxvj^{s} viijd' (79). Perhaps all the prices were by 'estimacion'.

Thomas Brygg in 1494 requested a 100*s* stone for himself at the Norwich Greyfriars, and for relatives in other places, three at 26*s* 8*d*, and one at 13*s* 4*d*. He was clearly distinguishing between these three prices (59).

In 1502 John Cobbe of Pulham St Mary ordered a 30*s* stone (85). In 1485 William Grigges of Hoxne, Suffolk, requested churchyard burial, and 'that my executors provide for a stone to be leid upon my grave ij fote in height and on wiche the pictur of my person my wiff and my childern to the value of xxxiij^{s} iiij^{d} ($2\frac{1}{2}$ marks)' (86).

There are seven examples priced at 40*s*. Two of these (87, 88) simply ask for a single stone, and another (89) requests churchyard burial with the stone over a man and his wife. Gregory Fyllyng (90)[6]* expected a stone, image and writing for this price. In 1503 William Nottyng, priest, requested burial in St Leonard's, London, and expected a stone and his name written on it (91). John Ayleward's will priced the stone at 40*s* (6). His stone measures 5 feet 4½ inches by 2 feet 6½ inches (164 by 77 cm), and is marginally less than 'normal' size but contains more brass work than a simple inscription. Roger Tymperley of Ipswich in 1498 requested burial in the churchyard of St Mary le Tower, and 'I wyll have a gravestone of Marbyll for me and my wyff w[t] ij images and Armys at the head and at the feete And on bothe sydys on the Toumbe accordyng to y[e] value of xl[s]' (92), evidently a tomb-chest coverstone with brass work on top and on the sides. The testator distinguished the work of the marbler from the brass engraver.

One example cost 46*s* 8*d* (3½ marks). In 1518 Henry Mownford, clerk, requested burial in St Mary Coslany, Norwich, and to 'have a ston of marble w[t] I Epytaphy in verses which I have wretyn in a bil to the price of xlvj[s] viijd or more aftur the advise of my executours to lye upon my grave' (93). The verses remain on an inscription, 5 by 26¼ inches (13 × 67 cm) in the care of the Norwich Museums. The slab has gone.

There are three examples at 4 marks (53*s* 4*d*). William Wright of Stockton in 1513 requested 'a gravestone to cover my grave and a scripture of my name ther in price liij[s] iiij[d]' (94). In *c.* 1605[7] a brass to William Wright was noted as a gowned man with a foot inscription, and despite minor inconsistencies, this can be identified with the will and with the extant indent, which measures 7 feet 1¼ inches by 3 ft 6½ inches (216.5 × 108 cm). In 1525 William Reve, priest, of Capel St Mary, Suffolk, requested 'that a graveston of marbylle be bowht & leyd on my fathers grave & myn w[t] a plat of latyn sett on the seyd ston on the whiche I wyll have writyn *Orate pro animabus Willielmi Reve & dni Willielmi Reve Clerici eius filii* On the whiche ston I wylle that myn executors do bestowe liij[s] & iiij pens' (95). John Colyn probably expected to be buried at St Mary le Tower in Ipswich and to have a stone with a 'scriptor' for this price (96).

Of the nine examples at 5 marks (£3 6*s* 8*d*), three simply request a gravestone (97, 98, 99). I imagine that either these stones were very large, or were embellished with brass work. In 1528 Thomas Browse, probably buried in St Crouch, Norwich, requested 'a stone laide apon my wyef and me with workmanship the price of v markes' (100). The unspecified reference to *workmanship* probably refers to a brass composition. In 1519 James Jermy was more specific, requesting burial by his wife at Earl Soham, Suffolk, and 'a grave ston for me & my wyff w[t] owre pyctours & Armes therupon of V marcs' (101). Edmund

Holkham was Robert Clyppesby's executor in 1451/2. He made his own will in 1484 requesting burial at St Benet-at-Holme, and (in Latin) 'a gravestone of marbyll priced five marks *ad similtudine de Clyppesbes graveston* with four shields in the corners and in the middle an image of an angel standing in a cloud holding in his hands a roll with a scripture *Orate pro anima Edmundi Holkham armigeri qui obijt die mensis Anno dni M^lo^CCCClxxxiiij^to^*' (102). The other three examples all refer to churchyard tomb-chests (20, 54, 103).

The next price is the 100*s* for Thomas Brigg already mentioned (59). Bartholomew Reed, knight, alderman, citizen and goldsmith of London, was a man of considerable wealth. In 1505 he requested burial 'w^t^ in the Cloyster of the Charterhouse of London that is to sey in the side of the Cloyster ther betweene twoo arches or moynelles of stone directly ageyn the dore ledyng or openyng owte of the choer ther into the said cloister . . . and I will that myn executours doo make a tombe of stone of the value & cost of xx^li^ w^t^ the Image of the Trynitie and of a dede corse knelyng therunto...' (104). Sir Roger Le Strange's fine brass, with weepers in the sideshafts of the canopy, remains on the coverstone of a lavish tomb with brass shields on the sides at Hunstanton (fig. 72). He requested in his will in 1505 that his executors 'cause a tombe to be made whereupon I will they shall bestowe xxvj^li^ xiij^s^ iiij^d^ to be made w^t^ in a twelfmonethe or ij yeres next aftir my decesse' (105).

From 4*s* to £26 13*s* 4*d* is a wide range of prices from which a general picture emerges. What is remarkable is that no brass is priced separately from the stone.

When was the Memorial Laid Down?

Eight examples requested stones to cover graves soon after death (79, 81, 106–11). Henry Pye of Northwold in 1529/30 requested a stone 'against mye vij^th^ daye' (112). In 1526 Alexander Skarburght, parson of Rockland, requested a 'grave stone Laied upon my grave w^t^ in the space of a monithe the price V markes ensuyng my dethe' (98). Thomas Salter in London in 1558 also expected the elaborate stone to be laid over him in a month (113).[8]* It is doubtful that the marblers could have reacted so quickly. There are two wills requesting three months (114, 115), and one six months (116). Ten examples, being all the rest but one that stipulate a time for completion, request a year (36, 54, 80, 117–23). The exception is the one or two years requested by Roger Lestrange for an elaborate and fine memorial (105).

Two of the 'within a year' wills request a black cloth to cover the grave (121, 122). In 1545/6 Henry Vincent of Westfield requested his executors to 'cover my grave w^t^ a grave ston of marble wherupon I wyll have graven my name and the daye of my buryell in brasse. Item I wyll

72 The splendid heraldic brass of Sir Roger Le Strange, 1506, at Hunstanton, Norf., of the 'Norwich 4' style.

that my executors Immediatelye after my buryall daye shall leye uppon my grave a blacke clothe to cover it w^{t} all and a candell to stonde brenning therupon of a quarter of a pownde of waxe by the space of one yere untyll the saide ston be layed upon my saide grave' (122).

In 1528 Robert Boston of West Winch requested his executors to 'bye a grave stone of marble for me the price of xxvj^{s} viij^{d} and it to be redy prepared *agaynst my yere daye* with my name redy written in brasse and a fygure of me in brasse above the wrytyng of the same' (80). The *yere daye*, or *obiit*, was the anniversary service for the dead. That such a disproportion of the wills should stipulate a year probably reflects the importance of this ceremony rather than the time needed for a stone, with or without a brass, to be ordered, made and delivered. At the other end of the scale, the *against mye vijth daye* of Henry Pye represented another such service. The 'month's mind' service will probably account for the hopes of Alexander Skarburght and Thomas Salter. This leaves the three wills requesting three months and six months. Perhaps this was the time in which the marblers could reasonably be expected to do their work, and gives a guide to the accuracy of dating by style. It was not prices but convenience and transport costs that made the local workshops attractive.

Many examples refer to burial beneath a stone already prepared. Ten of them (124–33) are widows seeking burial under their husbands' stones. This necessitated the lifting and replacing of the stone as anticipated by Cecylye Nark in 1530/1 'to the haynyng of the grave stone and layng of the grave stone agayne I gyve v^{s}' (133). Two husbands requested burial under their wives' stones (134, 135). Other relatives figure too. Peter Petirson, beer brewer of Norwich, in 1512 requested burial 'in the church of the Freer prechours in Norwich next the sepulture of my modir And I bequeth to the seid place for my buriall in the seid church soo that they ley that ston over me that now lieth over my modir xxvj^{s} viij^{d}' (136). In 1505 Thomas Marowe, serjeant-at-law, requested burial 'in the parisshe church of seynt Botolph wt out bisshopesgate of London w^{t} in the vaute under the tombe there where the body of William Marrowe my fader lieth buried Item I woll that myn executors provide a plate to be graven w^{t} scripture shewing the place of my burying and that plate to be sett upon the piler of the said tombe' (137). Why did Jasper Blake, gentleman of Wimbotsham, request in 1547 that he be buried 'under the stone of Nycholas Cornwallys next unto the sepulchre of my wyff' (138)? Perhaps Nicholas Cornwallis was his wife's first husband.

Eight examples of graves were prepared by male secular testators before their death (7, 83, 139–44), and another seventeen by priests (32, 145–59). Robert Arburgh alias Crane of Pulham Magdalen in 1543/4 requested his executors 'to leye the graveston which is Redy bowte wher as I shalbe buryed at such time as thei shall sse [sic] most convenyente' (144). William Wingfield's stone was waiting in the 'Priory' and not on the grave (7). George Pooly, parson of Attleborough, in 1540 wrote, '...& the ston y[t] lyeth w[t]in my howse to be leyd uppon me' (155). Perhaps the examples from the 1540s indicate testators taking advantage of ecclesiastical spoil.

Why was it necessary to prepare a memorial before death? There is a widespread belief that executors were untrustworthy. I have not gained that impression from reading thousands of wills. The whole testamentary procedure would have been impossible if this were the rule. Also, there is a difference between the disposal of property and the more personal preparation of the grave. Often priests had no close family ties, but enjoyed more intimate connections with the church building. This probably accounts for the disproportionate number of priests who prepared their graves before death. There are no references to the fashion for a *memento mori*. The delay in covering a grave is recorded in the Paston letters.[9]* Margaret Paston's husband died in 1466 and twelve years later nothing had been done. However, it is the stated unacceptability of this delay that points to its being exceptional. Margaret Paston is said to have requested that her gravestone and brass be prepared within a year as a reaction to that delay (117). Mainly for religious reasons a year has been demonstrated to be by far the most usual request.

There was the problem of dealing with the date of death before the testator had died. One way was to leave the brass undated. There are many undated brasses in Norfolk. The inscription for William Wingfield (7) bears no date. A second way was to have a plate added after death. This was probably more usual in the later sixteenth and seventeenth centuries. John Browne, whose undated will was proved in 1602/3, willed to be buried in St John de Sepulchre, Norwich, 'under the same stone as my well-beloved sister Mrs Winefride Browne at the cost and charges of my executor. Item I will that my executor shall cause to be engraven on a plate on the same stone best for the same purpose, my age, day of death and Anno domini, and that the said executor shall pay to him that shall do it, so as it is done fair and well, 10*s*' (161)[10]* (fig. 18). A third way was to leave blanks to be filled in later, especially suited for husbands buried after their wives. Robert Bunne in 1521/2 requested burial at Ranworth under his wife Beatrice's stone (135). The brass inscription remains, and the blanks for his date of death have not been completed (fig. 73). The brass can be dated by style to *c.* 1505–13, when Beatrice doubtless died and the stone and brass were prepared. Perhaps John Lowym, priest of Outwell, was alluding to adding dates in 1505: 'I geve to the belman for to amende my frendes graves 1[d]' (162). Adding a plate or adding a date was possibly indicated by Master John

73 Robert Bunne, d. 1521, and wife Beatrice, Ranworth, Norf., a 'Norwich 6a' style inscription.

74 Thomas Hoont, chaplain, 1510, Bintry, Norf.; a 'Norwich 6a' style chalice and inscription (notice the subtle differences between this and the 'Norwich 6' example, fig. 69).

Campe, parson of Cockfield, Suffolk, in 1525: 'I wyll that the scripture of my grave stone be made in true date' (147).

Detecting added dates, often completed in a different size or style, is not always easy. At Bintry, Thomas Hoont, rector, is commemorated by a chalice and a Latin inscription, dated 1510 but bearing no month (fig. 74). Style confirms this date. His will, dated 1536/7 and proved 1537, requested burial 'under my marbill stone in the chancell' (32). Clearly the brass was laid down long before his death. What had previously escaped detection is the small space following the final 'ten'. With Roman numerals he could have died from 1510 to 1548 necessitating only minor additions. The final superscribed 'o' in 'x^{o}' was a misleading mistake by the engraver.

New Perspectives

There is more that could be said – we have hardly touched on the part the relatively humble brass played in the journey of the soul – the elaborate funeral processions, the setting up of chantries, the religious bequests, and then the *orate pro anima*. Sometimes it seems people found it necessary to be remembered in curious ways. There are four examples (163–6) of testators making specific provision for people to lean or sit on their tombs. In 1513 Nicholas Beaupre of Outwell requested a vaulted altar tomb 'wth a marbill ston of iij fote in brede and in lenghe as the space will serve yt so that my grave be made as hye as the benche y[s] now and adionyng to the wall for the pepyll to syt upon wth scripturis and scochins accordyng as I have causid Thomas Gladwyn to peynt a clothe to ley upon my grave...Also I will that my iiij coshons coveryd w[t] greys skynnys Remayn in the churche one in my Deske and iij upon my grave stone to sit on' (163). One of the most important ways that wills can help the study of brasses is by giving new perspectives.

Abbreviations used in the Appendix

M.S. Mill Stephenson's number in his *A List of Monumental Brasses in the British Isles*, 1926 (Appendix 1938).

M.S.R. Mill Stephenson Revision number in the Monumental Brass Society's on-going work.

NcAC The Norwich Archdeaconry Court wills, kept in the Norfolk and Norwich Record Office in Norwich.

NCC. The Norwich Consistory Court wills, kept in the Norfolk and Norwich Record Office in Norwich.

PCC. The Prerogative Court of Canterbury wills, kept in the Public Record Office in London.

pd. proved.

Appendix of Will References

For each will is given the testator, the date of the will and the date it was proved, and the reference.

1. Roger Pall, bachelor of phisike, 30 May 1504, pd.?, PCC. Holgrave 13.
2. Thomas Powneder, 20 October 1525, pd. 15 December 1525, NCC. Brigges 204r [brass now at Christchurch Mansion Museum].
3. John Symondys the elder, 8 July 1502, pd. 3 August 1502, NCC. Popy 135.[M.S. IV at Cley but M.S. date wrong.]
4. Agnes Symondes, widow, 4 January 1511/2, pd. December 1512, NCC. Johnson 210r. [M.S. V at Cley.]
5. John Symons the elder, 8 July 1502, pd. 10 October 1502, PCC. Blamyr 20 [clearly the same as no.3.]
6. John Ayleward, parson, 17 July 1503, pd. 30 November 1503, NCC. Popy 380d.
7. William Wyngfeld, esq., 28 February 1509/10, pd. 29 April 1510, NCC. Spyltymbre 257r.
8. William Fak, 1485, pd. 24 January 1498, NCC. Multon 110r.
9. William Fuller, 24 September 1523, pd. 7 November 1523, PCC. Bodfield 14. [M.S. I at Castleacre.]

10. William Lamyn, parson, 16 March 1500/1 and pd.?, NCC. Popy 78r.
11. Elizabeth Swardeston, widow, 12 April 1507, pd. 1 May 1507, NCC. Rix 482r.
12. Robert Burnham, chaplain, 7 May 1512, pd. 12 July 1512, NCC. Johnson 138d.
13. John Sandwich, 14 April 1500, pd.?, NCC. Popy 2d.
14. John Ston, 6 May 1507, pd. 16 July 1507, NCC. Rix 439r.
15. Henry Larke, 6 April 1528, pd. 6 April 1529, NCC. Alpe 160r. Also at NCC. Godsalve 47, where 'I wyll that my grave be pavid wt flynt stone with a hart stone of marble in the middes therof wt a superscripcon of my name'.
16. Agnes Chamberlayn, singlewoman, 2 September 1539, pd. 28 October 1539, NCC. Cooke 18r.
17. Thomas Smyth, parson, 1524, pd.?, NCC. Brigges 169d.
18. William Nellson, curate, 15 January 1531/2, pd. 9 May 1531 (sic), NCC. Cooke 4d.
19. John Foxe, 3 September 1499, pd. 18 October 1502, NCC. Popy 169r.
20. John Rushburghe, 11 November 1518, pd. 19 September 1519, NCC. Gylys 174r.
21. Thomas Sharrington, esq., 15 October 1519, pd. 12 January 1524/5, NCC. Brigges 152d.
22. Thomas Gausell, esq., 14 September 1500, pd. 27 November 1500, NCC. Cage 117r.
23. Cecily Cannold, widow, 26 December 1503, pd. 9 January 1503/4, NCC. Popy 401d. [M.S. II at Poringland.]
24. William Wynne, 25 October 1505, pd. 18 November 1505, NCC. Rix 232r. [M.S. V at Upton.]
25. John Bukton, 29 January 1511/12, pd. 6 April 1512, NCC. Johnson 129d. [M.S. I at Wilton.]
26. John Isbellys, 28 March 1521, pd. 7 April 1521, NCC. Robynson 19r. [M.S.R. 38 at Norwich Museums, formerly M.S. I at St Etheldreda, Norwich.]
27. Robert Markant, 1 February 1522/3, pd. 26 September 1525, NCC. Brigges 175d. [M.S. II at Brisley.]
28. William Spriggye, 8 January 1534/5, pd. 16 April 1535, NCC. Godsalve 22r. [M.S. V at Strumpshaw.]
29. Robert Riches, 6 June 1534, pd. 21 June 1534, NCC. Platfoote 109d. [M.S. VII at Ludham.]
30. John Mottes, 3 March 1533/4, pd. 10 June 1534, NCC. Platfoote 115r. [M.S. I at Thorpe-next-Haddiscoe.]
31. Henry Magys, 28 September 1520, pd. 6 October 1520, NCC. Coppinger 33d. [Lost brass, M.S.R. 10 at Aldeby.]
32. Thomas Hunt, parson, 20 January 1536/7, pd. 25 Oct.1537, NCC. Underwood 5d. [M.S. I at Bintry.]
33. Robert Hemmyng, citizen and alderman, 8 April 1541, pr. 26 April 1541, NCC. Hyll 127r. [Lost brass but noted by Revd Francis Blomefield in *An Essay towards a History of Norfolk*, 2nd and more complete edition 1805 to 1810.]
34. John Garneys, 20 July 1522, pd. 8 August 1524, NCC. Brigges 138r. [M.S. I at Kenton, Suffolk.]
35 Thomas Chyld, 14 January 1509/10, pd. 17 March 1509/10, NCC. Spyltymbre 235r.
36. Thomas Abbys, 7 March 1532/3, pd.19 February 1538/9, NCC. Cooke 159d.
37. Edmund Wethyr, 10 February 1524/5, pd. 6 May 1528, NCC. Heyward 156d.

38. Thomas Gerard, parson, 26 July 1504, pd. 7 August 1507, NCC. Rix 464r. [M.S. III at Stokesby.]
39. John Smyth, parson, 11 May 1536, pd. 1 August 1537, NCC. Godsalve 234r.
40. Elizabeth Thompson, 17 October 1514, pd.15 December 1514, NCC.Coppinger 58.
41. Henry Bothom, 20 December 1512, pd. 14 March 1512/13, NCC. Johnson 157d.
42. Katheryne Toddenham, 8 October 1509, pd. 30 April 1510, NCC. Spyltymbre 255r.
43. John Felde, parson, 14 July 1508, pd. 10 October 1508, NCC. Spyltymbre 101r. [M.S. II at Belaugh, near Wroxham.]
44. John Flatman, 12 July 1520, pd. 18 August 1520, NCC. Robynson 130.
45. Robert Worlysth, 1 July 1517, pd. 14 October 1517, NCC. Brigges 51r.
46. William Alexander, 1 February 1524/5, pd.7 September 1525, NCC. Heyward 16d.
47. Juan Carre, vicar, 19 December 1530, pd. 6 April 1532, NCC. Attmere 204d.
48. John White, 20 August 1529, pd. 12 March 1530/1, NCC. Platfoote 29d.
49. Nicholas Purdy, 18 January 1489/90, pd.?, NCC. Wolman 37d.
50. John Glaven, 13 February 1504/5, pd. 27 January 1505/6, PCC. Holgrave 42.
51. Nicholas Nobbis, 28 January 1514/15, pd. 13 November 1515, NCC. Spurlinge 137d.
52. Thomas Johnson, 2 June 1533, pd. 5 September 1533, NCC. Platfoote 133.
53. Thomas Stywarde, gent., 26 March 1511, pd. 6 May 1511, NCC. Johnson 29r.
54. William Rushburgh, 22 October 1512, pd. 23 July 1513, NCC. Johnson 169d.
55. Geffery Aldwen, 18 June 1521, pd. 28 June 1521, NCC. Alblaster 57r.
56. Richard Harrye, 28 February 1434/5, pd.?, NCC. Godsalve 176d.
57. Robert Stywarde, 23 January 1536/7, pd. 1 June 1537, NCC. Underwood 67r.
58. Thomas Fuller, 9 December 1534, pd. 17 December 1540, NCC. Cooke 82r.
59. Thomas Brygg esq., 21 May 1494, pd. 12 November 1494, NCC. Wolman 202d.
60. Thomas Lynsted, 20 September 1520, pd. 31 October 1520, NCC. Alblaster 8d.
61. Marion Belaws, 20 September 1501, pd. 24 January 1501/2, NcAC. Fuller als. Roper 334r
62. John Baret, 3 December 1500, pd. 9 January 1500/1, NCC. Cage 151d.
63. Robert Franceys, 16 January 1505/6, pd. 2 April 1506, NCC. Rix 320d.
64. Richard Goodman, parson, 1 March 1514/5, pd. 13 April 1515, NCC. Brigges 5r.
65. William Brette, vicar, 17 June 1521, pd. 29 July 1521, NCC. Alblaster 70r.
66. William Bale, clarke, 20 March 1542/3, pd.?, NCC. Cooke 217d.
67. William Hagges, 6 June 1537, pd. 21 July 1537, NCC. Mingaye 130r.
68. Edmund Wright, 24 May 1505, pd. 5 June 1505, NCC. Rix 175r.
69. Robert Deen, 21 October 1496, pd. 4 January 1496/7, NCC. Multon 30r.
70. Richard Davy, parson, 4 August 1535, pd.?, NCC. Godsalve 185r.
71. Nicholas Gegebald, 12 May 1460, pd. 18 July 1466, NCC. Brosyerd 192d.
72. John Revis, parson, 20 June 1518, pd. 10 July 1518, NCC. Brigges 62r.
73. Dame Jone Blakeney, widow, 16 March 1502/3, pd. 20 June 1503, NCC. Popy 315d.
74. John Nunne, 23 June 1503, pd. 6 May 1504, NCC. Popy 465r.
75. William Wynne of Upton, 25 October 1505, pd. 18 November 1505, NCC. Rix 232v.

76. John Bukton, 29 January 1511/12, pd. 6 April 1512, NCC. Johnson 129d. [M.S. I at Wilton.]
77. Richard Heyhow, 17 May 1509, pd. 20 April 1513, NCC. Johnson 239r.
78. Ellen Dorand, widow, 8 November 1514, pd. 14 December 1514, NCC. Spurlinge 38r. [M.S. II at Barnham Broom.]
79. John Thurston, 12 August 1519, pd. 17 June 1522, NCC. Alblaster 133d.
80. Robert Boston, 3 May 1528, pd. 12 June 1528, NCC. Palgrave 23d.
81. Thomas Bevys, 10 August 1535, pd. 20 September 1538, NCC. Attmere 312r.
82. John Knapys, 27 December 1532, pd. 22 January 1532/3, NCC. Mingaye 29d.
83. Robert Carvile, citizen and mercer of London, burial at St Benet-at-Holme, Norfolk, 26 October 1504, pd. 10 March 1504/5, PCC. Holgrave 27.
84. Jeffery Nors, 26 August 1505, pd. 12 November 1505, NcAC. Fuller als. Roper 371d.
85. John Cobbe, 29 May 1502, pd. 12 November 1502, NCC. Popy 179d.
86. William Grigges, 16 January 1485, pd. 7 March 1499/1500, NCC. Wight 61r.
87. Robert Foster, 23 May 1507, pd. 16 August 1507, NCC. Rix 487r.
88. John Sabern, 2 May 1521, pd. 21 February 1521/2, NCC. Heyward 41r.
89. John Jewell, citizen and alderman, 16 March 1499/1500, pd. 19 May 1500, PCC. Moone 2.
90. Gregory Fyllyng, 13 May 1494, pd. 27 July 1494, NCC. Wolman 184d.
91. William Nottyng, priest living in London, 1 June 1503, pd. 22 November 1503, PCC. Blamyr 30.
92. Roger Tymperley, 14 September 1498, pd. 2 May 1499, NCC. Sayve 11d.
93. Henry Mownford, clerk, 10 September 1518, pd. 20 September 1518, NCC. Gylys 82r. [M.S.R. 57 at Norwich Museums, formerly M.S. I at St Mary Coslany, Norwich.]
94. William Wright, 26 May 1513, pd. 15 July 1513, NCC. Johnson 225d.
95. William Reve, priest, 22 April 1525, pd. 28 June 1525, NCC. Brigges 168d.
96. Jhon Colyn als. Thetford, 12 May 1538, pd.?, NCC. Mingaye 183d.
97. John Beteson, clerk, vicar of Northales, Suffolk, 6 April 1531, pd. 17 July 1532.
98. Alexander Skarburght, parson, 25 July 1526, pd. 29 July 1531, NCC. Platfoote 24d.
99. Thomas Mason, 1 August 1540, pd. 16 May 1542, NCC. Cooke 139d.
100. Thomas Browse, 6 July 1528, pd. 22 October 1528, NCC. Palgrave 34.
101. James Jermy, gent., 9 February 1518/19, pd. 1 April 1519, NCC. Gylys 120d.
102. Edmund Holkham, esq., 10 April 1484, pd. 10 January 1484/5, NCC. A Caston 229r.
103. Richard Ferror, citizen and alderman, 18 December 1514, pd. 20 December 1515, NCC. Spurlinge 168d.
104. Bartholomew Reed, knight, citizen and alderman of London, 19 October 1505, pd. 26 November 1505, PCC. Holgrave, 40, 41.
105. Roger Lestrange, kt, 7 October 1505, pd. 12 February 1505/6, PCC. Adeane 2.
106. Robert Framoos, 27 January 1513/14, pd. 8 November 1514, NCC. Spurlinge 34d.
107. Elyn Elwar, 26 March 1526 !, pd. 1 May 1525, NCC. Groundesborough 127d.
108. William Attemere, 18 April 1531, pd. 5 May 1531, NCC. Alpe 65r.
109. Lewes Brady, vicar, 28 February 1533/4, pd. 3 April 1534, NCC. Attmere 226r.

110. Thomas Parker, 2 July 1537, pd. 3 November 1537, NCC. Underwood 32r.
111. Godfrey Lawter, Yeoman of the Crown, gent., 10 May 1544, pd. 15 March 1545/6, NCC. Punting 189d.
112. Henry Pye, 26 February 1529/30, pd. 17 March 1529/30, NCC. Attmere 98r.
113. Thomas Salter, clerke, 31 August 1558, pd. 19 December 1558, PCC. Welles 13.
114. Elizabeth Yaxley, 25 January 1530/1, pd. 25 March 1533, NCC. Platfoote 104d.
115. James Cootes, 11 November 1536, pd. 23 November 1536, NCC. Hyll 56d.
116. Richard Gogney, 14 September 1539, pd. 16 December 1539, NCC. Godsalve 275r.
117. Margaret Paston, widow, 4 February 1481/2, pd. 18 December 1484, NCC. A. Caston 224d.
118. Hawica Stubbe, 8 January 1489/90, pd. 28 March 1505, NCC. Rix 126r.
119. William Harmer, 28 July 1517, pd. 11 August 1517, NCC. Gylys 31r.
120. William Wright, 3 October 1525, pd. 3 January 1525/6, NCC. Brigges 183r.
121. John Wroote, 4 January 1533/4, pd. 20 January 1533/4, NCC. Platfoote 97d.
122. Henry Vincent, 20 February 1545/6, pd. 20 May 1546, NCC. Whitefoote 155d.
123. Christopher Spratt, 10 May 1546, pd. 23 May 1546, NCC. Deyns 242r.
124. Joan Harneys, widow, 12 May 1492, pd.?, NCC. Wolman 150d.
125. Katherine Kerre, widow, 22 April 1497, pd. 6 June 1498, NCC. Multon 89d.
126. Joanne Methwold, 2 February 1497/8, pd. 19 February 1499/1500, PCC. Moone 6.
127. Margaret Shelton, 23 December 1499, pd. 3 December 1500, NCC. Cage 99r.
128. Agnes Tymperley, widow and gentylwoman, 1505, pd. 20 January 1506/7, NCC. Garnon 103r.
129. Katerine Bukenham, widow, 7 January ?, pd. 21 May 1510, NCC. Multon 166r.
130. Alice Hattar, widow, 14 November 1508, pd. 10 October 1511, NCC. Johnson 76d.
131. Alice Crome, widow, 4 May 1516, pd. 12 January 1518/9, NCC. Gylys 94r.
132. Dame Elizabeth Gelgit, vowess, 25 May 1528, pd.?, NCC. Palgrave 295d.
133. Cecylye Nark, widow, 11 February 1530/1, pd. 3 February 1530/1 !, NCC. Alpe 15d.
134. Thomas Irby, 20 April 1504, pd. 18 February 1504/5, PCC. Holgrave 26.
135. Robert Bunne, 21 January 1521/2, pd. 5 February 1521/2, NCC. Alblaster 152r. [M.S. IV at Ranworth.]
136. Peter Petirson, 1 September 1512, pd. 31 August 1513, NCC. Johnson 236.
137. Thomas Marowe, 31 March 1505, pd. 10 April 1505, PCC. Holgrave 27.
138. Jasper Blake, 17 July 1547, pd. 22 August 1547, NCC Wymer 70d.
139. William Calthorpe, knight, 31 May 1494, pd. 27 November 1494, NCC. Wolman 206d.
140. John Glemham, 4 August 1499 ?, pd. 31 March 1500, NCC. Wight 74d.
141. William Payne als. Paynot, London, gent., 26 April 1508, pd. 2 June 1508, PCC. Benett 1.
142. John de Veer, Earl of Oxford, 10 April 1509, pd. 10 May 1513, PCC. Fetiplace 11.
143. John Parsey, 28 May 1509, pd. 20 November 1509, PCC. Benett 22.
144. Robert Arburgh als. Crane, 20 January 1543/4, pd. 18 September 1546, NCC. Whitefoote 260d.

145. Richard Braunche, clerk, Master of the College of St Mary at Mettingham, 31 May 1506, pd. 19 October 1507, NCC. Spyltymbre 33r.
146a. John Gosselyn, 10 June 1505, pd. 6 September 1505, NCC. Spyltymbre 82r.
146b. John Dow, parson, 25 July 1518, pd. 31 July 1518, NCC. Gylys 65d.
147. John Campe, parson, 11 September 1525, pd. 20 January 1525/6, NCC. Brigges 184d.
148. John Skarlet, rector, 1526, pd. 20 July 1526, NCC. Heyward 33r.
149. John Radclyffe, parson, 18 December 1523, pd. 14 January 1523/4, NCC. Herman 38r.
150. William Richers, vicar, 2 January 1530/1, pd. 3 May 1531, NCC. Alpe 84–87.
151. John Oxcliff, parson, 30 August 1533, pd.?, NCC. Godsalve 40r.
152. John Gylys, priest, 28 August 1533, pd. 1 March 1535/6, NCC. Godsalve 135r.
153. Raffe Portar, parson, 28 September 1540, pd.?, NCC. Attmere 337r.
154. Robert Porter, parson, 18 May 1545, pd. 11 February 1545/6, NCC. Attmere 415d.
155. George Pooly, parson, 25 September 1540, pd.?, NCC. Hyll 146d.
156. Peter Dye, parson, 20 February 1545/6, pd. 16 October 1546, NCC. Hyll 242d.
157. Henry Taylor, priest, 1539, pd. 5 August 1540, NCC. Cooke 49r.
158. Robert Porter, parson, 18 August 1545, pd. 12 February 1545/6, NCC. Punting 196r.
159 John Neell, dean of St Mary in the Fields, Norwich, 15 November 1497, pd. 12 August 1499. NCC Wight 4d.
161. John Browne, ?, pd. 21 January 1602/3, NCC. Candler 178.
162. John Lowym, priest, 21 April 1505, pd. 15 April 1506, NCC. Rix 344r.
163. Nicholas Beaupre, esq., 21 December 1513, pd. 29 January 1514/5, NCC. Spurlinge 93r.
164. Edmund Jenney, knight, 1522, pd. 21 December 1522, NCC. Brigges 108r.
165. William Ugge, parson, 7 October 1560, pd.?, NCC. Jagges 172r.
166. William Wutton, Baron of King's Exchequer, 16 January 1526/7, pd. 11 November 1528, PCC. Porch 40b.

CHAPTER 5

The Analysis of Style in Monumental Brasses

MALCOLM NORRIS

The systematic study of style in monumental brasses, and the classification of brasses by style in preference to social groupings, costume similarities or period, is arguably the most important development in the subject's research since the Second World War, and the most far-reaching in its potential influence. While analysis of and controversies over style have concerned only a small number of scholars, the findings have already profoundly changed our understanding of brasses, and are belatedly altering well-established interpretations.

What style is, and why its perception is important, are not essentially difficult questions. As Greenwood has written, 'In theory, analysing brasses by style is simple, the putting of like with like, but the large number of brasses, the difficulty of deciding which features are stylistically significant and which are merely a fashion of the locality or period, complicate the matter'.[1] The term 'style' in the context of brasses refers to the particular idiosyncrasies and conventions of an artist or workshop in the design of figures, accessories, and the arrangement and lettering of inscriptions. Style has its origins in the artist's or craftsman's observation and representation, reinforced by repetition on the part of the originator, or by others copying models given to them, or following the training they had received in the course of a disciplined apprenticeship. As Emmerson has argued with good evidence, 'how a craftsman drew the design depended as much on his training as on any precise model in front of him. When the old training ceased to be given . . . an older craftsman could continue much as before, but younger men sought models elsewhere'.[2] There is plentiful documentary evidence of patterns being used in the Tournai workshops, and the use of drawings in allied crafts in Britain such as that of glass painting.[3] No large-scale design of a brass has survived, though the proof of the use of a reversible template for two independent shroud brasses of *c.* 1510 is almost conclusive,[4]* and the subtle modification and adaptation of designs indicate most convincingly the existence of detailed references. Once style is established and surviving examples related to it, the product of an engraver or an association of engravers is given clear definition.

A difficulty which has caused a reluctance to accept the validity of stylistic differentiation is that style is concerned with the manner in which for example faces, hands, drapery, canopy crockets, grass and lettering are portrayed, not necessarily the overall design or arrangement. Page-Phillips has pointed out that: 'Characteristics of a style ... often lie in a small detail such as the method of showing mail. Links of mail are not only small but tedious to engrave, and different shorthand was adopted by different artists to convey the same original',[5] and he went on to use the varying treatments of tasset hinges to illustrate such contrasts. Especially instructive are the pages of besagews, gauntlets, poleyns, sabatons and other details illustrated by Kent, the revealing arrangements of drapery folds and distinctive facial features contrasted by Emmerson and Badham, and the inscription lettering compared by Greenwood.[6]

Particular arrangements were popular with certain workshops and it is easy to regard them as part of the style. The presentation of female gowns caught up in front or back to facilitate walking, the placing of shields directly below and in contact with inscription plates, and the presentation of hands held wide open as an *orans* with the palms exposed, are good examples, frequently attributed to provincial, especially East Anglian, provenance. But these features can be misleading. Richard Amondesham (*c.* 1490) at Ealing, Middlesex, is an excellent case of the last, but is an undoubted London product on the evidence of style. Likewise a small woman at Aldenham, Herts. (*c.* 1535), though with the provincial characteristics of mob cap and raised gown, is unmistakably a London series brass.

Style is concerned with the detail of treatment and it is accordingly difficult to simulate. Once identified, its message is uncompromising. It is accordingly surprising how such an important aspect of the subject, and a basic tool of art historians, should have been neglected for so long. It is in part explained by conservatism and the demands of alternative interests, and in part by the slow and partial development of the study of style in brasses itself until the mid-1970s. A summary of its evolution helps to explain what has been achieved.

The most important nineteenth-century book on brasses, Haines' *Manual* (1861) (see fig. 19), was a broadly focused study, its introduction primarily classifying brasses by period and costume. But despite his objective to present the subject as a whole, Haines was a very shrewd observer of his resources, and his descriptions and footnote lists were frequently concerned with stylistic peculiarities even though he did not fully grasp their implication. Statements such as 'the bascinet is no less acutely pointed, the part over the forehead, the lower edge of the gorget, the cuffs of the gauntlets etc, are often elegantly ornamented with trefoils, the gauntlets frequently do not cover the last joints of the fingers' and 'the edges of the armour are represented with double lines',[7] record a particular manner of presentation, which Kent was later to identify as peculiarities of the London 'D' workshop. Similarly Haines made a brief but very perceptive summary of the characteristics and probable sources of provincial work, one which is particularly impressive in the context of present knowledge.

Unfortunately this excellent start was not consolidated. Druitt, properly concerned with armour, dress and vestments in his *Costume on Brasses* (1906), made no attempt to investigate the problems of sources, contrasting London-made brasses with those of the provinces and dismissing the latter – 'The most important school of engravers was that settled in London, who supplied the greater number of brasses. Provincial engravers, as a rule, show inferior workmanship...'[8] His position was reinforced by Macklin (fig. 20) in 1907, who emphasised the 'great similarity between brasses of the same style and period, although geographically they may lie far apart'[9] and attributed this to a famous workshop responsible for the 'normal type', divergencies from which were assignable to the provincial centres. Consistent with this view Macklin gave little attention to provincial styles, considerably less than Haines.

Between the two world wars the study of brasses in Britain was most effectively led by Stephenson (fig. 21) and Griffin, the former having an unusual familiarity with the examples, and consequently developing an expert perception of associations and comparative dating. It is nevertheless a fact that both were more familiar with brasses in the Home Counties than those of the north-east and east, and neither methodically recorded or quantified their stylistic observations. The result was an intuitive analysis, very effective when concentrating on the familiar, less so when attention was reduced. Mill Stephenson's *List*, (1926), uses the terms 'local', 'Eastern Counties type' and 'East Anglian school' without specific definition, and in some cases erroneously. Uncertainty was concealed with generalised dating of *c.* 1510 and *c.* 1520, and in some entries the unusual provoked confusion. An important case is the treatment of the rectangular plate brasses at St Peter, Colchester, two of which, to John Sayre and his wife Elizabeth, 1530 (see detail, fig. 75), and Agnes Woodthorpe, 1553, were clearly engraved *c.* 1575 and laid retrospectively, though with notable attempted antiquarianism in the first. Elizabeth Sayre wears a butterfly

75 John Sayre, Alderman, of Colchester, is shown on this family brass at St Peter's church in that city. Although he died in 1509, the brass was not made until about 1575, and attempts to show him and his family in correct costume for their time (detail).

head-dress, and all the figures have a late fifteenth-century appearance. What is conspicuously absent are the stylistic peculiarities of any series of brasses of the second quarter of the sixteenth century. Interestingly, Agnes Woodthorpe's first husband, Alyn Dister (d. 1537), shown on her Colchester brass, has his own memorial at Lavenham, Suffolk, and Stephenson correctly rejected the 1534 date there, proposing *c.* 1560. In their joint *List of Kent Brasses* (1923), Griffin and Stephenson had an opportunity to examine Kentish local work in detail, which they declined, attention to the subject being general and brief, confined to effigial and cross-brass evidence, and consequently including as 'local' a seemingly indifferent London product of 1532 at West Malling.

Insofar as there was a conscious approach to style it was attempted by d'Elboux and Esdaile with research into seventeenth-century brasses, and by Torr who associated brasses unsystematically but on a stylistic basis, noting significant similarities.

The immediate post-war period brought published cases by Torr, interesting studies by Linnell on Norfolk chalice brasses, which drew attention to style and lettering, and the identification by Owen Evans of the 'Fermer' series of brasses (e.g. fig. 76), in which association of the obverses was motivated by a desire to inspect the reverses! The really important contributions, however, were the article by Kent, 'Monumental Brasses – a New Classification of Military Effigies', (1949), and the lecture and study by Page-Phillips, 'A Sixteenth-century Workshop' (written in 1958, publication still forthcoming). The primary purpose of Kent's analysis was to refute Druitt's 'London school' hypothesis, stating 'I hope . . . to show that during the period under consideration the brasses generally attributed to London were not the products of any "school" but of several unconnected firms. Each had its own traditions of design, and its effigies developed along lines independent of those of its competitors'.[10] Avoiding the difficulties of analysing the earliest brasses, which did not appear to survive in sufficient numbers to establish series, and the great number and confusion of early sixteenth-century memorials, Kent confined his analysis to the armed figures from the period *c.* 1360 to *c.* 1485. Though limited, this was a seminal work, in which he identified convincingly six series of London engraved brasses designated 'A' to 'F', and identified a number of unusual cases requiring further explanation.

Page-Phillips, influenced by Kent, and by Evans' success in identifying the Fermer series, made a detailed study for the period *c.* 1535 to *c.* 1612, grouping brasses of London origin not in terms of a number of workshops but as the evolution of styles within a major workshop of evident integrity, its products united not only by style but the common use of earlier brasses derived from the dissolution of religious houses and chantries. His investigation ended with the apparent assumption of

76 *The brass of Richard Fermer and his wife Anne, 1552, at Easton Neston, Northants., after which the 'Fermer' series of brasses is named.*

the workshop and its engravers by the emigré Gerard Johnson and his sons. Whereas Kent had only examined armed figures, Page-Phillips listed all brasses, drawing attention to the value of inscription lettering for typographic analysis.[11] The findings were surprisingly different, Kent establishing rival firms, Page-Phillips the dominance though not monopoly of a single source of production, suggestive of radical organisational change during the sixteenth century.

The lack of interest among the older members of the Monumental Brass Society was unfortunate, as no prominence was given to these studies, and that of Page-Phillips has not, as yet, been published. Yet in contrast the interest of younger members was very strongly aroused. Some reference was made to the value of stylistic analysis by Bouquet in *Church Brasses* (1956), but his approach to style was speculative and confused, not only failing to benefit from Kent's work, but introducing bizarre associations, and attributing evident London products such as Oulton, Suffolk (1478), and Rougham, Norfolk (1472), to East Anglian sources. The intention was good, but the effect regressive. Attention to Kent's work, and to the benefits of focusing on style and wider comparative sources, was finally drawn by Norris in the widely circulated *Brass Rubbing* (1965). This publication both coincided with and reinforced a strongly shared interest among a group of members of the Monumental Brass Society, whose exchanges, differences, yet purposeful collaboration made style since 1970 a leading issue in the study of these memorials.

The article 'Haines's Cambridge School of Brasses' (1971)[12] by Greenwood set new standards in the examination of provincial work, considering all the evidence then available, examining the style of the examples identified with particular regard to lettering, including a distribution map and illustrations chosen to exhibit points of style, rather than general artistic merit. Greenwood followed this by a profusely illustrated chapter in *The Brasses of Norfolk Churches* (1976), establishing a total of seven series produced by Norwich engravers, subdividing these to permit highly accurate stylistic dating, and providing a framework on which to link documentary evidence relating to marblers. One page integrates the series divisions and subdivisions, estimated periods of production, sample lettering and examples of chalice brasses or indents belonging to each series. This chapter further discussed brasses of Cambridge and Suffolk workmanship in the county, and another by Norris described and classified brasses from London sources.

A further important innovation in 1976 was the modestly – but effectively – produced *Specimens of Lettering* by Badham, Blair and Emmerson, approaching style through lettering relating to early separate-inlay Lombardic letters (fig. 53), lettering from London series *c.* 1420–75, and lettering from the York and Suffolk workshops, all in preparation for more extensive research. Blair's analysis established for the first time that the separate-inlay letters had been cast in quantity by independent suppliers.

More general works gave style a greater emphasis, reflecting the growing interest. Page-Phillips in the concise and popular revision of *Macklin's Monumental Brasses* (1969) used two chapters to describe London and provincial workshops. Norris in the Europe-wide study *Monumental Brasses – The Craft* (1978) and *The Memorials* (1977) – attempted to establish stylistic guidelines for most English brasses. The particular value of the presentation lay in the extent of the coverage, the integration of what had been fragmented, the wealth of illustrations with series references included on captions, an initial revision of faulty dating, and examination of neglected periods, notably the early sixteenth-century London brasses, and provincial work in the north-east, the west and Kent. While concentrating on armed figures, series were traced more widely and typical civilian, ecclesiastic, shroud and emblem examples identified. The limitation of the analysis lay in its unevenness, some regions or periods having been researched in depth, others being the findings of original but limited investigation, concentrating on effigies.

Further accomplished specialist studies reduced the uncertainties, benefiting from a widening range of resource evidence. Emmerson in the article 'Monumental Brasses: London Design *c.* 1420–85'[13] returned to the fifteenth-century brasses originally examined by Kent, but classified all figures, illustrating his development of series with excellent details of faces, drapery, canopy ornaments and lettering, and relating documentary evidence of known marblers to the time-span of the series. Not only did he consolidate part of Kent's work, ensuring more accurate dating, but he also made important observations on the implications of changes of style, most especially in the confusion following the decline of a well-established workshop, as apparently happened after the decease of the notable marbler, John Essex, in 1465.

Badham in *Brasses from the North East* (1979), reappraised a group of provincial workshops, for the first time clearly differentiating York products from those of workshops probably in Boston, and identifying survivals from separate sources in Northumberland and Durham. Four York series were listed (e.g. fig. 77) to which another was subsequently added.[14] Two series were described from the Fens (e.g. fig. 78), the first of which is of unusual interest, being derived from London patterns. This association had already been established, but the scale of production had not. Further work revealed that incised slabs were made to the same patterns.[15] Badham was an innovator in the extensive use made of indent evidence and of rubbings of brasses now lost or

77 *At Allerton Mauleverer, Yorks., this brass from the 'York 1' workshop tradition depicts Sir John Mauleverere, d. 1400, and his wife Eleanor. Posture and draughtsmanship distinguish it from contemporary London brasses (e.g. fig. 98).*

damaged, that at North Witham (1421) being of critical value to Fens dating. The same author in 'The Suffolk School of Brasses, (1980),[16] further analysed the various series from 1475 to 1556 attributed to workshops in Bury St Edmunds (e.g. fig. 79), again making particular use of old rubbings and records, as well as the identification of significant conventions and letter forms.

The most recent analysis of style, greatly advancing understanding of the oldest and in many respects the finest brasses in Britain, is the centenary volume of the Monumental Brass Society, *The Earliest English Brasses* (1987). Style is examined by Binski and Blair, the former giving particular emphasis to stylistic connections and comparative art references, the latter greatly enriching the small number of surviving brasses with a wealth of indent evidence, demonstrating how informative indents are in the light of stylistic awareness. The whole is given particular force by the care and scholarship of the writers, and the

78 A prosperous wool-merchant, Nicholas Robertson, shown with his wives Isabel and Alice in a locally made 'Fens' style brass at Algarkirk, Lincs., of 1498. The Virgin and Child appear above.

breadth of resources, especially lost memorials, sculpted effigies and, to a limited extent, incised slabs. It is interesting to recall that Kent avoided this period on account of the paucity of examples, yet its latest assessment is an admirable extension and refinement of the approach that he initiated. It is one that is currently under further review in the light of a detailed analysis of incised slabs. The study of style has advanced greatly in twenty-five years, and with it understanding of brasses in their monumental and artistic context.

The benefits of the awareness of style and its systematic observation and analysis have many aspects. The primary and general benefit has been to focus and discipline the examination of individual brasses. Brasses are studied more rigorously and an apparently uninteresting piece of shop work is likely to attract far more attention than in the past. The style-conscious observer examines the brass as a whole rather than its superficial attributes, because it belongs to a particular series or group within a series. It reinforces what is known of the series, or by its discrepancies expands our knowledge of the series. Benefits can, however, be more specifically defined in terms of origin, dating, guidelines to the identity of engravers, indent analysis, re-used brass analysis and antiquarianism in monumental brass design.

There is now a far clearer perception of what is English and what foreign, and what is London and what provincial work pertained as late as 1960, and the study of style has made an essential contribution. Sir James Mann and others argued that the Septvans brass at Chartham, Kent (fig. 117), was French,[17] and Hartshorne concluded after a very detailed examination that Sir Hugh Hastings (d. 1347) at Elsing, Norfolk (fig. 131), was foreign, 'possibly Flemish but more likely French work'.[18] Both are now recognised as English, the current argument over Elsing being London versus East Anglian provenance. In contrast the now obviously foreign inscription of Sir Alexander de Irvyn of Drum (d. 1457) at St Nicholas East church, Aberdeen (fig. 80), was not noted as such. The inscription of Sir Ralph de Knevynton (d. 1370) at Aveley, Essex (fig. 23), is seen as of English origin in contrast to the Flemish plate with the effigy. Classification of brasses on the continent of Europe has similarly benefited. The clear differentiation of English provincial products from those of London and each series from others has changed the description of many brasses.

Reference has been made to Stephenson's reliance on experience and judgement rather than on a precise typology. Advances towards the latter have justified many revisions. Edmund Grene and wife (*c.* 1478), Hunstanton, Norfolk, is a notable case, a slightly unconventional representation but undoubtedly London 'F' series. Its location encouraged a 'local' description. In contrast early Norwich series examples at Sall (1453 and d. 1441) were treated as London work. Ralph Elcock (d. 1510) at Tong, Shropshire, was attributed to a local source, presumably because the brass is indifferently engraved, but there is nothing Midland about its style. Anthony Hansart (d. 1507) at March, Cambs., was apparently designated 'local' on the appearance of the inscription, which is unusual, but the figures are evidently London 'F' (fig. 34; cf. fig. 68).

The progress made is admirably illustrated in our understanding of the brass of Joan, Lady Cromwell, Tattershall, Lincs. Stephenson dated this splendid brass *c.* 1470, and explained its obviously Norwich style inscription as 'added', unable apparently to accept that so fine a figure could be provincial. Norris by 1966 was, on general figure style principles, convinced of its Norwich provenance, and so described it, but had not made the series analysis to correct the dating. Greenwood has shown the 1492 date of the inscription to be entirely consistent. A comparable evolution of uncertainty has occurred with the Fens 1 series, first treated as London products with the odd provincial copy, but now shown by Badham to be a coherent series, probably engraved in Boston between the dates *c.* 1408 and *c.* 1435.

Greater accuracy in dating has been an even more extensive benefit than the classification of origins. Broadly, systematic analysis has established a number of well-defined series, which may be summarised

79 A Suffolk-style brass, the heraldically garbed Henry Everard, 1524, at Denstone. Although he is clearly standing in a field, his head rests on a crested helmet (cf. fig. 31).

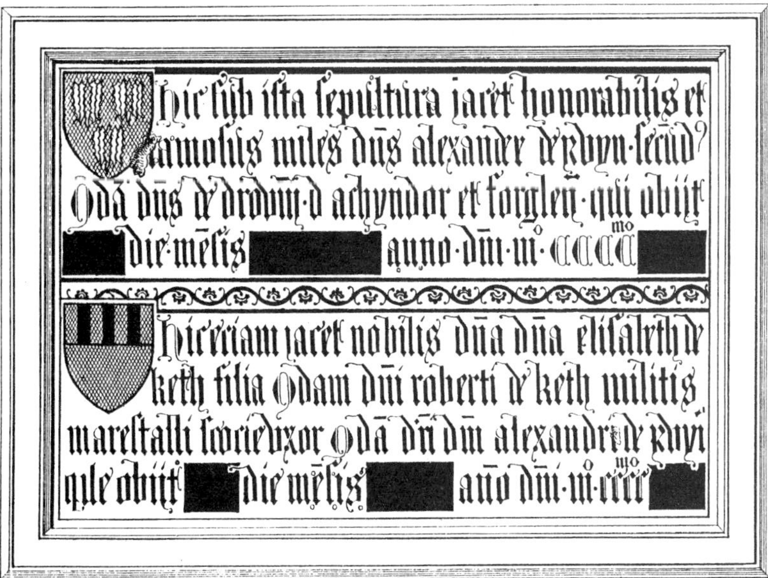

80 A curious inscription of Flemish origin in Aberdeen. It was ordered for Sir Alexander de Irvyn and his wife before his death in 1457, but no one in Scotland could be found capable of filling in the dates to match the rest of the lettering.

as follows, though the first four, 'B' since 1420, 'D', 'E', 'F' up to *c.* 1485, and the latter stages of 'G', have been the most highly researched. Notwithstanding, the findings are being tested, and 'Seymour' for example seems likely to have had an earlier beginning.

London series		
Ashford	*c.* 1273–1305	e.g. figs 7, 63
Camoys/Septvans	*c.* 1305–1335	e.g. figs 5, 9, 10, 117
Seymour	*c.* 1333–1350	e.g. fig. 6
Hastings	*c.* 1347–1348	e.g. figs 118, 131
'A'	*c.* 1358–1410	e.g. figs 44, 81
'B'	*c.* 1360–1467	e.g. figs 1, 2, 16, 25, 32, 35, 82, 98, 120
'C'	*c.* 1380–1410	e.g. figs 24, 31, 83
'D'	*c.* 1410–1498	e.g. figs 22, 29, 37, 40, 46, 84, 95, 96, 99, 122
'E'	*c.* 1420–1452	e.g. figs 85, 94
'F'	*c.* 1475–1535	e.g. figs 30, 33, 34, 59, 86, 97
'G'	*c.* 1500–1585	e.g. figs 14, 41, 45, 67, 75, 76, 87, 96, 123, 127–8, 129, 132–3
'H'	*c.* 1555–1585	e.g. fig. 88
Southwark	*c.* 1585–1640	e.g. figs 15, 18, 43, 89
Marshall	*c.* 1630–1660	e.g. figs 36, 42, 90

During this span periods of unusual inconsistency have been identified, namely *c.* 1348–*c.* 1355, *c.* 1410–*c.* 1415, and most particularly *c.* 1463–*c.* 1476 (Emmerson's 'Sub B' group, e.g. fig. 3), the first in the aftermath of the Black Death, the others apparently following the decline of important workshops. Series 'F' and 'G' appear to integrate *c.* 1535, and that of 'G' is absorbed by the Southwark workshop of Gerard Johnson, probably as a consequence of the dissolution of the Marblers Company in 1585. There are of course a small minority of brasses that fall outside these classifications, and the period *c.* 1500–*c.* 1535 has only been approached.

In the provinces the following series and groups of similar brasses have been established:

York

0. *c.* 1352–1385
1. *c.* 1380–1435 e.g. fig. 77
2. *c.* 1443–1475
3. *c.* 1480–1491
4. *c.* 1493–1503

81 A typical knight of the 'A' series, Sir John de Mereworth in Kent, 1366. His figure and canopy should be compared with the 'B' style knight in fig. 82.

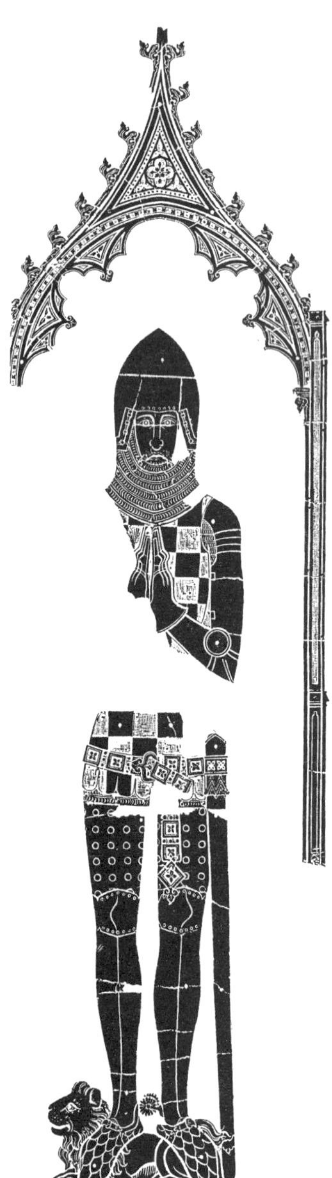

82 A typical knight of the 'B' series, Sir Adam de Clyfton, d. 1367; Methwold, Norf. This badly damaged brass was rescued from a tinker's cauldron, though much of it had already been melted down.

Fens (? Boston)
1. *c.* 1408–1435
2. *c.* 1488–1510 e.g. fig. 78

Norwich
1. *c.* 1450–1479 e.g. fig. 27
2. *c.* 1480–1497
3. *c.* 1485–1507 e.g. figs 95, 131
4. *c.* 1505–1522 e.g. fig. 72
5. *c.* 1502–1506 e.g. fig. 68
6. *c.* 1506–1557 e.g. figs 69, 71, 73, 74
7. *c.* 1497

Suffolk (? Bury St Edmunds)
1. *c.* 1475–1483
2. *c.* 1501–1521 e.g. fig. 70
3. *c.* 1515–1534 e.g. fig. 79
4. *c.* 1532–1556

Midlands (? Coventry)
1. *c.* 1467–1492 e.g. fig. 91
2. *c.* 1500–1511
3. *c.* 1512–1566
4. *c.* 1517–1522

Cambridge	*c.* 1510–1540	e.g. fig. 92
Kent	*c.* 1480–1545	e.g. fig. 93
South West	*c.* 1530–1535	e.g. fig. 26

In addition, indents and isolated examples record identifiable early products from Exeter, Lincoln, Newcastle, Shrewsbury and York (fig. 28); mid-fifteenth-century brasses from Durham, and sixteenth-century brasses from Lancashire and possibly north Essex. Most of the major series have clearly defined subseries, invaluable to dating.

The coverage of this analysis is as yet incomplete and uneven, but it has enabled a major and sound revision of dates. It has not of itself proved the date of any particular brass, so much as proved relationships, so that conclusions drawn of some extend logically to others. The radical re-dating and regrouping of the earliest brasses in England has been in part the product of documentary evidence, but style has been critical, especially in its interpretation of indents and related incised slabs. Yet this is but one period. Illustrative later examples of revisions in dating are Hampton Poyle, Oxon., 1424 to *c.* 1435; Mugginton, Derbys., *c.* 1475 to *c.* 1490; Feltwell, Norf., 1479 to *c.* 1520;

83 Large figures from the minor 'C' workshop, to Sir William and Margaret Bagot, 1407, at Baginton, Warwicks. Costume and armour can be compared with the contemporary 'D' style in fig. 84, with fig. 1 for the 'B' style.

84 A typical 'D' style knight under canopy to compare with figs 81–3 and 98, John Bedgebere, 1424, at Goudhurst, Kent.

Sawbridgeworth, Herts., 1484 to 1448; St Columb Major, Cornwall, 1545 to *c.* 1565, and Budock, Cornwall, 1567 to *c.* 1600. An illustrative case is that of part of a figure to a member of the clergy, probably from Bayham Abbey, and now in the Kent County Research Office (fig. 94). When published it was dated *c.* 1470, but the treatment of the face and hands show it to be of series 'E', and any post-1453 date is highly unlikely.

Attention to style has exposed a few cases of composite brasses, most interesting being that of Tomesin Tendryng, Yoxford, Suffolk, showing her and some of her children shrouded in a London 'D' brass of 1485, but attended by two daughters in normal dress, Norwich 3 additions of *c.* 1495 (fig. 95). It has also called into question well-established assumptions on costume, the Hampton Poyle brass being reputed as the earliest to show tassets on the unjustified acceptance of the inscription date. It has also clarified the preferences of purchasers, as in Emmerson's discussion of the brasses at Stamford, Lincs., to the Browne family, raising interesting questions as to why patrons adhered to or removed business from a particular workshop.[19]

The identification of series has been of value in giving guidance and support to the identification of particular engravers. Showing that a series of brasses arose during the active working life of a marbler does not of course prove his association to them, but affords corroboration to documentary evidence. The identification of Adam of Corfe by Blair is wholly consistent with the span of the Camoys series.[20] Emmerson's association of William West with London series 'B' is consistent with the development of that series and with the brass to William's father, *c.* 1435 at Sudborough, Northants., on which William is prominently represented.[21] At Norwich, Greenwood has shown that the work and death of Richard Foxe accords precisely with the Norwich 2 series. The stylistic examination of related art work can also support the evidence of the series, linking for example William Heyward the glazier, a proven maker of brasses, to the Norwich 3 series.[22]

While analysis of style rightly focuses on detail, series have their own peculiarities in outline, of the greatest value to the interpretation of indents. A London 'A' series armed figure is leaner and longer in the leg than that of 'B', whereas a 'C' figure will have more widely splayed feet and slimmer legs (compare figs 81, 24, 83). Cambridge series figures are readily discernible from those of Suffolk by their outlines (figs 79, 92), and both easily distinguishable from their contemporary London 'G' counterparts (fig. 96). Badham and Blatchly's recent analysis of the bellfounder's indent at St Edmundsbury Cathedral, Suffolk, with its comparisons with the existing Coket brass (d. 1483) at Ampton, Suffolk,[23] demonstrates how precise a guide the indent may be. An appraisal of the numerous indents at Aldeburgh, Blythburgh and St

85 The earliest English shroud brass, from the 'E' workshop, shows Joan Mareys, with her shroud elegantly slipping off her head; in her hands she holds a heart. From Sheldwich, Kent, 1431.

Mary's, Bury St Edmunds, all in Suffolk, and at Great St Mary's, Cambridge, is constructive, leaving the informed viewer with little doubt of what was once there. Thanks to established analysis of style indents compensate substantially for the loss of the latten inlays.

Analysis of style has benefited the study of re-used brasses considerably. It has for the reverses eliminated incorrect associations, and by stylistic relationships of the obverses assisted the exploration for re-used material. Kent's disassociation of the feet and tabard of Sir John Popham on the reverse of Walter Barton (1538) at St Lawrence, Reading, Berks., is a case of the first.[24] Owen Evans' linking and planned examination of the Fermer style brasses, a subsection of London 'G', illustrates the second. (The Fermer brasses are analysed

86 This little style 'F' brass to a baby in swaddling clothes at Hornsey, Middx., about 1520, prays 'Jesu Christ, Mary's son, have mercy on the soul of John Skevington'.

and described in detail by Hutchinson and Egan.[25]) The linking by Norris of the re-used woman *c.* 1530 at the Museum of Archaeology and Ethnology at Cambridge with other damaged figures at Aldenham, Herts., revealing a common reverse, was prompted by the treatment of the obverses. Attention to style has ensured that reverse fragments are appropriately dated and provenanced, so assisting links with others.

The identification of appropriated figures has been considerably advanced. Some of these, as at Ticehurst, Sussex (*c.* 1380 and 1503) are well known and require no more than sensible observation. Other cases are less obvious, and have only been recognised as a consequence of precisely defined series. In South Creake, Norf., John Norton (d. 1509), with his father and mother, is a proven re-use of Norwich 1 series figures of *c.* 1470, and Thomas Capp (1545), St Stephen's, Norwich, has a Norwich 5 series figure of *c.* 1505. The figure of Ele Buttry (d. 1546), also at St Stephen's, was long recognised as an appropriated female of *c.* 1410, but the mound beneath her feet with bedesmen was regarded as added, whereas stylistically it can only be part of the original. Among the most interesting examples is that of a civilian and two wives at Newnham, Herts (fig. 96). The man is

87 A peculiar brass made in London in the 'G' series, placed at Sefton, Lancs., for Sir William Molyneux and wives, about 1570. He wears a mail hood two and a half centuries out of date; captured banners are shown on his achievement of arms.

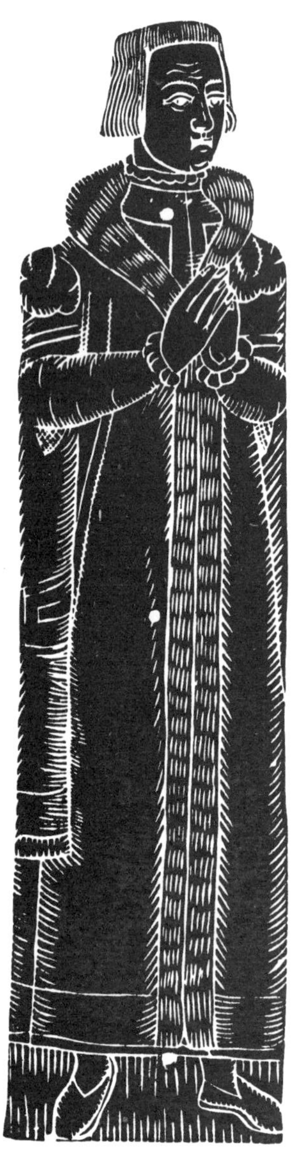

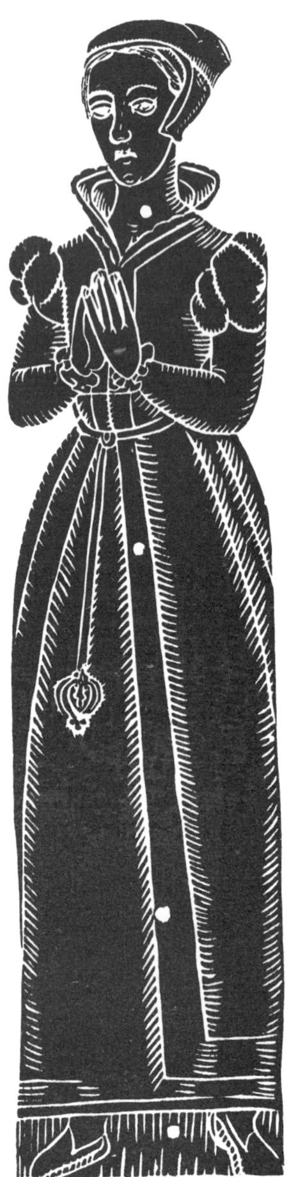

Of yo' charytie pray for ẏ soule of Edwarde
Crane & Elizabeth his wyf which Edward deceased ẏ
xxviii day of Marche A° M v° lviii whose soule god pdo

88 *A rare example of a civilian brass from the small 'H' series, Edward and Elizabeth Crane, from Stratford St Mary, Suff., 1558.*

89 A late brass from the Southwark tradition, Robert Coulthirst, 1631, shown with the arms of the Merchant Tailors' Company at Kirkleatham, Yorks.

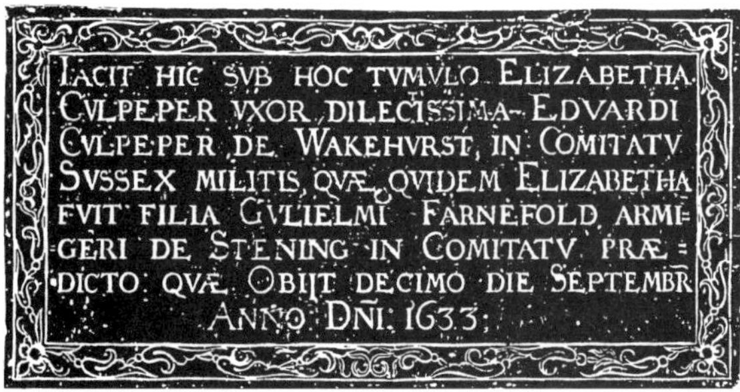

90 *Elizabeth Culpeper, 1633, from Ardingly, Sussex; a typical brass from the Marshall workshop.*

evidently an early London 'G' series figure of *c.* 1500, but the wife on his right is of London 'D' origin of *c.* 1492, wearing a typical sagging butterfly head-dress, and with simple coarsely executed drapery, with a characteristic bold V-shaped fold heavily shaded. The wife on his left was made with him, but the engraver cunningly repeated the butterfly head-dress to match the appropriation. This is an important brass, but one until recently ignored.

A further value of observed style in this context has been to establish what are really 'wasters'. A notable case is that probably of Abbot William Albon (d. 1476) at St Albans Cathedral, Herts. (fig. 97), engraved on the reverse of a late fourteenth-century woman. The obverse was long attributed to Abbot John de la Moote (d. 1401), contemporary with the reverse. Analysis by Goodall of the style of evangelist symbols first drew attention to the faulty attribution and relationship.

A particularly interesting contribution of stylistic perceptions is in recognising antiquarianism in brasses. The use of retrospective details by Elizabethan engravers has been well established, notably at Thames Ditton, Surr. (1580 and 1582), with the use of gable head-dresses (fig. 45), and at Sefton, Lancs. (*c.* 1570), with the surprising wearing of a mail coif (fig. 87). These however are obvious cases, and a clearer establishment of a workshop's conventions has exposed more subtle attempts.

The most important is at Little Casterton, Rutland (fig. 98). Thomas Burton (d. 1381) is depicted wearing a bascinet and aventail, and with a jupon covering breastplate and fauld. His wife is artistically presented, her hair arranged in late fourteenth-century manner. Yet the entire execution of the plate, the fineness of the lines, the treatment of the lion and dog, and of details such as the sword hilt leave no doubt that this is fifteenth-century London 'B' series work, dated by Emmerson *c.* 1420. The brass of William West and wife (1415), Sudborough, Northants., looks plausible as the man is depicted with a hood thrown back, but the style is London 'B' of *c.* 1435, and the brass was obviously laid retrospectively by his marbler son. At Chalfont St Peter, Bucks., the brasses of the William Whappelodes (1446) show the elder William wearing round besagues, presumably included to indicate age as they were no longer part of London 'B' design. The interesting Colchester examples have already been mentioned.

Lastly the analysis of style in the design of brasses is not self-contained, and can assist to relate brasses to other monumental and art sources and vice versa. Controversy over the origin of Sir Hugh Hastings has drawn effigies, manuscripts and painted glass into the arguments. Following the publication of Greenhill's *Monumental Incised Slabs in the County of Lincoln* (1986), attention has turned to the stylistic

91 A Coventry-made brass, Thomas and Emme Andrewe, 1490, at Charwelton, Northants., shown with their eleven children.

92 A small brass from the Cambridge workshop; a Master of Arts, probably that recorded by Dowsing as 'Mr Culiard, a fellow', at Trinity Hall, Cambridge. It must date from about 1530.

93 A brass of Kentish origin, Raff Brown, alderman and mayor of Canterbury, 1522, now in St Gregory's church in that city.

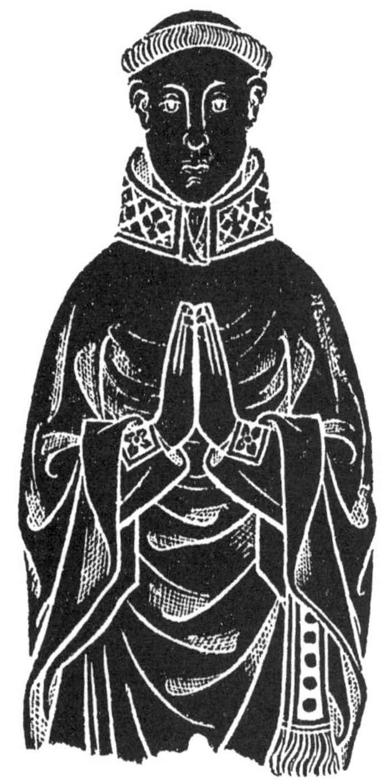

94 A damaged brass to a priest, about 1450, from the small 'E' series, found at Bayham Abbey, Sussex, now in the Kent Record Office.

affinity between Fens brasses and incised slabs, and from them to early Purbeck slabs and brasses of London origin.[26] The precise dating of series of scripts in the workshop is likely to prove of value to other related crafts.

It is appropriate in conclusion of this chapter to consider the future of this aspect of monumental brass research. Emphasis has been placed on what has been achieved, but the work is far from complete. The period *c.* 1350–*c.* 1420 needs consolidation with reference to all brasses. An immense amount of work is needed on brasses of the sixteenth and seventeenth centuries, in which provincial series of inscription plates are particularly numerous. The problems of the early sixteenth century are complex, requiring not only comparison of brasses, but even of the component figures and inscriptions as series do not appear to be discrete. More work is required on the minor provincial groups, and research by Bayliss has at the time of writing extended and revised

95 *Shrouded figures of Thomasina Tendryng, 1485, with five of her children, made in London in the 'D' series; two surviving daughters in normal dress were commissioned in Norwich to complete the brass. At Yoxford, Suff.*

96 A style 'G' civilian with his wives at Newnham, Herts., about 1500; the wife on the left is an appropriated figure ten years older than the others, and from a different series, 'D'.

97 The sadly mutilated brass of an abbot of St Albans, probably William Albon, d. 1476. A rare example of a fine canopied brass from the 'F' series. Lost parts have been added from old rubbings or drawings.

current assessments of the Midland series. Progress to date has been partial, and the use of different schemes of identification, by names, by letters and by numbers reflects the differences of individual approaches, which should in the end be standardised.

These are general areas, and there are individual brasses that do of themselves invite special study. Sir John Russell (1405) at Strensham, Worcs., is one on which Kent and Norris have recorded different views, the former regarding it as a later fifteenth-century copy. The very recent discovery of a fine 'A' series waster on the reverse of the figure is important new evidence. Philip Mede (*c.* 1475) at St Mary Redcliffe, Bristol, is of London quality, but may be a one-off survival of a Bristol workshop. Robert Whyte (d. 1512) at South Warnborough, Hants. (fig. 99), is challenging, so obviously late London 'D' in style, and similar to Nicholas Gaynesford (*c.* 1490) at Carshalton, Surrey, and yet confusing in the extravagance of the armour, and the uncompromising sixteenth-century date of the inscription. Emmerson's 'sub B' group contains brasses of widely differing quality, and possibly source.

There is also the provocative question as to whether association in style is necessarily in all cases exclusive to a workshop. The assumption of stylistic analysis is that it is, and it is for practical purposes a necessary

98 Sir Thomas Burton died in 1381, and by the time this brass was made by his wife Margery in about 1420 fashions had changed; here the engraver, from the 'B' tradition, tries to portray an earlier style of armour. It is at Little Casterton, Rutland.

99 *An elegant kneeling figure in armour, style 'D', at South Warnborough, Hants., apparently made some twenty years earlier than the inscription of 1512*

and useful assumption, but the Fens 1 series has exposed how derivative an engraver could be, and there may be subsidiary products to be identified. There is a great deal more to be learned about the organisation of workshops, and the study of style will continue to contribute to it.

Among those interested in brasses, there is at times expressed a certain weariness of the discussion of stylistic points, and the keen exchanges of writers who nevertheless have the common goal of establishing the facts. It is occasionally alleged that style has taken too prominent a place. This is not the case, if judged by its contribution to the subject and what is as yet undone. But it is, like any form of study, not isolated. Its consolidation requires further documentary evidence to confirm the general findings, and to exploit the clues. We know for instance that John and Henry Lorymer engraved brasses at a workshop near the Blackfriars, but which series? Emmerson has suggested series 'D', the dates of which fit conveniently with John Lorimer's death.[27] Where does the 'cunynge marbler' near St Dunstan's in the west, known from the Thomas Salter will, fit in? The study of style cannot provide all the answers, and its conclusions necessarily need confirmation. It has notwithstanding contributed greatly to the understanding of the memorials that remain and that are lost, and will continue to do so. Its painstaking observation, comparison and analysis is focused on the truth of these monuments, and this is of great worth to those who seriously enjoy and value them.

CHAPTER 6

Palimpsests – Re-used Brasses

JOHN PAGE-PHILLIPS

The word 'palimpsest' was first used in the seventeenth century to describe parchment that had been written on, rubbed out and written on again, like a slate; the palimpsest was the earlier writing, still partly legible. Because many of these manuscripts were in Greek, it was appropriate, for those who studied them, to describe the earlier writing as palimpsest, the combination of two Greek words, *palin* = again, and *psestos* = rubbed smooth.

The word was not applied to re-used monumental brasses until the 1840s, and was not, in its literal Greek meaning, very appropriate, because the re-use was mostly on the back of the sheet of brass rather than on a 'rubbed smooth' front. An unsuccessful attempt was made to use the word 'retroscript', but that too would have been misleading. The brass meaning of 'palimpsest' remains, but covers several categories of brass re-use, as listed below.

In examining a brass for signs of re-use, the overall design, style and date are important, but each component piece of brass, and the stone slab too, if it survives, requires separate assessment, on both sides if possible. Since brasses are generally riveted to their slabs, and slabs are very heavy, their backs only come to light by chance. One piece of brass, and one piece only, may come loose, leaving many other portions firmly fixed. Years later another piece may yield its secret. This gradually unfolding story is part of the fascination of the subject, and this chapter will soon need updating.

Types of Palimpsests

One brass can have component parts that are, disappointingly, not palimpsest, and others, as hinted above, parts that come under several different categories of palimpsest. Here are the four categories of palimpsest brass, and the number of examples of each, discovered in the British Isles up to 1989:

1. Wasters, Doodles and Laying Numbers – 81 examples

Essentially hidden on the back, these are scratches and engravings made by the same marbler or workshop that produced the front; the engraving is therefore contemporary with, and likely to be stylistically similar to, the front.

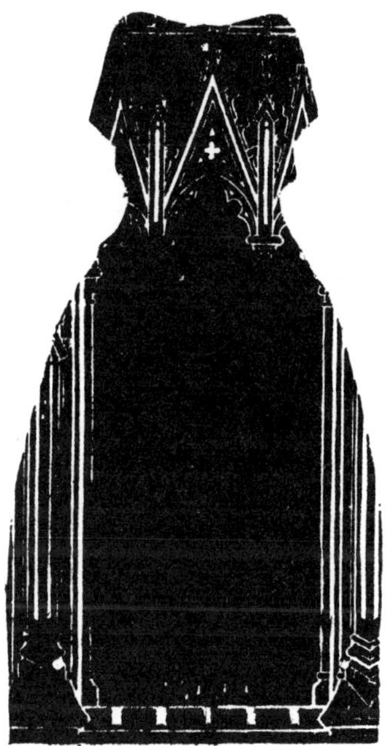

100 Offard Darcy, Hunts., c. *1440. A 'waster' – an unfinished super-canopy, from the London workshop making ladies (note the silhouette) like fig. 102.*

Wasters

In any workshop there must have been errors of engraving, misunderstood heraldry, misread inscriptions or details unacceptable to the executors. They might change an instruction or fail to pay. We can be sure that the metal was carefully kept, some for melting, but larger pieces, if blank on the back, for re-use on that side. Such palimpsests are *wasters*, recognisable because the engraving is incomplete (fig. 100) or faulty, although the engraving may not seem faulty on the fragment that survives. None the less, if the style and date of the engraving on both sides tally, the palimpsest is likely to be a waster.

The Waller brothers, who made brasses in London in the nineteenth century, commented that 'spoilt metal from the workshop must have been of frequent occurrence, as experience in the manufacture of similar memorials proves'. Several Waller wasters have been discovered (fig. 101), including pieces marked on the back with their monogram.

101 Thorncombe, Dorset, 1437. When Messrs Waller restored this brass around 1860 there was an indent for a lost shield. Not knowing the lost arms they placed a blank plate in the indent. In 1976 further restoration was necessary, and the back of the shield turned out to be a Waller 'waster'.

Doodles

Some palimpsests show that a marbler or apprentice has experimented with a burin or compass, engraved a difficult letter, or sketched out some design. The back of Trotton, Sussex, M.S. I, *c.* 1310 (fig. 5), has a sketch for a canopy finial. Such *doodles* might be found on any sheet of brass, otherwise blank or already bearing earlier engraving.

Laying numbers

A less common form of palimpsest is where pieces of metal bear *laying numbers*. There are examples of marginal inscriptions with numbers on the back (e.g. Southwick, Hants, M.S. I, 1548). The weepers of the Hastings brass (fig. 131) are numbered. An illiterate mason might otherwise find difficulty in laying the pieces correctly.

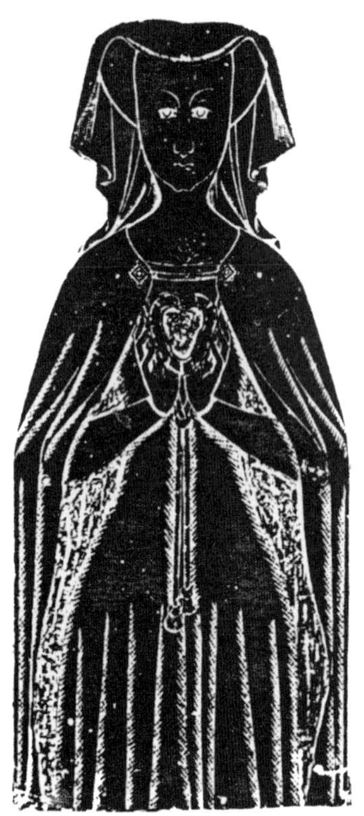

102 Great Ormesby, Norf., 1538. A London engraved lady, of about 1440, appropriated by a Norwich engraver, who softened the bold lines with shading for Dame Alice, second wife of Sir Robert Clere.

2. Palimpsests made from earlier brasses – 1,168 examples plus 85 appropriations

These fragments have been taken from one brass to form part of another. They bear engraving that is earlier on one side than the other, possibly in a much earlier or even foreign style. The 're-using' workshop generally hid the earlier engraving, but occasionally incorporated it face upwards as an *appropriation*. Large plate area compositions, such as many of the Franco-Flemish brasses, could be turned over and cut into several smaller ones. The 1,168 examples show that this is by far the most important category of palimpsest. These fragments are like jigsaw pieces, waiting to be put together. This possibility was recognised by both W.H.J.Weale (1832–1917), the distinguished art historian, and T.E. Sedgwick in the 1890s, when fewer fragments had been discovered. They would have been delighted with such palimpsest reconstructions as those shown on figs 109 and 110. The more that are discovered the greater the chances of finding pieces of jigsaw that fit together.

Appropriations

Some appropriations, such as groups of children or canopies, were made without additional engraving, but, if fashions and styles of engraving had changed, then the appropriated engraving might be updated (fig. 102). Groups of children were often appropriated. In order to gain the correct numbers of boys and girls at Westerham, Kent, M.S. VIII (fig. 103), the workshop had to appropriate, add and subtract children to and from the groups.

3. Non-monumental first use – 3 examples

Although there are so few examples, it is useful to distinguish this rare category of palimpsest and isolate it from category 2 above. Essentially, the first use of the sheet is non-monumental and only in re-use does it become part of a monumental brass. It has its opposite in category 4 below.

The marblers were most likely to re-use old brasses, but, in the course of their work, might have the opportunity to purchase sheet from other sources. These, though all so far religious in subject matter, bear unusual engraving for brasses. The top of a Crucifixion at Easton Neston, Northants., M.S. I, 1552, may be part of a metal icon or reredos. The 'Death of King Sweyn' (fig. 104), may have been held in a wooden screen containing scenes of the life and miracles of St Edmund.

A

B

C

103 Two groups of children (A) from Westerham, Kent, 1566, and the reverse engraving. For the first group, four sons c. *1520 (C) have been halved; two serving as 'appropriations', and two as 'palimpsests' behind one daughter. The second group of children were engraved on the back of more children of* c. *1510, and part of the figure of a lady of* c. *1520 (B).*

104 Frenze, Norf., 1551. Presumably this was one of a set of panels depicting the life and miracles of St Edmund, engraved c. 1470 to go on or near the shrine in the Abbey of Bury St Edmunds. It depicts one of the miracles of St Edmund when he freed the people of Bury from having to pay tribute (the money bag) to King Sweyn, who reaches out and is transfixed by Edmund's spear.

4. Non-monumental second use – 16 examples

These are parts of monumental brasses, where re-use is in a surprisingly miscellaneous collection of non-monumental settings.

A monumental brass could be cut up and re-used anywhere, if all that was required was a piece of brass sheet. A recently discovered example, probably found in Thames mud and purchased by the British Museum in 1988, forms the underside of a Tudor weight (fig. 105). Others became the backs of clock faces, a sundial, weathercock, foot-scraper, fireback, keyhole cover and a mason's angle (fig. 106). A brass rubbing (*c.* 1840?) in the Ashmolean Museum has recently been identified as showing the complete brass from which the mason's angle was cut.[1]

One of the strangest re-uses was discovered when the London (Fermer style) brass at Blatherwycke, Northants., M.S. I, 1548, was restored in 1970. The brass was either sent without a slab, as at Atherington, or the original slab broke in transit. For some reason the brass had to be fixed to a local stone by a mason unused to fixing brasses. He bored holes for the brass dowels right through the slab, poured in a wasteful and ineffective cascade of lead, and used brass dowels *that were cut from a brass*. Two of the dowels laid side by side form part of a face.

105 A weight of 50.76 gm, countermarked with a crowned 'h', c. 1540, cut from a brass. The reverse showing three lines of a Latin inscription ending in 'AMEN', c. 1490. Purchased by the British Museum in 1988.

Re-used slabs

The slabs that held brasses were also liable to be re-used. One or two appropriated brass canopies appear to belong to their slabs. In other words an old slab with a brass canopy was re-used by adding a new brass figure and inscription (e.g. Burwell, Cambs., M.S. I, 1542). As soon as old slabs had lost all the metal from their indents, if they were at floor level, their unevenness and anonymity meant that they were likely to be removed. Many were re-dressed on one side or another, and re-used as flagging or building material, e.g. to support a cloister pillar in Old St Paul's, or to floor a mill race at Eynsham, Oxon. But monumental masons were keen to recycle old tomb slabs and many lost-brass slabs have evidence of double use. Even when the old surface was shaved down to remove evidence of an indent, the bottoms of old dowels often remain, as at Ashby St Ledgers (fig. 127). From their pattern the general design of the earlier brass can sometimes be plotted. Sometimes there was no need to shave down an old indent if the new brass completely covered it, as at Cople, Beds., M.S. X, 1590 (fig. 107). Where an earlier indent remains, and appears strange and unsightly today, it is likely that it was once filled with composition. At Blewbury, Berks., M.S. VI, 1548, an earlier empty indent of a lady, between John Latton and his wife, is strangely misleading, and has been described by Mill Stephenson (in his *List*) as a second wife.

106 A mason's angle, obtained by the Society of Antiquaries of London in about 1940, which was cut from an inscription plate to Richard Crook, d. 1549, made c. *1580, from Brightwell Prior, Oxon. (A rubbing of* c. *1840 in the Ashmolean Museum, Oxford, shows the complete inscription.)*

There is an interesting parallel with category 3 palimpsests, where the first use was non-monumental. There are a number of brass-bearing slabs that have once been altar stones, the consecration crosses still remaining. In several instances re-use coincided with an order from Elizabeth I for the removal of stone altars (e.g. North Mundham, Suss., M.S. I, 1558).

The Development of Interest in Palimpsests and Appropriations

Awareness of palimpsests has grown rapidly from the 1840s as more and more have been discovered. Two summaries of palimpsest knowledge have been attempted, the first in 1900–03 by Mill Stephenson, and the second in 1980 by John Page-Phillips.[2] The quantity and area of palimpsest engraving more than doubled between the two summaries. Now, in 1989, nearly 500 obverses provide us with 1,268 palimpsest fragments.

The earliest was noted in the seventeenth century by the antiquary Anthony Wood (1632–95) in St Mary Magdalen, Oxford, 'Note yt wn the brass . . . was some yeares ago taken up, I read this french inscription engraven on the other side [inscription given]. So yt by this it shewes yt the said brass had been fixed to another grave, but whether it lay'd here or in another church I know not'.[3]

By 1750 another antiquary, Tom Martin, in his church notes,[4] drew both sides of the priest in Thrandeston, Suffolk, but only five others had by then been noted – and they were unknown to him, tucked away in other people's church notes. The value of Martin's church notes and several other early records of palimpsests is that they are the only records that survive; the brasses have since disappeared.

Gradually, with the introduction of heelball in the 1840s, the better recording of brasses, the publication of textbooks on brasses, such as Revd Herbert Haines' *Manual* (1861), and the bringing together of like-minded people in brass-rubbing societies (Cambridge, 1887 and Oxford, 1893), an awareness of brasses in general and palimpsests in particular developed. In a letter to the Oxford Society Mill Stephenson revealed that, 'for some years I have been collecting material towards a complete and exhaustive paper' on palimpsests.[5] His work was eventually published by the Cambridge Society, by then the Monumental Brass Society, and fills much of Volume 4 of their Transactions.

Although the First World War halted the activities of the MBS and there was a long period of dormancy until 1934, palimpsests continued to be uncovered at an average rate of two discoveries a year. Helping in the revival of the MBS were several palimpsest enthusiasts, no longer purely church note-takers, but practical engineers who, in their spare time, were ready to repair brasses; Reginald H. Pearson (1879–1961), Major H.F. Owen Evans (1898–1966) and more recently Dr H.K. Cameron (1906–85).

Two active brass conservators today, Brian Egan and William Lack, owe much to the skills of these predecessors, and share with them a special interest in and responsibility towards palimpsests. Thanks largely to them we can be sure that new discoveries will be recorded with rubbings, photographs, metal thickness measurements, and the production of polyester resin facsimiles of interesting discoveries.

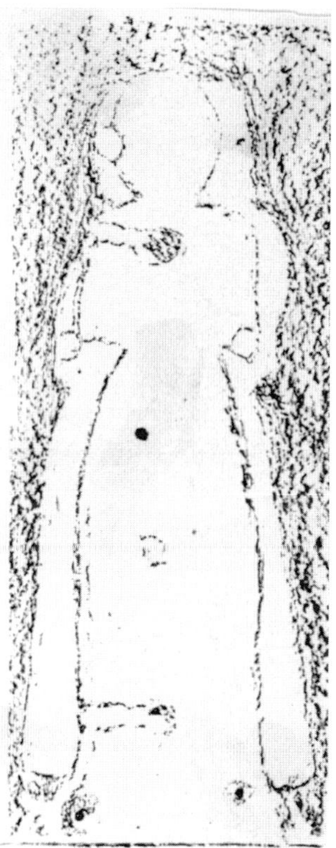

107 Cople, Beds. An appropriated slab; the indent for a larger 1590 lady reveals how it once completely hid the indent of an earlier sixteenth-century lady.

Historical Causes of Palimpsests

This section examines palimpsests in the second category above. These are the majority of palimpsests. If one looks at the dates when these palimpsests were re-used, over 80 per cent fall within the period 1535 to 1585. The period of greatest re-use must have coincided with a period when a great number of church monuments were destroyed.

The first years from 1535 were the beginning of the Reformation in England. The break with Rome gave Henry VIII the opportunity to convert the rich possessions of the Catholic Church into money for himself. Monasteries were dissolved and in 1536 the Court of Augmentations was set up to handle the sales of church lands and all moveable contents. This included church metals – bells, candlesticks, brasses. Some palimpsests from this period bear proof of their monastic origins. For example, a 1539 brass at Haddenham, Bucks., M.S. III, has a palimpsest inscription to a prior of Bisham Priory; and there are plenty of anonymous monastic figures, such as a life-size *c.* 1310 figure

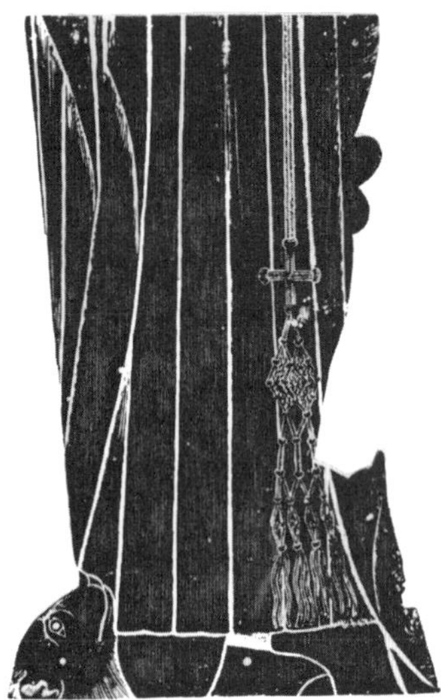

108 A rubbing of the discovery made on fig. 128, showing the lower half of an ecclesiastic, c. *1430, wearing a pendant of the order of St John of Jerusalem, his feet on a lion, probably from St John, Clerkenwell, London.*

of an abbot at St John Maddermarket, Norwich M.S. X, 1558, probably removed from St Benet's Hulme. Many of the palimpsests are of secular figures, and some of them too came from monastic churches. Parts of one to Sir John Popham, a famous fifteenth-century soldier, showing him in armour, were removed from the London Charterhouse and now form palimpsests in Reading, St Lawrence, Berks., M.S. III and Friston, Sussex, M.S. I, both engraved *c.* 1542. The palimpsests have been identified as Sir John Popham's brass because they include his name on an inscription and part of his arms on a tabard. (Another piece of an armoured figure on the back of the same brass at Reading has been proved by stylistic analysis not to be part of Popham's brass: see Kent, 1949.)

Following the Dissolution of the Monasteries came further money-raising operations; the dissolution of all chantries, colleges and hospitals. Palimpsest evidence of the suppression of the military order of the Knights Hospitallers of St John of Jerusalem comprises fragments from their church of St John Clerkenwell, London, all being used up *c.* 1546 (Ellesborough, Bucks., M.S. I; Lambourne, Essex, M.S. I; Harlington, Mdx., M.S. II; St Mary Islington, M.S. II). To this list can be added the brass at Ashby St Ledgers (fig. 108), illustrated at the moment of discovery in fig. 129.

Many churchwardens' accounts of Edward VI's reign record inventories of church goods and sales, which include church metals. The purchasers can sometimes be identified as founders or marblers. Only the latter would be likely to make palimpsests of their purchases. The accounts of St Dionis Backchurch refer to brasses as 'marbelers mettall'. They were sold by weight, roughly 3d per pound.[6*]

Mary returned the country to Rome; Cranmer and other Protestant martyrs were burnt, including Rowland Taylor of Hadleigh in Suffolk in 1555. When Elizabeth was on the throne and England was Protestant once more, the people of Hadleigh remembered their martyr and set up a brass inscription in about 1580. This leads us to consider a very different historical cause for the vast majority of palimpsests behind brasses made between 1570 and 1585. The martyr's inscription, like most English brasses of the period from 1570 to 1585, is palimpsest with Flemish engraving on the back. At first sight this is not remarkable; Flemish brasses had a formidable reputation among those who could afford them in England, and there are notable imports in Kings Lynn, St Albans, Newark and elsewhere. But these Elizabethan palimpsests have not previously been laid down in England; they bear foreign heraldry and many of the fragments of inscription are in old Dutch (e.g. fig. 109). They are nothing to do with the Reformation in England; they have been shipped across the Channel and we must look to events there for an explanation.

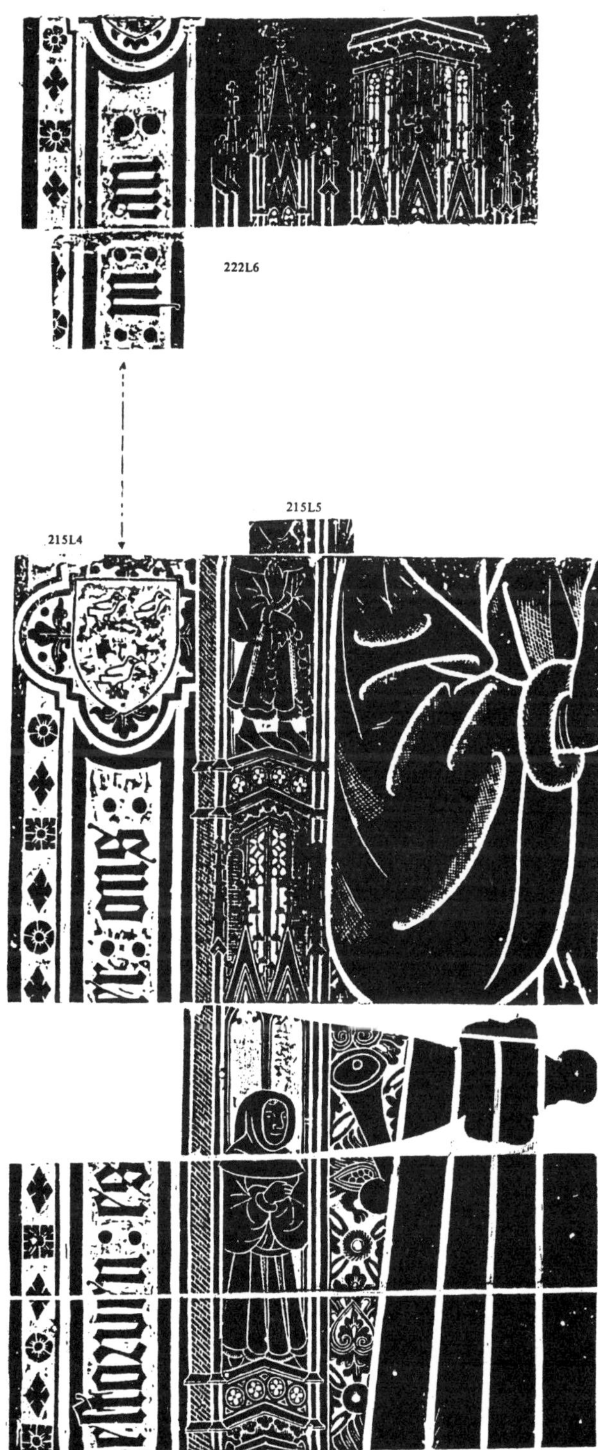

109 Fragments of a large Flemish brass to a civilian, with a dagger at his waist, standing in front of a tapestry under a canopy with weepers in side shafts and a marginal inscription in old Dutch, with a shield. These seven pieces are hidden behind three English brasses: (1 & 2) Goodnestone-next-Wingham, Kent, 1558; (3 & 4) Barrow, Suff., 1569; (5–7) Boreham, Essex, 1573.

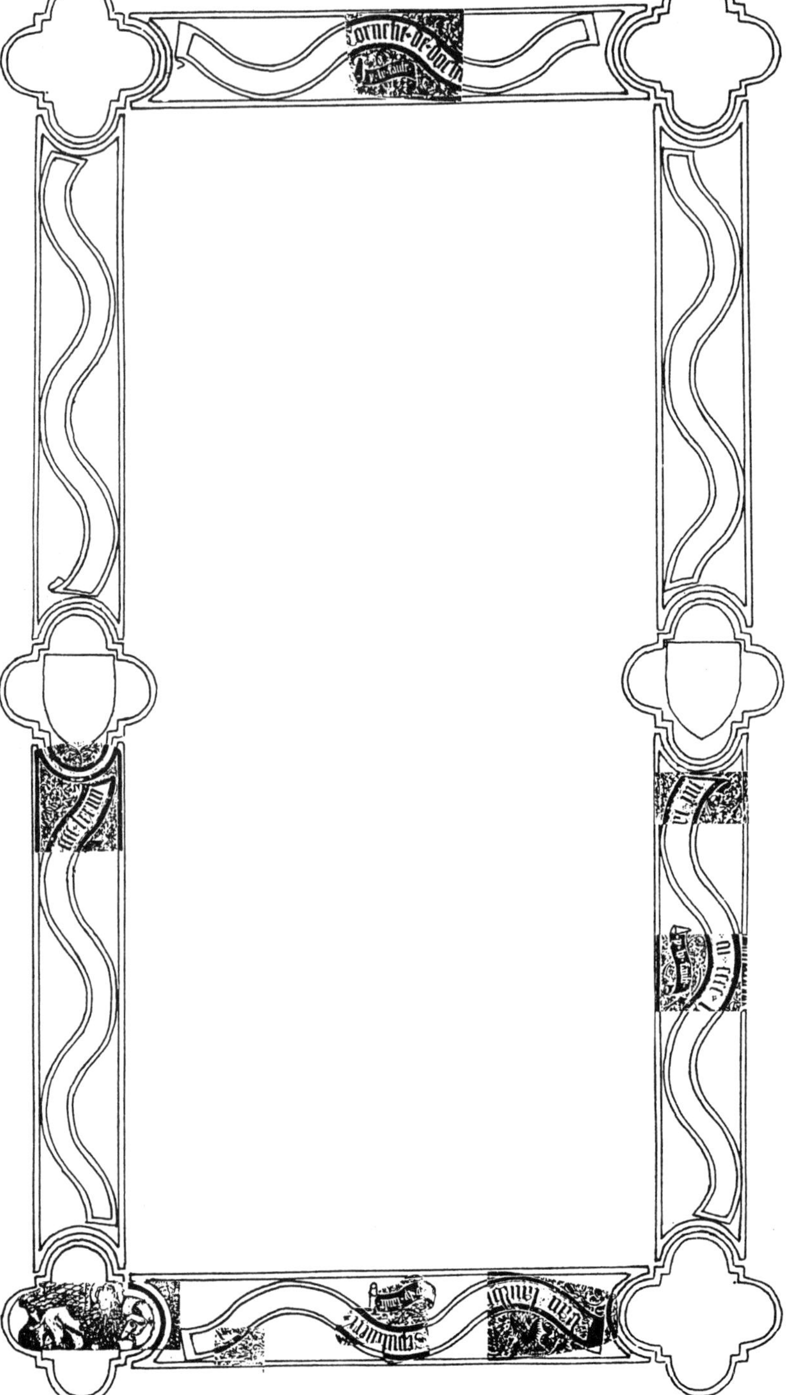

110 A palimpsest reconstruction. The backs of four brasses of 1582/43 hide eight numbered palimpsests that belong to one Flemish brass of 1489, from the now destroyed church of Our Lady, Oudenburgh, near Ostend. A surviving record of the complete inscription enabled William Lack to make this reconstruction. The four obverses are located: (1) Whichford, Warwicks., 1582; (2, 4–6, 8) Walkern, Herts., 1583; (3) Marsworth, Bucks., 1583; (7) Lee St Margaret, Kent, 1582. The inscription reads: [Hier lecht joncfr] Cornelie de doch[ter van Jan de Bloc, Tristran van Hallewin wyf was, die verseet] int ja[er ons Heeren] M CCCC L[XXXIX, den derden dach] van lauw[e +] Sepultuere [van Tristran] van [Hallewin Willems zone die versceet int jaer M] CCCC LXXIIII [up den XXIIIsten dach in meye. Bidt God over de ziele.] Translation: 'Here lies the lady Cornelie, daughter of Jan de Bloc. She was Tristran van Hallewin's wife. She died on the last day of January 1489. Here lies buried Tristan van Hallewin, William's son, who died on 23 May 1474. Pray to God for their souls.'

The Netherlands were under Spanish rule, Catholic, harsh and unpopular. Gradually opposition to Philip II and his regent, Margaret of Parma, gathered under the Protestant flag of William of Orange (the Silent). The first outbreak of violence in Low Country churches was iconoclastic, purely destructive, but soon William realised that church metals were tradeable and could be used to raise money for the war against the Spanish. Many Dutch people had fled from Spanish vengeance in 1566, and sought refuge in England. Via the network of Dutch churches in exile, the 'churches under the cross', he sought to raise money by church collections, but he also sent pirated goods and church brasses to England to be sold there. One Amsterdam refugee of 1566 was Garrat Jansen (1541–1612, usually known by his English name, Gerard Johnson) whose workshop style is recognisable on many London-made brasses of the 1570s and '80s. He would have been a sympathetic purchaser of these Flemish brasses. There is evidence too that some of this Flemish scrap reached Norwich marblers. The Hadleigh inscription to Rowland Taylor is on the back of Flemish scrap that has passed through Johnson's Southwark workshop; but Flemish scrap behind 1577 brasses in St Margaret de Westwick, Norwich, and Reepham, Norfolk, has passed through a Norwich marbler's workshop.

It is satisfactory to be able to pinpoint exactly where some of these Flemish scrap imports once lay. By chance, a record of the full inscription of a brass that once lay in the church of Our Lady in Oudenburgh, near Ostend, survives,[7] and from this evidence, the jigsaw of figure 110 has been constructed by William Lack. It draws on eight palimpsest fragments from four 1582/3 brasses in England.

Each palimpsest is a fascinating challenge. What is the engraving a part of? What style? What date? Are there other palimpsests that can be linked or associated? Given names, dates or heraldry, can the deceased person be identified? Does documentary evidence, such as a will, exist to prove where that person was buried? Success with this sort of research has an element of luck, but a growing number of palimpsests can be run to earth.

111 An inscription to William Wryghsley (Wriothesley), York Herald, 1509, probably from St Giles, Cripplegate, where other members of his family were buried, on the reverse of a brass to John Spelman, 1545; Narborough, Norf.

Inscriptions that have been traced include ones to a herald, skinner, armourer and fishmonger (figs 111–14). Heraldic shields include one perhaps from Fladbury, Worcs., and one from Arundel, Sussex (figs 115, 116). The collective evidence of identifiable palimpsests suggests that the marblers generally obtained their scrap material from local sources, London workshops from London churches, Norwich from round Norwich and Suffolk from round Bury St Edmunds. The sudden imports from the Low Countries are an obvious exception to this conclusion. For several years the Flemish imports dominate palimpsests, and then they vanish by 1586. This sudden stop may have been because the Flemish supply came to an end, or equally because a cheaper alternative brass sheet had just come on to the market, for it was just after 1584 that London-made brasses began to appear using thin 2 mm hammer-beaten brass plate. This thinner plate should have made a cheaper product, but it was made from calamine ore that had to be carted all the way from the Mendip hills in Somerset to a battery mill at Isleworth just off the River Thames. The carriage costs were high. Moreover John Brode, the manager of the mill, frequently squabbled with his partners. He ran out of money and the mill probably closed

112 Inscription to Richard Swane, skinner, d. 1492, and his wife Joan, known to have been buried in St Mildred Poultry, London; on the reverse of a brass to William Myddilton, 1557; Westerham, Kent.

113 Inscription to Richard Pecok, armourer, and wife Isabel, c. *1450; also known to have been buried in St Mildred Poultry, London, on reverse of a brass to Robert Bryckett; Barley, Herts., 1566.*

114 Inscription to Thomas Hastings, fishmonger, d. 1506, and wife Agnes, d. 1500, recorded as buried in Greyfriars, London; on reverse of a brass to Richard Sharp, 1553; Northiam, Sussex.

about 1598. A 1607 map calls the site a paper mill. Nonetheless, for several years, 1584–98, the thin brass sheet from Isleworth all but ousted palimpsests.

Progress with research on palimpsests is haphazard and slow. The discovery, on average, of between two and ten a year, still leaves hundreds of brasses, thousands of fragments, unexamined. However, it should be possible to examine palimpsests using an ultrasonic transducer, without any need to remove the brass from its slab. The engraving on the back would be scanned and recorded without disturbing the front. The obstacle to achieving such an archaeological scoop is probably only cost.

Finally let us return to the fronts of brasses. What are the backs telling us about the fronts, about the marblers and the workshops that engraved the obverses? We have very little documentary evidence of marblers and workshops, and the outputs from each are known mainly from the brasses themselves, and their surviving distribution. We recognise the hand of an individual designer in a face or in lettering, and can begin to build up lists of styles (see chapter 5). Palimpsest links between so many brasses in the 1535 to 1585 period are therefore immensely important in confirming common workshop origins and in suggesting that the linked obverses were engraved at about the same time. The date of engraving can differ widely from an obverse date of death, as we see on the wide range of death dates represented on fig. 109.

The underlapping criss-cross pattern of palimpsest links is extensive and does not exactly match lists of styles. In other words, for example, palimpsest links may suggest that two different obverse lettering styles belong to one workshop. Were there two designers/marblers at work in one workshop at the same time? Palimpsest links are most important in any study of sixteenth-century workshop styles.

115 Part of the arms of Throckmorton impaling Spiney, probably from brass to John and Eleanor Throckmorton, 1445, Fladbury, Worcs.; on reverse of a symbol of St Mark, sixteenth century, now in the British Museum.

116 The back of a once-painted shield, placed, with two others, at a 1664 restoration of the tomb of Archbishop Chichele, d. 1443, in Canterbury Cathedral. The tomb was again restored in 1897, when this palimpsest was discovered. The heraldry suggests that it came from the brass to Henry, d. 1579, the last Fitzalan Earl of Arundel, in Arundel, Sussex. Now in the care of the Society of Antiquaries, London.

CHAPTER 7

Brasses in their Art-historical Context

NICHOLAS ROGERS

It is a measure of the extent to which English monumental brasses have been neglected by most art historians that until now only one doctoral dissertation on the subject has been completed.[1]* Writing in 1932, Elfrida Saunders rightly observed that 'no acccount of English medieval art would be complete without a reference to the memorial brasses which are a justly famous branch of English handicraft'.[2] Yet her treatment of the material is summary, a couple of pages embedded in a chapter entitled 'Metal-work, Ivories and Tiles'. Certainly no one who had more than the slightest acquaintance with brasses would have made such an assertion as: 'Attempts have been made to divide the brasses into different schools according to their style. They are, however, very conventional in their treatment, and do not differ greatly'.[3] Joan Evans, in her volume on the period 1307–1461 in the *Oxford History of English Art*, which is unsatisfactory in many ways, presented a *réchauffé* of Macklin, treating brasses primarily as social phenomena and making no attempt to relate them to works of art in other media.[4] A refreshing novelty of approach was shown by Lawrence Stone in 1955, in *Sculpture in Britain: The Middle Ages*. Here, drawing with profit on the researches of J.P.C. Kent, he integrated brasses in a general stylistic chronology.[5] In so doing he tentatively questioned the accepted dating for the early knights.[6] It was some time, however, before this new approach was followed up by other art historians. As late as 1973 the catalogue of a major exhibition of East Anglian art held at Norwich managed to avoid all mention of brasses in the region, with the significant exception of those of Sir Hugh Hastings (fig. 131) and Robert Braunch.[7] A consideration of the brasses produced in Norwich and Bury St Edmunds would have facilitated an assessment of local style in the late fifteenth and early sixteenth centuries.

Kent's 1949 article was essentially archaeological in its typological analysis.[8] However, later writers such as Sally Badham, Robin Emmerson, Roger Greenwood and above all Malcolm Norris, who have developed the same approach so successfully, have shown an increasing awareness of the importance of comparisons with works in other media.[9] More general works published in the last twenty years have also, with varying degrees of success, attempted to relate brasses to other works of art.[10] In this process of re-evaluation a valuable contribution has been made recently by art historians who normally specialise in other media. Lynda Dennison has used her unrivalled knowledge of fourteenth-century English and Flemish manuscript illumination to place brasses in their stylistic context.[11] Paul Binski has shed new light on familiar figures by applying the analytic techniques he has elsewhere employed for panel and wall paintings.[12] The Age of Chivalry exhibition saw the acceptance of brasses as more than fashion illustrations.[13]

A prerequisite for the art-historical analysis of brasses is a consideration of their aesthetic. In his 1980 thesis Michael Nitz dealt with medieval attitudes to gold and brass and innovations in light metaphysics.[14] However, his argument that there was a close causal connection between such philosophical developments and the genesis of brasses is at best speculative, and is marred by a wayward dating of the monuments. It might indeed be objected that patrons were concerned only with the utilitarian aim of obtaining an effective form of commemoration befitting their social status. Workshop wasters point to the care usually taken over the presentation of heraldry or official dress. John Gage's correspondence with Gerard Johnson reveals a critical patron's awareness of the visual impact of minutiae of fashion.[15] The clearest evidence of an appreciation of good design is provided by the Paston Letters. Edmund Paston, ordering his brother's tomb in 1489, wrote: 'It is told me that the man at Sent Bridis is no klenly portrayer; [the]r for I wold fayn it myth be portrayed by sum odir man, and he to grave it up'.[16] Though many of those who ordered their brasses from Flemish workshops rather than English must have done so because of their mercantile contacts with that region or their desire to have a monument which more fully manifested their opulence, some clients, such as Abbot de la Mare of St Albans, must have been motivated by aesthetic considerations in their choice, preferring the more refined draughtsmanship and richer surface effect of Flemish brasses, more closely akin to precious metalwork.[17] Thomas de la Mare, Edmund Paston and John Gage, and the craftsmen who worked for them, all had a conception of the qualities of a good brass. However, over the centuries of brass production there were significant aesthetic as well as stylistic changes, as designers realised new potentialities of the medium.

Panofsky's dictum that 'brasses evolve from the 'monumental effigies' of which they are, if one may say so, linear or graphic abstractions' is a

117 A knight of the Septvans family, made about 1310 for the place of honour in the new chancel of Chartham church near Canterbury. One of the series of early knights in mail armour, cross-legged in the English style.

useful generalisation applicable not only to the earliest brasses but to their successors right down to the seventeenth century.[18] Brasses and sculpted effigies often emanated from the same workshops and not unnaturally shared formal and stylistic characteristics. We should however be aware that designs could be copied by more than one workshop; the Septvans brass at Chartham, for instance, is very similar to the effigy of a de Ros now in the Temple Church, London, but originally from Kirkham Abbey, Yorkshire, and a product of the York workshop.[19]* Certain types of effigy, most notably the more contorted figure poses, were rarely if ever translated into two-dimensional terms. Conversely, the designers of monumental brasses soon adopted patterns which would have been difficult to render in three dimensions. The lance-carrying pose of Sir John II d'Abernon is unknown in contemporary monumental effigies, but can be matched on incised slabs, as well as in stained glass and painting.[20] The closest parallels to the Septvans figure (fig. 117) are also to be found in incised slabs and paintings. Paul Binski has characterised the similarities with the work of the Madonna Master in the Psalter of Robert de Lisle and the Westminster Abbey sedilia of 1308.[21] These stylistic connections are so close as to invite speculation about the involvement of the one artist in all three works.[22]* A dating to the years around 1310, which is supported by the figure's close formal relation to French incised slabs,[23] would favour the traditional identification of Robert de Septvans (d. 1306), rather than William de Septvans (d. 1322), as has been suggested recently.[24]*

As a general rule, and with significant early and provincial exceptions,[25]* English incised slabs were not produced by the workshops which executed brasses. They did not enjoy the prestige of continental examples. Nor was there, after the early period, the same readiness to mix materials. Therefore the best-known examples of the use of common patterns by craftsmen in the same workshop working on different types of two dimensional monuments are to be found among the fourteenth-century Flemish incised slabs in this country. Despite neglect, Boston preserves the finest range of these monuments. That of Wessel Smalenburgh, originally in the Greyfriars there,[26] can be seen as a simplified version of the pattern used for such brasses as that of Adam de Walsokne (d. 1349) at King's Lynn.[27] In both cases the bend of the knee is expressed by a short diagonal line. Elements of the Smalenburgh composition are to be found on other incised slabs presumably from the same Tournai workshop: the dog with its head turned back occurs on another slab at Boston, and a priest at Ashby Puerorum is under a much-worn version of Wessel's canopy.[28]

Close affinities of design can be discovered between certain early cross-brasses and their incised or low-relief contemporaries. However, the greater detail possible in engraved brass encouraged a more pictorial treatment of the cross-head. How this motif could be transformed by a talented artist is well illustrated by Sir John and Ellen de Wautone at Wimbish (fig. 118). Nitz has stressed the move away from monumentality in these figures, whose interrelating poses capture a moment of reality.[29] Dennison has argued convincingly that there are remarkable similarities between Wimbish and Elsing and manuscripts produced in East Anglia, most probably at Cambridge, in the late 1340s, such as the Brescia Psalter and the first campaign of the Vienna Bohun Psalter.[30] In both media there is an interest in perspective and figures are lively, often displaying a marked *déhanchement*. As David King first noted in 1973, this soft, mannered style is also to be found in the Ely Lady Chapel glass.[31] The art-historical evidence surely points to an East Anglian source for the Hastings style designs, and the distribution pattern of brasses and indents in this style suggests that they may also have been produced somewhere in the region.

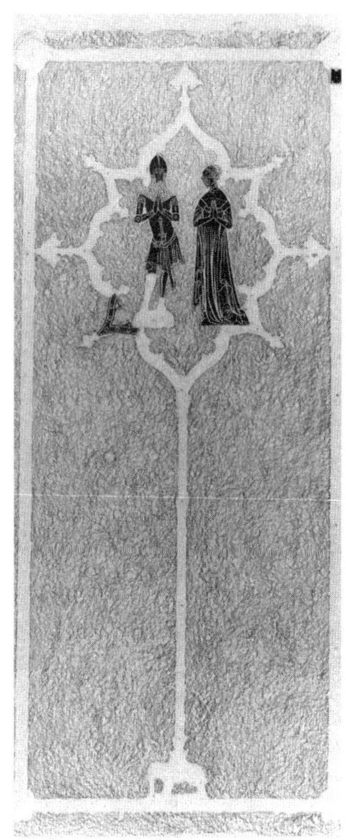

118 Sir John and Ellen de Wautone, 1347, in the head of a cross founded on an elephant, at Wimbish, Essex. From the same workshop as the Elsing brass, but a very different iconography.

The painterly Hastings style was short-lived, probably one of the many victims of the Black Death; but the latter half of the fourteenth century shows an increasing awareness of the possibilities of two dimensions. The period saw the most imaginative development of canopy designs, in which the engraver was unrestrained by the structural considerations which inhibited the sculptor.[32] More work needs to be done on the relationship between the architectural forms on brasses and their full-scale counterparts. The most famous example of the exploitation of the pictorial qualities of the medium is the Wyvil brass at Salisbury.[33] Scarcely less startling in its idiosyncrasy of design was the brass of Thomas of Woodstock, formerly at Westminster Abbey, which was evidently laid down at the time of the transfer of his remains to St Edward the Confessor's chapel in late 1399 or 1400.[34*] The surviving indent is inaccessible, but something of the appearance of the brass can be gained from an engraving in Sandford (fig. 119). The motif of the deceased surrounded by his kinsfolk provides an immediate link with the adjoining tomb of Edward III. John Orchard, latoner, who was probably responsible for the latter's gilt-bronze effigies, may have been involved in the production of London brasses.[35] On the Woodstock brass we are presented with what is in effect a secular Tree of Jesse, a concept even more clearly stated in contemporary glass.[36*] The compartmentalisation suggests a comparison with a miniature executed for a member of the Bohun family into which Thomas had married.[37] However the overall effect most closely resembles a Perpendicular window such as the great east window at Gloucester. Of surviving brasses, that of Walter Pescod (d. 1398) at Boston most closely reflects this elaborately tabernacled composition.[38]

It is not unnatural that there should be close links between monumental brasses and stained glass, which often had a memorial function. Both crafts involved large-scale graphic design, and in both

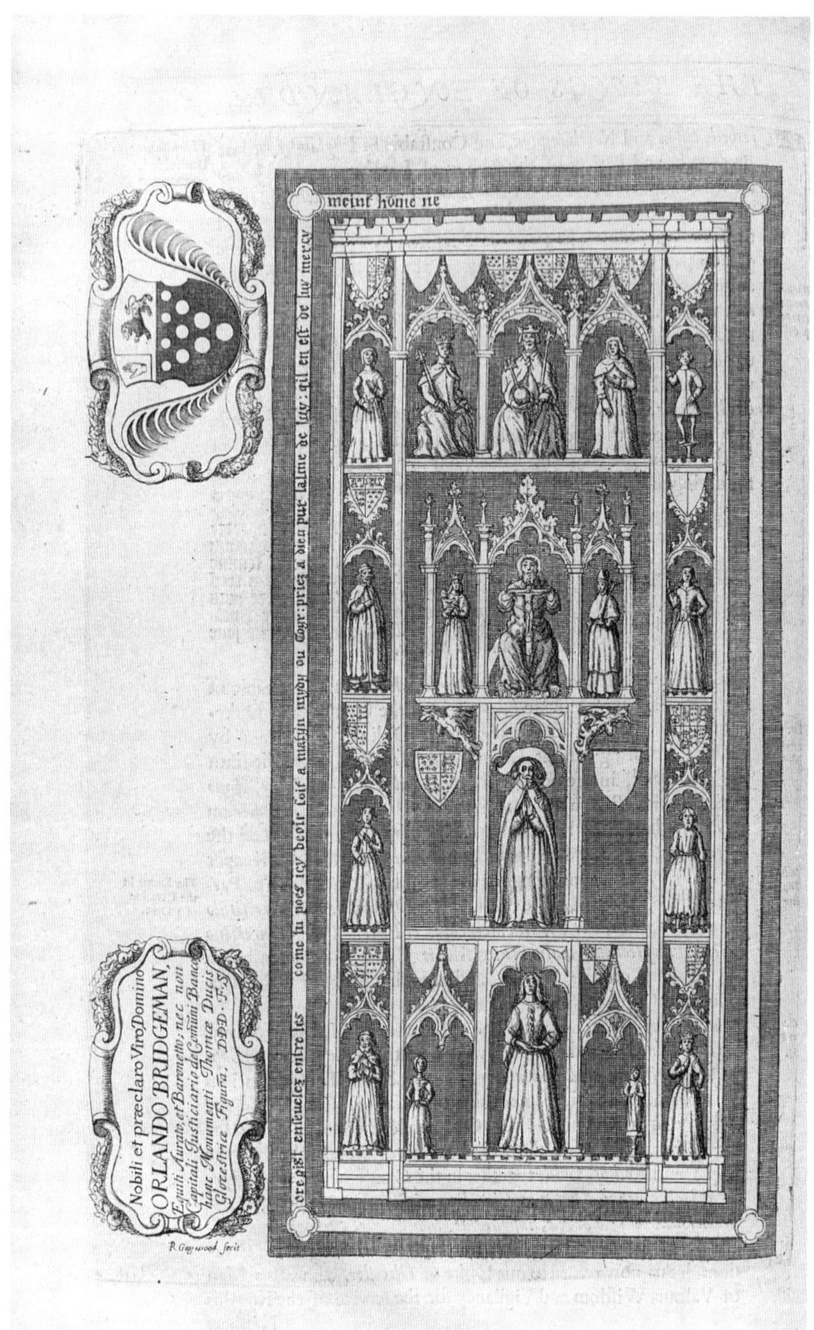

119 An eighteenth-century engraving of the magnificent lost brass to Duke Thomas de Woodstock, 1397, once in the Confessor Chapel at Westminster Abbey. The duke's figure is comparatively small, no larger than those of his family and ancestors who surround him.

cases standard patterns were often employed. As early as 1936 J.A. Knowles drew attention to the links between York glass and contemporary brasses, though his arguments were vitiated by his belief in a German origin for brasses which are in fact either local or Flemish products.[39] In fact, there is firm evidence that there were workshops which produced both brasses and stained glass. The London marbler and glazier Richard Stevens has been associated with Series 'D' brasses.[40] The elaborate colouring of a fine 'D' brass, that of the Earl and Countess of Essex at Little Easton, and even its construction of small plates, recalls the appearance of stained glass. William Heyward of Norwich (d. 1506), who was responsible for the best-designed local series of brasses, also functioned as a glazier. Windows at both East Harling and St Peter Mancroft, Norwich, have been attributed to him.[41] Some of the York brasses may have been produced as a sideline by men whose primary business was glazing.[42] One type of brass, in which the deceased is shown as a kneeling figure, is undoubtedly derived from stained-glass design. It is instructive to compare the priest and St John the Baptist at Aspley Guise, Beds., of *c.* 1410 (fig. 120) with a panel by Thomas Glazier of Oxford at Winchester College Chapel, depicting

120 Kneeling figures of a priest in academic dress before St John the Baptist, of about 1410, at Aspley Guise, Beds. This style 'B' brass is closely related to the window shown on fig. 121.

121 A stained-glass window in Winchester College, showing Richard II and St John the Baptist, providing an obvious parallel to the design of brasses such as that in fig. 120.

Richard II with his patron saint (fig. 121).[43] Usually the object of the kneeling person's devotion was represented either as an independent element above, as at Morley, or in a cross-head or on a bracket, as at Hildersham or Upper Hardres.[44] Sometimes, however, as in the case of the fine effigy of William Langeton at Exeter Cathedral,[45] that focus is taken to be a carved or painted image in the chapel where the brass is placed, thus integrating it more securely in the architectural setting.

Design links with other media are less easy to establish. Fine engraving may hint at the involvement of goldsmiths, and there are a few late instances where such involvement is documented.[46] A difficulty in establishing such links at an earlier date is the poor survival rate of English precious metalwork. Occupying a no-man's-land between branches of metalwork are objects such as engraved latten lecterns[47] and devotional panels. Remnants of several English equivalents of the Susa triptych survive as palimpsests. The most remarkable of these was found at Frenze, Norfolk (fig. 104).[48] The subject can be identified as the slaying of Sweyn by St Edmund. It is likely that it formed part of a screen or door near the saint's shrine at Bury. If so, it belongs to the repairs carried out after a disastrous fire in 1465, when the greater durability of a brass panel would have been especially appreciated.

Ronald Van Belle has drawn attention to the memorial function of several fifteenth-century Flemish paintings and their links with brass design.[49] English painted panels may similarly be seen as a chief source of inspiration for the mural brasses of the late fifteenth and early sixteenth centuries. Again, iconoclasm in both media has deprived us of much of the means of comparison. A particularly attractive survivor is the Annunciation at Fovant, Wilts., set up shortly after 1492 (fig. 122). The precise iconographic type, with the Virgin wearing a diadem and having her hands crossed, can be traced in London art back to the beginning of the century.[50] The involvement of the donor in the sacred action is a commonplace in Netherlandish painting, and can be found in English panels such as the Martyrdom of St Erasmus at the Society of Antiquaries.[51] The naturalism of the Northern Renaissance is reflected in the brass of Geoffrey Fyche (d. 1537) at St Patrick's Cathedral, Dublin, in which the canon is shown praying in a panelled oratory before an altarpiece of the Pietà (fig. 123). Similar illusionistic interiors can be found in contemporary manuscripts and early printed books.[52] The stylistic relationship between early sixteenth-century brasses and wood and metal cuts deserves to be explored in detail. The contrast between raised and incised drapery folds on the Fyche brass is reminiscent of a Wynkyn de Worde woodcut of 1519.[53] An earlier woodcut which evokes comparisons with brasses is that of Henry VI invoked as a saint, of *c.* 1490–1500, a single copy of which survives in

122 A small devotional brass of a type once common, showing the deceased, George Rede, as a 'donor' kneeling at the side of a scene of the Annunciation; Fovant, Wilts., 1492.

the Bodleian.[54] The kneeling supplicants in this image resemble Richard and Katherine Amondesham at Ealing.[55]

As Edmund Paston's letter implies, the brass engraver was not necessarily the originator of the design. The medieval artist might be required to prepare designs for a wide variety of media, as is apparent from the Pepysian Sketchbook and other medieval model-books.[56] Although it is not possible as yet to point with confidence to the originator of any of the standard patterns used by London workshops of the fourteenth and fifteenth centuries, in at least one case a probable design source can be suggested. Certain narrow-shouldered London 'A' military effigies of the 1360s, such as Sir John de Mereworth at Mereworth, Kent (fig. 81), or Thomas Cheyne at Drayton Beauchamp, Bucks., bear a close resemblance to wall-paintings of two military saints, dating from 1350 or 1351, formerly in St Stephen's Chapel, Westminster.[57] The studding of Thomas Cheyne's greaves and cuisses, and even the curious pendant bells below the knee, can all be paralleled on the image of St Mercurius. The Westminster figures were painted on narrow piers between windows, and represented as partly cut off by the surrounding niche. This spatial illusion was neglected by the adapter of the design, who consequently emphasised the compressed nature of the image.

123 A pictorial brass made in London in 1537, placed in St Patrick's Cathedral, Dublin, showing Dean Geoffrey Fyche kneeling in a panelled chapel before an altar with a painting of the Pietà as a reredos.

124 Margaret Svanders, 1529, shown shrouded behind a tablet held by angels on a brass probably designed by her painter husband Gerard Horenbout. Fulham, Middx.

Not until the early sixteenth century does one have the opportunity in England to assign a brass with reasonable certainty to a named artist and compare it with his work in other media. At Fulham is a lozenge-shaped Flemish plate commemorating Margareta Svanders (d. 1529) (fig. 124).[58] She was the wife of Gerard Horenbout (or Hornebolte), the 'most renowned painter of Ghent' (as the inscription styles him) and the mother of two other artists, Lucas and Susanna, and it is sensible to look to the members of this family, which had come to England in 1522, for the source of this noble representation of a shrouded figure. Lucas Hornebolte was to become King's Painter in 1534, and as a pioneer of the portrait miniature might be considered a likely creator of this intimate design. However his 1525–6 Fitzwilliam Museum miniature of Henry VIII, with its scrawny angels and clumsy lettering, does not inspire confidence in such an attribution.[59] There is an intriguing possibility that Susanna, who is prominently mentioned in the inscription, was responsible for the design. Albrecht Dürer had thought

125 One of a series of allegorical engravings by the eccentric Richard Haydock, this brass to Erasmus Williams, 1608, at Tingewick, Bucks., shows him framed by complicated symbols.

it worthwhile purchasing a miniature painted by her at the age of eighteen in 1521, but no surviving work can be attributed to her.[60] However the most likely candidate is Margaret's husband Gerard (*c.* 1465–1540), a panel-painter, miniaturist, and designer of ironwork, tapestries and stained glass.[61] The careful construction of the design with its strong symmetry and the classicising detail of the inscription

126 Sir John Wynn, 1626, at Llanwrst, Denbighshire, engraved by Robert Vaughan who had earlier engraved a portrait of him as a print.

tablet accord with his documented additions to the Sforza Hours. More precise comparisons may be made with a miniature in a book of hours now in the J. Paul Getty Museum.[62] As on the brass, the text on this page is placed on a tablet with a moulded edge held by two angels. Margaret's shrouded head is very similar to that of a matron saint on the left of the miniature.

Post-medieval brass design manifests a similar variety of influences to those noted above. Sculptors such as Gerard Johnson, Epiphanius Evesham and Edward Marshall adapted their styles to the demands of the medium as had medieval marblers.[63] Many late sixteenth- and early seventeenth-century brasses follow the forms of contemporary portraiture. This influence is particularly marked in a series of trapezoidal plates emanating from a York workshop.[64] Perhaps the most interesting productions of this period are the efforts of line engravers who were primarily book illustrators. The emblematic concoctions of Richard Haydocke, such as that at Tingewick, Bucks. (fig. 125), are the visual counterparts of the conceits of Jacobean poetry.[65] The finest examples of this genre are undoubtedly the portrait brasses of various members of the Wynn family at Llanwrst, executed by the Wrexham goldsmith Silvanus Crue and the London-based Welsh line-engravers Robert and William Vaughan.[66] Sir Richard Wynn's decision to incorporate brasses in the Gwydir Chapel is probably a case of conscious antiquarianism, in keeping with the historical interests of the family. But the forms devised are novel. Robert Vaughan's brass of Sir John Wynn (fig. 126) which began the series is closely related to the portrait engraving of Sir John which he had earlier executed for the family.[67] William Vaughan's rectangular plate commemorating Lady Sarah Wynn (d. 1671), a neglected masterpiece of English Baroque art, is conceived as a title-page. Judged by the aesthetic standards of the fourteenth century, the Llanwrst brasses are disasters. Judged by the standards of their own day, as they should be, they are effective and imaginative monuments.

In recent years art historians have become more aware of the need to look across the whole range of media when assessing the art of a period, disregarding the misleading division into 'major' and 'minor' arts. It is only when monumental brasses are viewed as part of that totality, and not isolated as antiquarian curiosities or manifestations of social history, that their true worth can be appreciated.

CHAPTER 8

The Care and Conservation of Brasses

MALCOLM NORRIS

The study of brasses and of what they can tell us about belief, fashion, heraldry and families, and about the craft that made them, may be based on records, the research of antiquaries and comparison with allied arts, but above all it is based on the actual surviving brasses themselves. The conservation of these memorials is a vital aim of the Monumental Brass Society and of all those truly interested in the subject. Conservation is therefore a relevant subject to include in this book.

What is meant by conservation? We would suggest that it can be defined as 'the preservation and care of brasses in their appropriate setting, preferably in their original position, and with regard to the patina and wear that ageing has inevitably brought'. (Respect for patina is no mere sentiment, as patina is an important defence against corrosion.) This is not overall a passive, *laissez-faire* definition. It is one that demands great commitment from all those concerned with these memorials, considerable discipline, and a respect for brasses as treasures of the church, in which past worshippers and benefactors have invested, confident that their successors will value their memory.

Surprisingly, in view of their apparent durability, brasses – and even more so incised memorial slabs – are very vulnerable. The reasons for their often deteriorating condition are various.

First, since they are predominantly floor monuments, they have been subjected and remain subject to much wear, depending on the position in which they lie. The Courtenay brass (*c.* 1410) in Exeter Cathedral and the Golafre fragments (d. 1396) in Westminster Abbey are sad examples of the consequences of being set in places exposed to heavy tread. An example of a badly worn, though not completely obliterated, brass, is that from Barnham Broom (fig. 71). This wear is not confined in its injurious effects to general scratching of the surface and obliteration of the design. Continual tread imposes flexing of the metal if there is any hollow below the brass plates, which is frequently the case if the bituminous mastic bedding has deteriorated. This leads to loosening of the plates and the eventual loss of component parts. An example is the famous brass of Sir Hugh Hastings at Elsing, Norf. (fig. 131) from which small pieces gradually worked loose and became lost over the last two centuries since the first rubbings were made. Important parts of the canopy, the inscription, shields, two angels and the legs of the figure became detached, were for a time left loose in the church chest, and gradually disappeared from the site, in a few cases to surface later in salerooms or museums, from which several have been restored to the church.

Second, because of their position (especially in the case of high tombs), brasses and incised slabs are not infrequently moved. Reasons may include changes in church layout, reorganisation of space following changes in liturgical fashion, the insertion of heating systems, or the relaying of whole floors. Sometimes brasses were carefully transferred together with their stone slabs, even moving to different churches, as at Cowfold, Sussex, moved from Lewes Priory, or Wappenham, Northants, from Biddlesden Abbey. In other cases they were grouped in a specific part of the church, as at Cobham, Kent. But more often such care is wanting; many high tombs were destroyed, usually on the grounds that they took up too much space, as at Iver, Bucks., 1508, and very large numbers of brasses have been removed from their slabs and mounted on the walls without regard for their context. In some cases this may have protected the plates from damage, but the divorce of brass from slab is quite inconsistent with proper conservation.

Third, a common result of the above practice is that brasses and incised slabs are often placed in positions which lead to their deterioration through damp penetration or contact with inappropriate material. Brasses set directly against lime-washed walls, or fixed with iron nails or bolts, can suffer severely from corrosion, which damages the surface of the metal and leads to loosening of the plates. Indents, or important fragments of incised slabs, are frequently simply discarded, or buried under concrete. At Iffley near Oxford a very fine fifteenth-century indent was long left exposed in the churchyard, and it is suspected that a portion of an early fourteenth-century incised slab from St Bartholomew the Great, London, was carted off in a sale of rubble. Moreover, ignorant attempts at care can make the damage worse: coarse matting laid directly over the brasses collects dust and grit, which can scratch the surface badly. Any sort of rubber or plastic-backed mat causes condensation, and may soon decay, sticking to the surface of the metal, and setting up dangerous chemical reactions. Polishing brasses with abrasive cleaners such as Brasso, while it may show local pride and concern for the brass, inevitably leads rapidly to the engraving being totally polished away.

Fourth, thefts from churches are becoming increasingly common. The isolation of many village churches, which are less frequently used by their communities as the numbers of resident clergy decline, makes this all the easier. Increased mobility makes it possible to remove stolen goods from the scene of the crime very rapidly, and the consistent refusal of governments to ratify the UNESCO convention on stolen art treasures means that once they have passed through a saleroom very little can be done to recover them. Churches near motorways or airports are particularly vulnerable to the calculating art thief. The loss of the important brasses at Brampton Ash, Northants., is but one example of a theft that was probably planned. Other thefts seem to be simple opportunism, encouraged by the overall insecurity of the target, often at popularly visited churches like Broadway, Worcs., where the Daston brass of 1572, after which a whole style of engraving has been named, was stolen a few years ago. Thankfully this one was subsequently recovered, but many small brasses have disappeared without trace.

Lastly, well intentioned but poorly informed attempts at restoration can make problems worse, even though in the short term these attempts may have preserved brasses that would otherwise have disappeared altogether. In 1994 the fine Wyndham brass of 1571 at St Decuman's, Watchet, Som., had to be completely re-laid, since in the nineteenth century the plates had been refixed with round-headed pins driven only into wooden plugs. The brass was, as a result, very insecure, and the lower half of one figure was quite loose. In the 1950s the major Flemish brass of Alan Fleming, 1361, at Newark, Notts., was riveted to a steel frame and laid directly on to wet concrete. This caused considerable corrosion, and has meant the need for complete re-laying. A remarkable case of undisciplined intervention which combined inappropriate restoration with additional engraving was the treatment of the two pairs of brasses at Fowey, Cornwall. Comparable ill-informed recutting of incised slabs took place at Prestbury, Cheshire, and Enford, Staffs.. Replacing lost parts of monuments may be an attractive and apparently positive action, but too frequently the end result only reinforces the need for caution.

Conservation is a challenge to continual vigilance, lest brasses become loose or vulnerable, be subject to heavy wear or abrasive polishing, be used for supporting damp flower vases or simply be forgotten as irrelevant relics of an unwanted past. There is a difficult balance to be struck between ensuring that these memorials are accessible for appreciation and study, and ensuring that they are not so exposed that they deteriorate. It may be argued that what is not seen is not at risk, but this is largely untrue. Brasses locked up and forgotten in cupboards or chests frequently 'travel' – as in the case of the fifteenth-century Melman inscription at Sall, Norf. The modern fashion of carpeting churches from wall to wall not only hides the floor memorials of all sorts but conceals their condition and indeed their continued existence. Two very important brasses at Merton College, Oxford, were recently discovered to be bright green with corrosion from rising damp which had been concealed from sight for years under a supposedly protective carpet. (In this case the discovery prompted the college authorities to have all the brasses properly conserved and re-laid in their original slabs, a welcome response.)

Conservation is also a challenge for collaboration and collective responsibility. Few parish churches have adequate resources to maintain the fabric, let alone elaborate fittings and accessories, as well as meeting pastoral demands. Even where there is strong interest and a keen sense of responsibility, there remains a severe conflict of interests. Parochial Church Councils are necessarily careful bodies, cautious in their deliberations, prudent in expenditure and resistant to the seemingly endless urgings of outsiders. They tend to move slowly and warily, which is quite understandable if they have become used to tolerating a situation for a long period because nothing could be done. Hence the central importance of funding agencies, whether well-established national bodies like the Council for the Care of Churches or English Heritage, private charitable funds like the Francis Coales Charitable Foundation, or controversial commercial ventures like the National Lottery. However, for any of these funds to operate, needs must be brought to their attention, and procedures carefully followed to ensure that the work is necessary, will be appropriate, and will be effectively carried out. Resources seem slim in the face of potential demand, and the very need to determine priorities can lead to delays which in turn increase the eventual expense. There are few skilled and experienced conservators of brasses, and since the work is rarely 'profitable' in a commercial sense, it is unlikely many more will be forthcoming.

Supervising bodies, like Diocesan Advisory Committees, have an important role in making recommendations on applications, yet it is not their task to take initiatives, but rather to react to them; they cannot compensate for lack of interest or initiative at parish level. Archdeacons are more assertive, but they have a very wide brief and are fully aware of the constraints under which parishes operate. It is not surprising therefore that the main responsibility devolves on the local clergy, who are in a position to perceive the needs, guide the interest and ensure some action; but they too have a many-faceted role with fiercely competing priorities. Some clergy in fact consider the care of historic monuments totally irrelevant to their vocation. Those who do not can find their position quite exasperating, as for instance one group of activists campaigning for the protection of bats insist that broken church windows must not be repaired, while others agitate to stop the damage inflicted by the bat droppings.

In this confusing and inhibiting situation, those who have a real interest in the preservation of brasses and incised slabs have potentially a very useful role, especially if their energies are channelled through a disciplined and resourceful society. The Monumental Brass Society aims at being such an organisation. Isolated individual action can be fruitless, if enthusiastic or judgemental complaints are continually made over a state of affairs of which the church authorities are fully aware, whereas a systematic monitoring of the situation in conjunction with those authorities can produce real results. Local secretaries of the Monumental Brass Society can receive information from individual members, and when appropriate pass it on to the clergy, using the Diocesan Advisory Committees. Advice can be offered by the society, backed up with information on potential resources, a willingness to assist in raising funds, and even access to a modest primary fund. An initial financial commitment, however small, very often opens access to more substantial resources. In some cases the society finds a total lack of interest, but in the majority of cases interest can be aroused once a course of feasible action can be identified, and the urgency of the problem explained. What is most necessary is awareness of good conservation practice, and the means of achieving and sustaining it. Many good practical measures are not expensive, as long as the situation is not neglected until damage becomes severe.

The following measures are suggested as reasonably practical for churches to follow, and fully in accordance with good conservation principles:

1. Brasses should be kept clean with a duster and a paraffin rag, with an occasional application of 'Renaissance' micro-crystalline wax, which helps resist corrosive elements. Any form of abrasive cleaner should be avoided. This, of course, demands restraint: visitors to Elsing have expressed disappointment at the drab appearance of the superb brass of Sir Hugh Hastings after its expert conservation, but keeping it like this is in the best interests of the brass.

2. Wherever possible brasses and incised slabs should be in positions where they are not exposed to wear. A case in point is at Northleach, Glos., where the brasses can easily be admired and studied without risk of tread and disturbance.

3. If brasses and incised slabs are not intrinsically protected by their position, they should be adequately covered with felt or some other very soft material. It may be necessary to cover this in turn with a

heavier carpet. Such covering – though never impervious, which would cause condensation – may also be necessary even on a high tomb if the church provides a home for large numbers of bats, as at Somerton, Oxon.

4. An alternative to covering, if the brasses are not located in main walkways and are available for inspection, is to protect them with a light wooden railing, or a rope sufficient to discourage careless walking. Good examples of such practice are at Exeter Cathedral and Stoke Fleming in Devon; Chipping Campden, Deerhurst and Northleach in Gloucestershire.

5. Ideally it should be ensured that brasses and incised slabs can be viewed without having to move heavy furniture or other equipment. In some churches brasses can only be seen after removing wooden covers; this was formerly the case at Elsing, where the heavy iron chains attached to the covers used to crash down on the fragile brass as the covers were replaced. The total permanent covering of monuments is especially deplorable, as it entirely disregards their purpose, and means that there is no way of

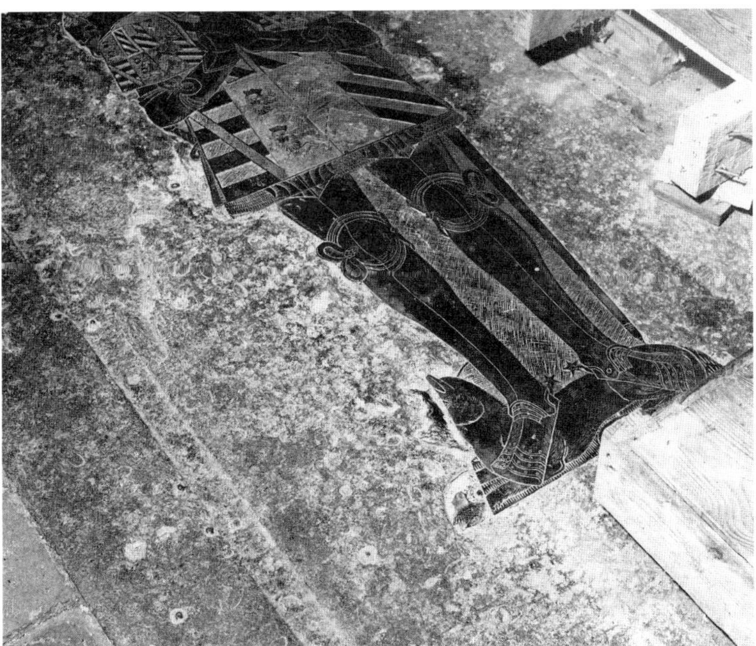

127 The brass of Sir Richard Catesby (his feet on a cat), 1553, at Ashby St Ledgers, Northants., under repair in 1972. The flooring has been removed to reveal the brass; dowel heads in the foreground (additional to those for his lost marginal inscription) prove that the slab once held an earlier brass, the indents for which have been planed away.

monitoring any corrosion or damp that is concealed from view. In some places only 'keyhole' access is available, as at Battle, Sussex, where the brass of William Arnold can only be seen through a trap door: this is an unsatisfactory compromise. Figure 127 shows how the important palimpsest brass at Ashby St Ledgers had to be liberated from its wooden prison before restoration could begin. A number of brasses are now concealed under fitted carpets – at Fressingfield, Suffolk, the church guide at the time of writing continues frustratingly to emphasise an attractive brass of 1489 which is covered in this way.

6. Where brasses and incised slabs are set on high tombs it is important, though difficult, to ensure that they are not used as bases for seasonal ornaments such as Easter gardens, or stands for water-filled vases full of flowers. There is need for care and tact here – the most formidable element in any parish can be the decorators, and high tombs are often positioned in key positions on either side of the sanctuary, where flower displays are seen to best effect. But the gradual damage to both stone and metal is very considerable. If the position must occasionally be used, some sort of protective covering should be made.

7. If brasses or slabs are attached to the walls, great care is needed to ensure that they are protected from damp penetrating the walls, and are isolated from corrosive elements such as limewash or iron. A brass nailed with iron nails on to whitewashed plaster will inevitably corrode badly, and innumerable such cases exist. The task of remedying this is enormous, and much still needs to be learned.

8. The pernicious influence of damp is greatly worsened if the monuments, whether on walls or floors, are not allowed to 'breathe'. This they can do if exposed to the air or covered only by soft carpeting. They cannot do so effectively if under glass, perspex or any impermeable carpeting or sheeting. Damp is trapped under the covering, usually first manifesting itself by clouding the underside of glass or perspex so that the brass becomes invisible in the fog. Unfortunately much expense has been incurred in the past in covering brasses in this way, nearly always to poor effect. The overall attractiveness of the monument is greatly diminished, especially if, as at Shorwell, Isle of Wight, the frame for the perspex pays no attention to the shape of the carved stonework around the brass. Among the most important brasses covered in this way are Lord Camoys at Trotton, Sussex, and the early Greenefeld brass at York (fig. 28), both on high tombs. There are many other

examples, particularly in Surrey. Even when the covering has been removed, holes for the bolts that formerly fixed it remain a permanent disfigurement on the slab, as at Buslingthorpe, Lincs. Covering with glass is not an appropriate method of conservation.

The measures described are essentially the prudent means of preserving memorials which are not in a threatening or severe state. Expert attention is needed when brasses are found to be clearly insecure, if green corrosion is visibly penetrating the metal or if the plates are lying very 'proud' of their slabs. In these cases a qualified conservator would be needed to remove the brasses, clean, re-rivet and reset them in their slabs. Brasses are often found in isolated insecure churches and in damp situations, so that their conservation, while carried out according to the modern practice of 'minimum intervention', must provide security from theft and protection from damp. The methods are analogous to the original medieval process, the plates being bedded on bituminous mastic which provides support and protects them from damp, while the new rivets are secured in the slab with inert resin rather than lead. Figure 128 shows the brass at Ashby St Ledgers, Northants., under repair, and the revealing of the palimpsest reverse.

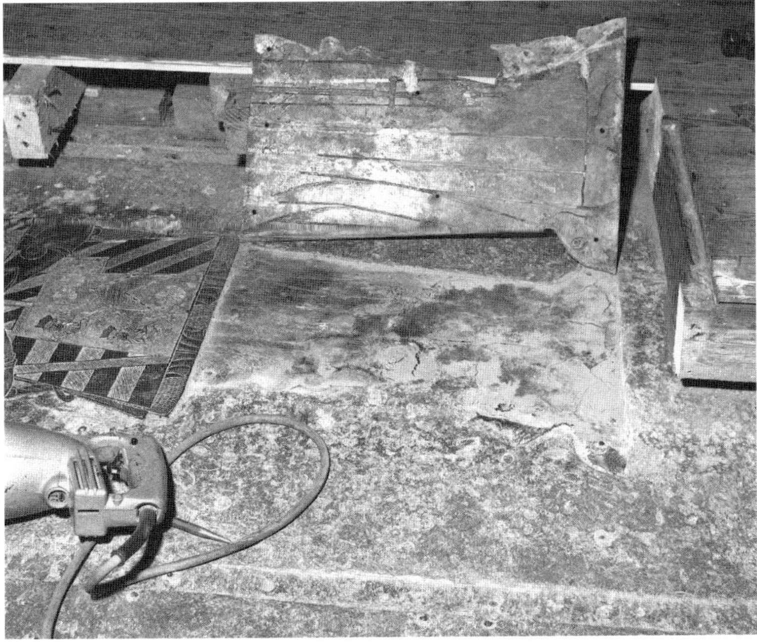

128 Sir Richard Catesby, Ashby St Ledgers. After centre tapping and drilling through the old dowel heads, Sir Richard's legs were raised to reveal a palimpsest (see fig. 108). The indent is still filled with pitch, imprinted with a mirror image of the palimpsest.

Brasses that have been divorced from their slabs and screwed to the wall need either to be set into suitable boards for mounting on the wall, or, if funds permit, re-laid in new stones, wherever possible ensuring the correct original alignment of the plates and outlining missing parts. Setting brasses on boards is often controversial, not only for the choice of wood (oak, for example, emits acids which are injurious to copper alloy) but also from the aesthetic viewpoint that the use of wood is an inadequate substitute for stone. Nevertheless the use of boards is a cost-effective solution which effectively removes the brasses from the source of corrosion and provides additional security. In some cases where brasses had been taken up from their slabs and placed on the wall it has been found possible to return them to their original slabs, a most satisfactory outcome. An example is at South Ockendon, Essex, where the Bruyn and Barker brasses (1400 and 1602 respectively) had been displaced for a century.

If a brass is seen to be in need of attention the correct response is to inform the Diocesan Advisory Committee secretary, and the Monumental Brass Society's local secretary, if there is one, or the general secretary. If adequate resources for the repair are not available locally this does not mean that they cannot be obtained. Under *no* circumstances should economies be sought by getting a firm inexperienced in the conservation of brasses to attempt a repair; this is likely to lead to much greater long-term expense, and can cause permanent damage to the brass. This is especially risky if the brass is of complex composition, such as with the enamelled copper inlays at Carshalton, *c.* 1490 (front jacket illustration), or on the shield of the elder Sir John Daubernoun at Stoke d'Abernon, both in Surrey. The rewards of specialist treatment are apparent, notably at Carshalton, where the removal of corrosion from the plates was placed in the hands of a specialist metalwork conservator. Another outstanding piece of recent work is at Christ Church, Oxford, where the apparently uninteresting Walrond brass of 1602 turned out to be surrounded with a most interesting painted framework, which was carefully restored by Anna Hulbert, a wall-painting conservator.

An important contribution to conservation can be made with polyester-resin replicas. These replicas, unlike the casts formerly found in such abundance in brass-rubbing centres, are precise copies made by taking a mould from the original, which moulds should only be made by an expert. Such replicas have a variety of uses which have not yet been sufficiently exploited. First, they can provide an alternative to the original for those seeking to make rubbings. Careful brass rubbing does no harm whatever to a brass providing the plates are well set,[1] but there are many instances where access to brasses can be difficult and inconvenient and creates possible risks, not by the rubbing process itself but the need to be in close contact with potentially fragile stonework. A good example is the Beauchamp brass of 1406 in St Mary's, Warwick, which was set in the seventeenth century in a stone frame high up over the doorway to the Beauchamp chapel. Rubbing the original would clearly be difficult and dangerous, so the provision of a replica is a good measure, which allows much better examination of the detail of this outstanding brass. For all but the most exacting scholarly purposes a polyester resin cast is an entirely accurate record of the design.

Second, such replicas afford a wholly satisfactory alternative to the exposure of both sides of a palimpsest brass. In the past access to both sides was often provided by mounting the plates in hinged frames, as at Harrow and Harefield, Middlesex, or St Lawrence, Reading. The intention is good, but the result is disfiguring, and the risk of damage or theft increased. Even more risky was the Oxford University Brass Rubbing Society's practice in the 1890s of refixing palimpsests with 'patent screws' which in theory could only be opened with a key, but in practice usually yielded to a penknife!

Third, replicas provide an alternative to restoring lost parts of memorials, which is always controversial in conservation terms. If the desire is to display the monument as it was when perfect, this can be well done by making a replica and incorporating missing parts from old rubbings or drawings. The brass of Sir Hugh Hastings was treated in this way, and the replica made available for display in the society's centenary exhibition in London. Another brass which invites such a reconstruction in replica is Lady Athol, 1375, at Ashford, Kent, whose now armless figure appears quite inexplicable.

Fourth, replicas can be used to protect valuable brasses. This approach is currently proposed at Gorran, Cornwall, so that the original brass can be kept in a locked vestry but the replica be displayed for casual visitors. The remarkable Spryng brass (1486) at Lavenham, Suffolk, could well be made more visible in this way, as could the swaddled infant of 1580 at Pinner, Middlesex, long hidden away in a safe.

What then of brass rubbing in the context of conservation? Suffice it to repeat that careful rubbing does not itself constitute a risk. Indeed, access to brass rubbers invites regular inspection, cleaning and observation which all too many brasses lack. There can be no doubt that the astonishing level of interest in brass rubbing in the 1960s and '70s put an unacceptable pressure on certain famous brasses, where queues for rubbing had to be introduced. However, the current decline in such interest is in some respects to be regretted, since it deprives churches of visitors, a modest source of income and an awareness of their treasures. Far more brasses have been stolen in the period since 1975, when brass rubbing was effectively killed off by high fees and the proliferation of 'brass-rubbing centres', than in the fifteen years of interest before then. There may of course be no connection, but the evidence is inconsistent with the not uncommon story that brass rubbers were responsible for thefts. In contrast, incised slabs present a very different picture: they are not really vulnerable to theft, but can be damaged by rubbing, for the condition of the stone may be unstable and friable. 'Dabbing' rather than rubbing (see p. 178) exerts much less pressure and may be suitable for slabs which are too fragile to rub. Rubbing of incised slabs should only be selectively allowed, and when the stone is deteriorating not permitted at all.

We conclude by considering the return of alienated brasses to their original positions, a rare but satisfying occurrence. There are many loose brasses or fragments, some in museums or private collections, others known only from rubbings in old collections, notably those of the Society of Antiquaries and the British Library. Among these displaced brasses are a pair of figures of national importance for their period, as well as fragments of brasses otherwise still in their churches. In some cases these loose plates may be best left where they are, either in the safety of a museum or in recorded private care. In other cases however the best interests of conservation are clearly to be found in restoring the brasses to their proper places. The Monumental Brass Society was able to take a leading part in restoring elements of the Hastings brass to its slab in Elsing, including a long-lost angel which was discovered by Claude Blair and Malcolm Norris in a London antique dealer's shop in 1961. Other brasses have been returned at Hinton St George, Som.; Marcham, Berks. and Little Chesterford, Essex, while the society is now engaged in restoring three fragments from the collection of the late John Page-Phillips through the generosity of his widow. The most spectacular of recent restorations has been the rediscovery of half a dozen huge brasses which were believed to have been destroyed in the Second World War. They eventually surfaced in the Hermitage Museum in St Petersburg, and are now back where they belong in Poznań, Poland.

This is an especially satisfying aspect of conservation, reversing the erosion of these memorials through theft and carelessness, and asserting confidence in the future and the pleasure and instruction people to come will have from them. But this focuses on a very unusual, if not romantic, aspect of conservation work; the real and regular business is to ensure that what we have remains safe, is kept in good order, and is carefully attended to. The task is one of regular monitoring, responsible initiative, and widening information, so that, with the addition of adequate funding, brasses and incised slabs will remain a feature of our churches for the future.

CHAPTER 9

Brass Rubbing, Reproduction and Collections

MARTIN STUCHFIELD AND PETER HESELTINE

The origins of brass rubbing are, regrettably, obscure. There exist a number of mid-seventeenth-century oil paintings which portray the interiors of old churches in the Netherlands with groups of children who, as in fig. 17, are gathered around a boy who is clearly rubbing something on the floor – presumably a brass or incised stone. The earliest brass rubbing which has been discovered lies among the papers of the seventeenth-century antiquary Edmund Gibson; these are preserved in the Bodleian Library at Oxford.[1] This interesting relic relates to the revision of Camden's Britannia and was taken from the curious brass commemorating Roger and Elizabeth Legh, 1506, at Macclesfield, Cheshire (fig. 129). To obtain this early rubbing Gibson's correspondent appears to have used a piece of graphite and two sheets of paper.

129 The oldest known brass rubbing, made by Henry Prescott in 1693 for Edmund Gibson, now in the Bodleian Library. It shows Roger Legh, 1506, from Macclesfield, Cheshire, with the well known 'Mass of St Gregory' devotional panel.

Another early impression is contained among the volumes of manuscript notes on Suffolk churches by the antiquary Thomas Martin (1697–1771), most of which are now kept in the County Record Office at Bury St Edmunds.[2] This important rubbing is of the lost inscription which was engraved to the memory of Thomas Melle, dated 1526, and originally laid in Kirkley church near Lowestoft. The rubbing was made with pencil on rough paper with the character outlines being subsequently delineated with pen and ink. Although undated it is likely that the plate was recorded at the time of Martin's transcription when he visited the church on 14 March 1754.

The antiquarian interest in brasses which blossomed in the eighteenth

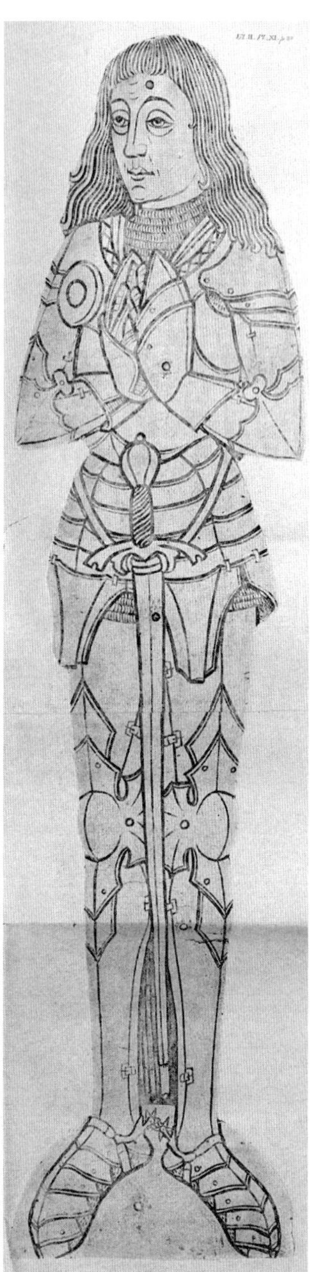

130 A print taken off the surface of the brass, bound into Gough's Sepulchral Monuments. *The figure is the only surviving part of a brass requested by William de Wingfeld, in his will of 1509/10, to depict himself with his two brothers, all in armour, at Letheringham, Suff.*

century led to the earliest collection of rubbings – or in this case impressions – by Craven Ord (1756–1832) and Sir John Cullum (1733–85). These are now preserved in the British Library[3] and are especially valuable since they include many parts of brasses which are now lost. Ord, in partnership with Cullum, started work in about 1780 and employed a technique that is unlikely to find favour with present-day clergy – nor with their church cleaners. In this somewhat messy procedure, brasses were covered with printing ink so that it flowed into the incised lines; the surplus was wiped off the flat surface and sheets of damp paper (dipping in the Thames was supposed to be singularly efficacious) were laid over the surface. With the aid of rags and cloths, pressure was placed on the paper to press it into the incised lines to make a reversed, albeit faint, impression. This pale image was later 'improved' with pen and ink or brush. The work of Ord and Cullum was inspired by Richard Gough (1735–1809) who produced his *magnum opus* between 1786 and 1799.[4] Contained in it are three folded sheets made in the Craven Ord method from Letheringham, Suffolk (fig. 130). Gough, however, cheated slightly as he took these brasses home to make the impressions. Only in comparatively recent years have some of the brasses he removed been returned to the church.

Brass *rubbing* as we know it today appears to have started when various methods were developed to produce an impression, including, for example, the use of a lead plummet, which, due to its extreme hardness, tended to tear the paper, and was indistinct. Our fig. 131 is a rubbing of 1838 made with graphite, which is also rather faint. The wax used by shoemakers for blackening the leather, called 'heelball', was found to be more satisfactory. The use of a special brass-rubbing wax was introduced by Messrs Ullathorne, of Long Acre, London, who perfected a heelball suitable for brass rubbing during the late 1830s. Ullathorne's wax, manufactured from a composition of beeswax, tallow and lamp-black, was available in a variety of hardnesses and in both stick and cake form (about the size of an old penny) to suit the particular condition of the brass. In collections of old rubbings Ullathorne's heelball can be easily recognised as, over the years, it acquires a whitish bloom which can be wiped off. Shoemakers' heelball, which was considered to be greasy and prone to produce a grey result, was ultimately superseded by a wax bearing the brand name 'Astral' which is produced by F. Ball and Co. Ltd, of Leek, Staffs., and remains widely used today – and still bears the traditional name 'heelball'. This harder wax includes shellac. Modern brass-rubbing wax is available in a number of colours, although even this fashion is not new – H. S. Richardson of Greenwich produced a gold heelball in the nineteenth century.

Interest in rubbing brasses has waned significantly since the boom of the 1960s and '70s. At its height, bookings for months in advance were

131 King Edward III and Lord St Amand, appearing as mourners for Sir Hugh Hastings, 1347, Elsing, Norf. This graphite rubbing was made by John G. Nichols in 1838.

required to gain access to the more popular brasses, while the proliferation of books on brasses strained the pocket of even the most ardent collector. Numerous articles appeared in the *Bulletin* of the Monumental Brass Society expressing concern that brasses were being rubbed excessively, citing examples of poor behaviour in church and warning of the dangers of commercialism. This popularity had the effect of causing many churches to restrict or ban rubbing even to the serious student. It had the accidental effect of stimulating interest in other forms of recording such as photography.

Undoubtedly the introduction of synthetic resin facsimiles has contributed to the decline in church brass rubbing, as much perhaps as the change in taste and the movement away from the black and white décor of the 1960s. For many reasons, possibly including the lack of atmosphere in a brass rubbing centre compared to the antiquity and serenity of a parish church, interest declined steadily throughout the 1980s with the resultant closure of those centres not situated in major tourist areas. It would be appropriate to take this opportunity to condemn centres which promote facsimiles of fictitious brasses to the uninitiated visitor. Those depicting 'Henry VIII', 'Elizabeth I' and 'William Shakespeare' do little to encourage a serious study of the subject. The best centres do, however, serve to ensure that the techniques of rubbing are learned on a replica, and from this start many people have gone on to develop a lifelong interest.

Before the procedure for rubbing a brass and the various methods of reproduction are discussed, that of finding the brasses and obtaining permission to rub them should be outlined. Many books contain lists, of varying accuracy, of churches containing brasses. The most comprehensive work is Mill Stephenson's *List* (1926), reprinted in 1964, but again out of print. It can be found in most reference libraries, and very occasionally turns up on the second-hand market. Since the early 1970s this essential reference work has been in the process of revision and updating by members of the Monumental Brass Society. The revisors are checking the accuracy of the original list and extending its scope to include nineteenth-century memorials, indents and an indication of the workshop or style of each brass. This material will be held on a computer data bank and is being issued in sheet form to members of the society.

In addition to the general books on brasses, most major brass counties have a publication listing the monuments in the county churches. These local publications are of varying age and usefulness. The majority, except the most recent, can be found listed in Richard Busby's *Beginner's* and *Companion Guides*. Among recent general works, John Page-Phillips' revision of Macklin (1969) includes brief revised lists and maps. A new endeavour, which is superseding the piecemeal revision of Mill

Stephenson's *List* is the publication, county by county, of a complete fully illustrated list of brasses by William Lack, Philip Whittemore and H. Martin Stuchfield, beginning with Bedfordshire in 1992.

It is essential, indeed there may even be a legal obligation apart from good manners, that a person wishing to take a rubbing first obtain permission from the relevant authorities. In most cases the incumbent (the rector, vicar or priest-in-charge) is the individual responsible. His or her name and address is given in *Crockford's Clerical Directory*, available at most reference libraries. It is recommended practice to obtain permission in advance as this can prevent disappointment on turning up unexpectedly – churches are used for other functions.

Some brasses cannot be rubbed because of inaccessibility – at Tilbrook, Beds. and Toppesfield, Essex they are covered by the organs. Brasses at Leighton Buzzard, Beds., Monkleigh, Devon and Waltham Abbey, Essex are impossibly high on the wall. One at Staverton, Devon, is on an external wall covered by a grille. Normally rubbing is not permitted on Sundays and on Saturdays the church may be in use for weddings. Funerals are an unpredictable hazard! One of the authors has watched a coffin and mourners process over his half-finished and hastily covered rubbing. A fee is payable and is normally fixed by the church although some clergy still request a donation – which should be realistic. When writing to the church, a stamped addressed envelope should be included for the reply.

Specialised materials are advised for brass rubbing and, as a general principle, these should be adhered to since they produce the best results and avoid damage to the brass and the church. The three essential ingredients are wax, paper and masking tape.

Waxes of varying quality can be obtained from a reputable artists' supply shop, and 'Astral' wax or heelball produced specifically for the job is obtainable from the Monumental Brass Society. Its main advantage over other waxes is its ability to produce a crisp, dark and even black image without the build-up over the lines resulting from the use of more greasy materials. Gold and silver heelballs are available but have some disadvantages in reducing the crispness of the image, and, because their use involves a thicker than normal black paper, a less clear impression of essential fine detail. Most rubbings for museums or serious collections are traditionally produced as black on white, as are most of the illustrations in this book. It is however fair to note that the main collections contain a number of rubbings in gold on black taken in the nineteenth century. Heelball is manufactured in two sizes, as a stick and as a cake the size of a bar of soap. Sticks are normally used although the larger cake is useful for large areas of brass. It needs to be carefully controlled lest it lead to spectacular tears. Hand-sized cakes can be purchased or made by melting down the remains of sticks of heelball and pouring the hot wax into a suitable container – egg-cups produce a very conveniently shaped cake. The molten wax should be cooled very slowly to avoid cracking.

The selection of paper can prove more of a problem. Ideally it should be tough, but not thick; it should be capable of withstanding storage for long periods of time without discolouring or becoming brittle. Wood pulp or recycled papers with high acid content are unsuitable. An all-rag detail paper, which is available in a variety of widths and lengths, is best suited for the purpose. Unfortunately it is expensive and the 60-inch wide paper which is needed to rub some of the larger compositions is becoming increasingly difficult to find. For most brasses the normal widths of 20 to 40 inches are sufficient.

The third prerequisite is masking tape – *not* transparent cellulose tape – which is needed to secure the paper to the floor or wall without damaging the surround, particularly if the brass is fixed to a plastered wall. The ordinary cellulose tape has been known to remove large chunks of whitewash, in fact most mural brasses are surrounded by little rectangles of plasterwork where paint has been removed by the inconsiderate. Nineteenth-century books on brasses recommend the use of 'wafers' – which were small sticky labels rather like postage stamps: a misunderstanding of this has led some people to absurd and irreverent attempts to make paper stick to a wall with communion wafers! It is worth remembering that many churches have prohibited brass rubbing because of irreverence, carelessness or the damage caused by using incorrect materials.

Other items which it is useful to transport to the church include scissors, a soft brush (for example a wallpaper-hanging brush), a small dustpan and a soft duster. Some people find it useful to have with them an illustration of the brass they are to rub, or a sketch-book to note the component parts. Once it is covered by the paper it is easy to forget the details of a complex design or the position of the protruding hilt of a dagger.

The actual procedure for rubbing is relatively straightforward once the brass has been found, which can sometimes be quite difficult. The church guide will often give the precise position and it may be necessary to remove furniture carefully or roll back a carpet, which should always be replaced on completion.

The following method of rubbing is one the authors have found successful; in time most people will build up their own variations.

1. Kneel by the side of the brass, never on it. Clean the brass and the stone or marble surround with the soft brush to remove all traces of grit, dust, bat droppings and other debris. If this is not done carefully, the brass may be damaged and the paper will almost certainly tear – traditionally in the last moments of rubbing.

2. Unroll the paper and cut off the necessary length, leaving a reasonable margin at top and bottom.

3. Secure the paper along the top edge and roll it down. Before fixing feel over it carefully with your hand to make sure all bits of grit have been removed. Stick the paper down by placing a piece of masking tape on to the paper at a downwards angle. Give it a slight tug before stretching it to the stone. Do this again on the opposite side of the paper to ensure the section is taut. Work down the edges of the paper using masking tape at about 6- to 8-inch intervals. On some large memorials it can be advantageous to secure 1 or 2 ft of paper at a time, completing the rubbing and then cleaning the brass and unrolling and fixing more paper.

4. Carefully outline the composition with your fingers so it stands out – this will help to show you where the edges are and avoid inadvertently rubbing over them. Unless a rubbing of the stonework is also being included, you will not want to leave marks on those parts of the paper which are intended to be white, although it is a common modern practice to rub the whole slab, brass and stone, to give the complete composition. Where there are missing parts indicated by an indent or recess in the stone surface, these should be carefully outlined and the position of any surviving rivets or channels shown.

5. Feel over the paper again and note where any protruding rivets are likely to tear the paper. It may be advisable to make a small hole at this point for the metal, to avoid tearing the paper and enabling it to lie flat on the brass. The hole can easily be repaired from behind when the rubbing is completed.

6. Hold the heelball fairly flat and begin rubbing at the top of the brass. To begin with it may be best to make an 'L' shape with the other hand by stretching out the thumb and laying the palm of the hand flat on the paper. By rubbing within the outstretched hand, it is possible to control the length of the rubbing strokes more easily. Try to rub in the same direction throughout – this is normally up and down, following the main lines of the engraving, going with them rather than across them. The aim is for a good even finish, not necessarily jet black (although many rubbers pride themselves on this) but one in which all the engraved lines are crisply and precisely shown. It will not always be possible to obtain a perfect rubbing – after all, the brasses were not made for artistic reproduction.

7. Finish each section before moving on. Returning afterwards is not always successful as the paper flexes and distorts slightly under the pressure of rubbing, or occasionally as a result of climatic conditions. A difficulty frequently encountered is a damp floor or wall and the consequent stretching of the paper. Due to its composition paper is particularly unstable, and rubbings are likely to blur and become indistinct. One solution is to put the paper down and leave it for 20 minutes, then tighten it up again before rubbing.

8. When the rubbing is complete, check that all the details have been included – even experienced rubbers can occasionally forget the small piece of sword which crosses behind the legs. Polish the brass carefully with a clean soft duster which will help to remove the marks of rubbing. Peel the masking tape off from the paper outwards to avoid tearing it. If any of the brass or stone has been obscured by the tape, rub beneath it before moving on to the next piece.

9. Finally, clear up. Sweep up any bits of heelball, masking tape, etc, and take them away with you.

This procedure is suitable for most floor brasses and many of the mural ones. Where a brass is recessed into a stone frame, other techniques may be necessary. Double-sided tape can be employed to secure paper which is cut to exactly the size to fit the frame. (Be very careful not to let the heelball slip off the edge of the paper and mark the frame.) Double-sided tape is also needed to rub brasses where parts are against a wall or step as at Tolleshunt d'Arcy, Essex, or recessed into the floor as at South Benfleet in the same county.

An alternative method of producing a rubbing is dabbing – a process which is much less popular today. It is still effective for recording brasses which are either worn or finely engraved and for indistinct slabs where the stone has flaked and the indent is not clearly defined. (For the latter a newer method is to use an archaeological grid and graph paper to produce a scale drawing.) The first step is to prepare a dabber by wrapping chamois leather round rags to make a ball or pad. This should be firm and with a flat base.

Prepare a paste of even consistency from powdered graphite and either olive oil or linseed oil. Spread this on to a piece of cardboard. Cover the brass or stone with tough white tissue paper as you would for rubbing. Dip the dabber into the paste until an even blackness has built up on the dabber and apply it firmly and evenly to the paper to build up a dark grey impression. In certain circumstances, where the engraving is particularly fine, it may be preferable to wrap the chamois leather round a finger in order to provide the sensitivity necessary to bring out the fine detail. The results can be crisp but faint.

A third method of reproduction which achieved some popularity in the past is the reverse rubbing which involves producing an image where the engraved lines appear black and the rubbing white. Since this is another messy procedure it is advisable to experiment on small, clearly incised and relatively simple compositions. Initially, a rubbing is made in the normal way but using a white wax on white detail paper. It can be done with a white candle, but white heelball is more effective. At home the engraved lines should be filled meticulously with Indian or black waterproof ink and left to dry thoroughly. The wax is then removed with a paraffin-soaked rag to leave a reverse impression. This technique can be most rewarding for recording heraldic shields, where the intention is the accurate delineation of the tinctures with coloured paints and enamels. Although effective, the reverse rubbing requires considerable patience and skill.

Rubbings produced as historical records should not be cut out, mounted or touched up in any way. Damage and tears can be effectively repaired with a flour-and-water paste and paper which will not stain the rubbing in the long term. Rubbings should be clearly labelled and a system, for example a card index or loose-leaf folder, developed for maintaining records of the brass. This would normally cover the name and any personal details of the individual commemorated by the brass, the church and its location, the date of the rubbing, the dimensions of the slab and a note of any parts which were lost at the time of rubbing.

The storage of rubbings presents difficulties – most collectors and many local museums and record offices have still not found a satisfactory method. If photographic reproduction or exhibition is required, the rubbings should not be folded. An architectural storage cabinet is suitable for storing smaller rubbings while a 610 × 880 mm artists' portfolio can be used for transporting them. Various classification schemes can be developed including topographical order, date order, workshop styles or costume classification. For larger rubbings the possbility of rolling them up inside a plastic drain-pipe could be considered. The cardboard tube in the centre of a carpet or linoleum roll is another possibility.

In recent years the photographic reproduction of brasses and indents has become important to the recording and study of brasses. For some people a photograph is an essential adjunct to a rubbing as this sets the brass in its context in the church. For others, photography forms an alternative to the laborious task of rubbing, although the use of a camera is not straightforward.

The decision about whether to take transparencies or prints in colour or black and white depends on the use to which they will later be put. If the intention is to provide talks and lectures, the advantages of taking slides are obvious, especially as it is usually possible to take reasonable-quality prints from them if required. Colour film, whether prints or slides, is essential when recording the coloured enamel or mastic which still exists on many brasses (e.g. Little Easton, Essex; Broxbourne, Herts., or the one illustrated on the jacket). Intricate engravings, especially goldsmiths' work, as at North Crawley, Bucks., and Great Berkhamsted, Herts., as well as the colour and fossil structure of the stone into which the brass is set are notably suited to reproduction in colour. Such details are impossible to record with conventional rubbings. The contrast provided by black and white prints is essential for book illustrations, conservation reports and archive purposes.

Permission to photograph the brass will be required in exactly the same way as rubbing if ladders, tripods and lighting are to be employed. Wherever possible, it is preferable to photograph brasses with the aid of natural light while making sure that shadows from leaded or stained windows do not inadvertently obscure the brass. The use of a tripod is crucial, particularly with the long exposure which may be necessary in darker corners, since the slightest jolt or vibration will blur the image. Brasses on the floor should be photographed from overhead, and a step-ladder will often be necessary.

Many brasses are located in dark corners and an independent light source will be required. Flash units fitted to cameras have limited success since the direct flash can eliminate detail through excessive glare. An independent flash source or photoflood will give better results, although it will be necessary to obtain permission if using the church's power supply. Those new to the use of photography will find it advisable to experiment with different camera positions and exposures, keeping a careful record to compare the developed results.

The study of brasses is greatly facilitated by the existence of collections of rubbings dating back to at least 1800. Most local record offices and museums have a few, but great national collections exist at the Victoria and Albert Museum, the British Museum and the Society of Antiquaries in London. Outside London, the Cambridge University Library houses the huge Cambridge Collection and the Ashmolean Museum and Bodleian Library in Oxford hold smaller but valuable assemblies of rubbings.

Those in the British Library Department of Manuscripts tend to be older ones – such as those made by Ord and Cullum: they are valuable collections and very fragile. The Victoria and Albert Museum collection is extensive and organised topographically. Many of the rubbings arrived at the museum as discarded material from the Antiquaries, so the collection contains little or nothing which is not to be found elsewhere, but the catalogue has been published.

Oxford's Ashmolean Museum collection is good on Oxfordshire particularly, and contains quite a lot of material on lost brasses. The Bodleian holdings include a number of collections with some valuable older rubbings, but it is more noted for its manuscript drawings and antiquarian notes, which include references to many lost brasses. The British Library and the College of Arms are also extremely fruitful sources of such material. Many local record offices and libraries have little-known collections of church notes and rubbings which would repay research.

The two major collections are at the Society of Antiquaries at Burlington House in Piccadilly and at the University Library, Cambridge (formerly at the Museum of Archaeology and Ethnology). The Cambridge collection is nearly complete for the whole country and includes rubbings by many famous names. It has impressions of many lost brasses, few of which cannot also be found in the Antiquaries' collection. Rubbings in both collections are arranged topographically and stored flat in large portfolios. Those at the Antiquaries have recently been photographed by the Historical Manuscripts Commission and are available on microfiche. As all the collections are ageing, access to them is rightly restricted and only allowed to those with a genuine purpose in consulting them. The projected national repository of brass rubbings in memory of Malcolm Norris should be more accessible, although it is unlikely to be anything like as complete.

CHAPTER 10

A Case History

In this chapter a number of authors look at a single brass, one by no means spectacular, and indeed one that many would pass over as of little interest. The brass chosen is that of Sir John Bassett and his wives Elizabeth and Honor, at Atherington, Devon. It is not, at first sight, a spectacular or unusual composition, but a series of insights, from different aspects, show what an informative source this brass can be. The chapter provides a model for the study of individual brasses which could be applied to many other cases. The brass itself is illustrated in fig. 132, the tomb on which it lies in fig. 133.

I) Ordering and Later History
JON BAYLISS

Following the death of Sir John Bassett in 1528, his widow Honor married Arthur Plantagenet, Lord Lisle. He was appointed Lord Deputy of Calais in 1533, a position which kept the Lisles abroad and forced them to run their English affairs by correspondence. When Lord Lisle was arrested on suspicion of treason in 1540 his letters were seized by the Crown as possible evidence. Three of the letters to Lady Lisle report progress on the provision of a brass to Sir John Bassett, which she had ordered before she left for Calais in July 1533.[1]

Unfortunately, the name of the maker of the brass is not given. The first mention of it in the letters is of its despatch from London.[2] It went by carrier as a set of plates to the Bassett house at Umberleigh in Devon in November 1533. It was normal practice for a brass to be set in its stone in the workshop where it was made. However there are a number of instances where it is obvious that brasses were sent for laying locally, particularly in the further flung reaches of the country. Transport of the stone slab was a major expense if a brass was to be transported any distance from the workshop and examples may be seen in Wales and Yorkshire of London-made brasses laid in local stones. In the case of the Bassett brass, this cost-cutting measure must be set against the large sum of money, five pounds, asked for gilding the brass and colouring the

132 The London style 'G' brass to John Bassett, d. 1528, and wives Honor and Anne, made in 1533 and fixed by a local mason in Umberleigh Manor chapel, now at Atherington, Devon.

arms, which considerably exceeded the cost of engraving, thirty-three shillings and fourpence. This gilding, assuming it was indeed done, took place after the brass reached Devon.

The final stage in the process was the laying of the brass at Umberleigh, which was done by a local mason, Oliver Tomlyng, as reported in April 1534.[3] That Tomlyng was not entirely familiar with the practices of laying a brass is clear from the incorrect positioning of the two sets of children, which were set under the wrong mothers and thus look outward rather than inward as intended. The positioning of the figure of Sir John slightly further up the slab than his wives is also unusual. It was no doubt these two peculiarities and the use of local stone which formerly led to the brass being described as re-laid at a later date. It was not until July 1534 that George Rolle, clerk of the records of the Court of Common Pleas, a Devon man who had paid for the brass to be engraved, wrote to Lady Lisle to say that he had been reimbursed.[4]

The chapel of the Manor House at Umberleigh was demolished in 1818, and the rood-screen, monuments and some other fittings were moved to the nearby parish church of Atherington, where they remain to this day. As two of the letters describe the brass plates as being for a tomb, which was not a term used for a floor slab only, and the slab is now on top of a tomb-chest, this may also be the work of Oliver Tomlyng.

II) Analysis of the Style
MALCOLM NORRIS

The stylistic characteristics of the brass of Sir John Bassett present no problems, according predictably with the established date of the memorial. It is a good standard product of what is currently grouped as the 'G' series, a series first appearing at the very close of the fifteenth century, early dated examples being at Kedleston, Derbyshire (d. 1496) and Hempstead, Essex (d. 1498), though it is likely that both were engraved somewhat later. After *c.* 1530 the great majority of brasses attributed to London engravers can be related to this series until the 1580s, though with considerable variations in conventions and quality.

In many respects the 'G' series appears at its worst during this period, having lost the bold, if coarse, simplicity of brasses such as Thomas Brewse Esq and wife (1514) at Little Wenham, Suffolk, but preceding the improvements evident in Roger Gifford and wife (1542) at Middle Claydon, Bucks., which in turn were followed by those reflected in the far more accomplished 'Fermer' group of brasses, of which Richard Fermer Esq. (1552) at Easton Neston, Northants., is an excellent example[5] (fig. 76). The Atherington figures are inelegant, the lines strong but not perceptively drawn, and the male figure badly proportioned. Shading is applied inexpertly and heavily on the adult representations. In the memorial's favour the overall presentation is confident and the ensemble eye-catching. The children, who are very simply represented, would not appear out of place on a brass ten years earlier, but the arrangement of mixed groups, correct in numbers and gender, leaves no doubt that they were made with the adult figures.

A variety of stylistic features are typically 'G'. With regard to the people, the widely opened eyes, the mouths with strongly defined lips, and the clumsy hands, with finger-nails but no indication of bone structure, are notable. The apparently excessive length of Sir John's leg from knee to instep is a consistent 'G' peculiarity. The voluminous gowns of the women conceal any such idiosyncrasy. In terms of dress, certain aspects of equipment are distinctively 'G'. These are the simple rounded sabatons, the fastening of the tassets represented as segmented rectangles, and the sword belt with its looped end. A further distinctive detail is the representation of the grass in little clumps, expressed by a curving horizontal line supporting the blades.

An interesting brass for comparison is the rich heraldic composition of Sir William Gascoigne at Cardington, Beds., slightly later but, with the exception of the grass, having many similar details. While there remain a few contemporary brasses of probable west-country origin as at Hutton, Som. (1528) and Doynton, Glos. (1529), style alone would assert the London provenance of this brass notwithstanding the appearance of the local setting of the plates.

III) Armour and Arms on the Brass of Sir John Bassett

CLAUDE BLAIR

Sir John Bassett wears a conventionalised representation of a full field armour of the early sixteenth century, very old-fashioned for the time of his death; it is accompanied by a mail collar (standard) and a mail skirt, which would have been attached to a padded arming-doublet worn underneath the armour. The square-toed sabatons (matching contemporary civil footware), rounded one-piece breastplate and pauldrons with haute-pieces are all characteristic of the period. The Gothic one-piece tassets are particularly old-fashioned, though the evidence of graphic and sculptured sources, including brasses, indicate that these probably remained in use rather longer in England than on the continent. The same sources also suggest that the suspension of the tassets from the middle, rather than the edge, of the skirt of the cuirass was an English fashion. The weapons are a standard cruciform arming-sword with arched quillons, and a ballock-knife of a kind represented on a number of contemporary alabaster effigies.

The ultimate source of the design was probably an Italianate armour of generally similar shape and construction to Henry VIII's famous silvered and engraved armour in the Royal Armouries at the Tower of London (No. II 5), though without the latter's unusual steel parade-skirt. Inaccuracies in detail, however, leave no doubt that a drawing made from a real armour was a very long way removed from the one used by the engraver. There is no lance-rest, the tasset-straps and buckles are shown as hinges, the poleyns either have a side-wing on each side or a single one that completely encircles the knee – it is not clear which – both of which would be impossible on a real armour, the pauldrons appear to be made solid, so that they would have been quite inflexible, and their haute-pieces have been distorted and curtailed. They appear, in fact, to be misunderstood versions of the type of pauldron with a solid reinforcing-piece attached to the front.

IV) Costume of the Wives of Sir John Bassett
KAY STANILAND

The two wives of Sir John Bassett are shown identically dressed to denote their identical status, a typical convention in brasses. The women depicted are generalisations dreamed up by the engraver rather than careful portraits, and they show what he imagined a lady of the second Lady Bassett's standing might look like.

The dress of Lady Bassett is indeed typical of her status in Tudor society. Eschewing the very elaborate and extravagant fashions adopted by the noble ladies of the royal court, she displays a certain conservatism and conventionality while at the same time adopting one or two new fashions useful for demonstrating her rank as the wife of a country knight. Thus her gown's style is that established somewhat earlier in the century: a close-fitting bodice with wide square neckline, close-fitting upper sleeves and a fairly full skirt. Underneath she wears a linen chemise gathered into a neckband and probably fastening with a button or a small brooch. Her head-dress, the ubiquitous gable worn with a stylised English hood and stiffened back section, was already beginning to fall out of fashion; underneath, the edges of a close-fitting linen cap protrude.

Lady Bassett would have owned many gowns of high-quality English cloth. Fineness of spinning, weaving, dyeing and finishing were what was sought in these expensive woollen cloths, making them nearly as costly as the silk damask or velvet which would have been the only alternative for Lady Bassett. In her sleeves we find a concession to fashionable novelties, less practical than the rest of her dress. Her undersleeves, separate from the main body of her gown, were interchangeable, thus allowing variety in dress; they were probably of a rich material such as satin, with vertical stitching to hold padding in place. The wrist frills foreshadow the ruffs so soon to adorn fashionable necks and wrists. One of the most potent symbols of wealth and status was the lavish use of expensive imported furs such as sable or marten, and her large hanging fur cuffs bring Lady Bassett's ensemble more nearly up to date.

The use of gold or silver, either in embroidery or jewellery, were further indicators of wealth and status. The fret decoration on Lady Bassett's gable head-dress, for instance, probably took the form of couched gold or silver threads; noblewomen and royal princesses enriched this ornamentation further by adding pearls or precious stones. Girdles and belts also provided opportunities for rich display and were widely worn by both sexes. Lady Bassett is depicted wearing what is obviously an ornamented girdle from which is suspended a pouncet-box on a long chain. These perforated receptacles held pomanders or sponges soaked in aromatic vinegar and were used to ward off diseases and alleviate unpleasant odours, truly the accessory of a lady of standing and refinement.

Sir John Bassett's daughters are depicted uniformly dressed as adults, with gable head-dresses and gowns with simple turn-back cuffs of earlier sixteenth-century date. Their brothers wear the long gowns also more typical of earlier sixteenth-century male fashions.

V) The Heraldry of the Bassett Brass
JOHN PAGE-PHILLIPS

There were four brass shields on the Bassett memorial, as well as two carved stone ones on the north side of the tomb, designed to identify the families connected to Sir John Bassett and those of his two wives. On the south side of the tomb are five shields, one blank but with an impaling line, and four with initials 'S', 'I', 'K' and 'B', presumably for Sir John Bassett, Knight, reset out of order when the tombs were moved from Umberleigh (fig. 133).

On the brass, there is one missing shield that probably duplicated the one next to it. This bears I and IV: *barry dancetty or and gules* for Bassett, II: *barry of six vair and gules* for Beaumont; III: *argent a saltire vair* for Champernowne. The Beaumont quarter represents John Bassett's grandfather's marriage to Joan Beaumont, who had brought the Bassett lands round Umberleigh. The nearby cross-legged stone knight, *c.* 1240, is said to be a Champernowne, and the Champernowne arms are

133 The tomb-chest for the Bassett brass, Atherington, Devon, made by Oliver Tomlyng in 1533.

carved on the jupon of the late fourteenth-century effigy of a knight with his lady. (All these monuments were brought from Umberleigh chapel in 1818.)

On the shields below we have Bassett quartered as above, impaling *gules, three clarions or* for Grenville, under the dexter wife, and *azure, three battleaxes erect or* for Dennys under the sinister one. This agrees with the present arrangement of the children, even though they implausibly look away from the centre, for it is the first wife, Ann Dennys of the battleaxes, who had the one son and four daughters, the second, Honor Grenville of the clarions, who provided three sons and four daughters. The description of the Grenville arms as 'clarions' classifies them as musical instruments, hand-held Papageno pipes, although they have variously been described as rudders, brackets, lance rests, horseman's rests and other names. The two carved stone shields on the north face of the tomb repeat the impaled arms for the two wives. They may originally have been on opposite sides of the tomb, adjacent to the relevant figures, for the tomb as it stands is obviously something of a collage.

VI) The Life of Sir John Bassett
PAUL COCKERHAM

Coming from a wealthy family long established in the West Country, John Bassett was the eldest son and heir of Sir John Bassett, of Tehidy, in Cornwall. He succeeded his father in 1485, aged twenty-three, and inherited substantial estates both at Tehidy and at Umberleigh in Devon, with large houses at each.[6]

John is first recorded as one of the justices of the peace for Cornwall, in company with other members of the county aristocracy. As such, he was concerned not only with legal disputes and trials at the Sessions in Bodmin and Truro, but also with the administration of the king's policies in the area. During his years on the Bench, John must have experienced at first hand an increase in the level of lawlessness especially in the west of the county, centred around the poverty of the miners. It was unfortunate therefore that the heavy taxation voted by Parliament in 1497 sparked off two uprisings among the Cornish, in the year in which John was appointed Sheriff of Cornwall, and to whom therefore fell the task of dealing with the offenders.[7] Fortunately both rebellions came to nothing, though the house at Tehidy was severely damaged by the miners as a protest at John's loyalty to his position, and his involvement in the unpopular task of levying fines on the known offenders.[8]

For these services John was knighted in 1502, and he continued thereafter in the public role of local government incumbent on his status in the county, being appointed Sheriff twice more in 1518 and 1522, and Sheriff of Devon in 1524. In none of these periods of office however were his activities as noteworthy as before.

Domestically Sir John Bassett broke with family tradition and settled at Umberleigh, perhaps because Tehidy was too close to the mines and the belligerent miners. There he adopted the life of a country squire concentrating on his estates and rural pursuits rather than on affairs of state. Life would have been far from dull, as he was constantly engaged in a private war with his neighbours across the river at Brightly, who assaulted the Bassetts' servants, dammed up the mill sluice, poached salmon and generally created mischief.[9] No doubt Sir John retaliated in a similar fashion. More conventionally, however, he considerably developed his estates at Tehidy and Umberleigh, and also presented several priests to livings within his patronage, notably the advowson of Camborne, with its links with the rich and powerful Glasney College.[10]

Sir John first married an undistinguished local woman, Ann Dennys, who gave him no surviving male heir. In his fifties he married again, his bride this time being Honor, a daughter of Sir Thomas Grenville, whose estates were close to Umberleigh, just over the county border at Stowe.[11] Honor provided him with a second family before he died in 1529 leaving his son and heir John, aged only nine, to succeed him.[12] His widow remarried Arthur Plantagenet, Lord Lisle, and thereby capitalised on her new-found links at Court; for example her daughter Anne Bassett was a maid of honour to Jane Seymour, and was even rumoured to be a likely candidate for the king, just before, fortunately for Anne, he married Catherine Howard.[13] Lord Lisle died in 1541 leaving Honor again a widow, to die in relative obscurity over twenty years later at Tehidy in her native Cornwall.

VII) The Children of Sir John Bassett
JOHN PAGE-PHILLIPS

As well as illuminating the process of manufacture of the brass, the Lisle letters enable us to glimpse the lives of Sir John's second wife Honor Grenville and her children and stepchildren.[14] The relevance of the letters to the Atherington brass is that Honor Grenville, after a year of mourning for Sir John Bassett, married Lord Lisle, and the letters were all received by them. For Honor, this second marriage was a social lift. Lisle was a bastard son of Edward IV, brought up in the royal household and called variously Arthur Plantagenet or Arthur Wayte.

At first she moved with her children and some of her stepchildren to Lisle's home at Soberton in Hampshire, but in 1533 he was appointed Lord Deputy of Calais and moved into the Staple palace within the walls. The 'Lisle letters' are those received by the Lisles during the next seven years in Calais. They survive because they were seized as evidence for a trial that was never held.

The move to France was the opportunity for the two unmarried stepdaughters, Jane and Thomasine, to return to Devon to Umberleigh Manor, where their father's brass lay in the manor chapel, and where they had many nearby relations, including their two married sisters, Margery Marres and Anne Courtenay. Their one brother, probably John, is only known from the brass and must have died many years before. Jane, the eldest daughter, now in her forties, wrote to her stepmother asking for permission for her and Thomasine to stay at Umberleigh and have the pasture of one cow in the park. But there were arguments with Sir John Bonde, a priest responsible for the manor accounts, as well as the yearly obit for Sir John Bassett. Jane thought that he was too old and inefficient, defrauding Honor of fishing money. He may have been inefficient, with failing eyesight, but Jane was difficult. He complained that he had been locked out of the back door. Eventually Thomasine fled from her sister early one morning and sadly her death was reported eighteen months later.

However, as Lisle's wife, Honor was able to raise her own children above the simpler country existence of her stepchildren to the Court of Henry VIII. In France, she arranged for them to learn French. One daughter, Katherine, became a lady to Anne of Cleves, but another, Anne, became maid of honour to Jane Seymour, Anne of Cleves, Katherine Howard and Katherine Parr. She was an attractive girl and in 1542 was one of three in whom the king showed a marked interest. Another daughter Mary had been learning French with Madame de Bours and became involved with a young Monsieur de Bours without royal permission. She and Honor were arrested and caught throwing love letters down the 'jake'. Years later she married a local Devon man in Atherington church.

Of Honor's sons the eldest, John, went to Lincoln's Inn. The letters describe how he must be kitted out with clothes, bedding and fuel. He married his stepsister Frances, daughter of Lisle by his first wife Elizabeth Grey. We follow the ordering of wedding garments in London, a cap with a white feather and a chain of goldsmith's work for him, but Frances complained about sleeves that should have been turned up with tinsel and a kirtle that should have been silver. A year later a daughter was born and named Honor.

John's two brothers, George and James, both learnt French in St Omer. George was later to live at Tehidy, where his mother spent her last years. James became a servant to Gardiner, Bishop of Winchester, and later (1555) a gentleman of the Queen's Privy Chamber. He married Mary, daughter of Thomas Roper and Margaret, daughter of St Thomas More, an expert in Greek and Latin who translated her grandfather More's 'Treatise on the Passion of Christ'.

Arrested and taken to the Tower of London, Arthur Lisle eventually received a ring from the king as a token of forgiveness, and died of shock or joy. He had reached the age of seventy-nine. Honor, thirty years younger than him, had borne him no children, although a phantom pregnancy is recorded. After his death she went to live in the home of her first husband's ancestors at Tehidy, where she died in 1566. She was buried nearby at Illogan, but the Bassett brass there is to her grandson James.

If Anne Bassett came close to the Crown in 1542, her grandnephew had even grander thoughts. John and Frances, as well as a daughter Honor (above-mentioned) later had a son Arthur (1541–86). His son Robert, Anne's grandnephew, was one of sixteen claimants to the Crown of England in 1603.

Summary of Genealogical Information

Sir John Bassett 1462–1528
m. (by 1474) (1) Eliz. Dennis, d.1515; by her five children:

1. John(?) d. in boyhood pre-1515
2. Jane
3. Margery = William Marres
4. Anne, b. 1490/4 = James Courteney
5. Thomasine, 1490/4–1536

m. (1516) (2) Honor Grenville 1493/5–1566; by her seven children:

1. Philippa, 1516–82 = James Pitts
2. John, 1518–41 = Frances Plantagenet, b. 1518/20
3. Katherine, 1517/20–post 1558 = Henry Ashley, d. 1588
4. Anne, 1521–57 = Walter Hungerford
5. George, 1522/5–98 = Jacquet Coffin
6. Mary, 1522/5–98 = John Wollacombe
7. James, 1526/7–58 = Mary Roper

Notes

Abbreviations

Antiqs J: Journal of the Society of Antiquaries of London.
Arch J: Journal of the Archaeological Institute of Great Britain and Ireland.
CUABC (Cambridge University Association of Brass Collectors) *Transactions 1887–1893* (afterwards the *MBS*).
EEB: COALES, J. (ed.), *The Earliest English Brasses*, Monumental Brass Society, 1987.
ISSCM: International Society for the Study of Church Monuments, later the Church Monuments Society, *Bulletin*, 1979 –
JBAA: Journal of the British Archaeological Association.
MBS Bull: Monumental Brass Society Bulletin, 1971 –
MBS Port: Monumental Brass Society Portfolio, 1894–1914, 1934 –
MBS Trans: Monumental Brass Society Transactions, 1887–1914, 1934 –
M.S. Reference number of brasses in Mill Stephenson's *List* (1926 and Appendix).
M.S.R. Reference number of brasses in Monumental Brass Society's ongoing revision of Mill Stephenson's *List*.
Oxford J: Journal of the Oxford University Brass Rubbing Society, 1897–1912
PCC: The Prerogative Court of Canterbury wills, kept in the PRO.
PRO: The Public Record Office, London.
RCHM: Royal Commission on Historical Monuments.

Chapter 1

1. Kent, 1949.
2. *Antiqs J*, Vol. LXXII (1992), pp. 180–1.
3. *EEB.*
4. Boutell, *Christian Monuments*, 1849; Cutts, 1849; see also Ryder, 1985.
5. Panovsky, 1964, pl. 69.
6. *Arch J*, Vol. XV (1858), pp. 267–77.
7. Firle House, East Sussex, illustrated in Norris, *Craft*, fig. 74.
8. Norris, *Craft*, p. 43.
9. Adhémar and Dordor, 1974.

Chapter 2

1. Dante, *Purgatorio*, canto xii.
2. Busby, 1973; see also Briggs, 1974, and the chapter on Documentary Sources in Bertram, 1976, pp. 76–115.
3. College of Arms MS, RR 19 e/a, Hutton's Church Notes of 1619, f. 20.

4. Camden, 1586.
5. Philipot, 1960.
6. Eventually published as Ashmole, 1736.
7. Dugdale, 1656.
8. College of Arms MS 'Arundel I', RR 29/B, f. 3.
9. Stow, 1598.
10. Stow, edn of 1754, p. 534.
11. Weever, 1631.
12. Gough, 1983.
13. Gough, 1786–99; Bod MSS, Gough Maps 215–228*. (Coney G.M. 225, f.318.); see Badham, 1991.
14. Gough, 1786–99, Vol. I, p. 115.
15. See Wood, 1786, 1790, 1792–6. Mr Gutch was rector of St Clement's, Oxford, where he was assisted between 1824 and 1826 by John Henry Newman, Fellow of Oriel, who himself was to further the study of brasses by editing the Suffolk portion of Dowsing's journal in Wells, 1840.
16. Cotman, 1819.
17. Waller, 1842–64.
18. Cambridge Camden Society, 1840–64.
19. Haines, 1849.
20. Manning, 1846.
21. Boutell, 1847, 1849.
22. Cutts, 1849.
23. Haines, 1861.
24. See Malcolm Norris' analysis of Haines' work in Chapter 5.
25. van Biervliet, 1987.
26. Creeny, 1884, 1891.
27. Stephenson, 1926.
28. Greenhill, 1986.
29. Kent, 1949.
30. Lack, Stuchfield and Whittemore, 1992 onwards.
31. Cameron, 1971.
32. For the history of the M.B.S. and its works, see Busby, 1987.

Chapter 3

1. Useful introductory textbooks are: Blair, 1958; Norman, 1964; Norman and Pottinger, 1966.
2. See, for example, Franklyn, 1970.
3. For example, an inventory of the arms and armour at Farnham Castle in 1295 includes three bascinets, five pairs of plates (armour for the torso), two of which incorporated arm-defences, four plate chin and throat defences (*gorgeris de plat*), five pairs of plate gauntlets, two iron arm-defences (*vaantbras ferr'*), five pairs of greaves with knee- and thigh-defences of plate (*iambers ferr' et pulan' and quisser' de plat ferr'*). I am grateful to Mr Philip Brooks for this reference, which is from the Winchester Pipe Roll for 1295 (Hampshire Record Office, Winchester, Roll E.C. 159318, mem. 10v).
4. See the comparative illustrations pls VI (a) & (b) in Mann, 1939, pp. 276–98.
5. See Mann, 1931, pp. 88–95.
6. See Norris, *Craft*, figs 12, 74–5; *Memorials*, fig. 261.
7. Norris, *Memorials*, fig. 126.

8. Wagner, 1958, i, pp. 338–81; Galbreath, 1977, chs 1, 2; Holmes 1988, pp. 176–7.
9. M.S. II; RCHM, *Westminster Abbey*, pl. 57.
10. *Portfolio Plates*, 10.
11. Adhémar and Dordor 1974, p. 265 (Cordeliers, Nantes) and p. 279 (Abbaye d'Ourscamp).
12. PRO, PCC 15 Godyn, will of Thomas Dauberichcourt, 1466: the monument does not survive.
13. Hunter Blair, 1943, 1–26, esp. pls x–xiii; St John Hope, 1901.
14. PRO, PCC 27 Luffenham.
15. *Portfolio Plates*, 425.
16. *Portfolio Plates*, 326.
17. *Portfolio Plates*, 111 (Wixford); Norris *Craft*, p. 205 (Guildford).
18. Lind, 1894, Taf. xx. 3; xxv. 4; etc, all fifteenth century.
19. *Portfolio Plates*, 118–19, 200; Bruges Town Hall, *Souvenirs 'Britain in Bruges'*, 1966, p. 49 (a Yorkist collar from the brass to Josse de Bul); Lind, 1894, Taf. xxv. 2; xlv. 2, li. 2.
20. *Portfolio Plates*, 118; Cherry, 1969, pp. 38–53. See also Page-Phillips, 1969, p. 79.
21. St John Hope, 1913, p. 304 and fig. 184; Paris, Bibl. Nat., ms lat. 1158, f. 27v, reference supplied by Mrs D. Scarisbrick; Norris, *Memorials*, fig. 78.
22. Thomas Fetherston of Winchcombe, Glos., 1489, PCC 20 Milles; and Sir Thomas Burgh of Gainsborough, Lincs., 1485, PCC 30 Vox.
23. *MBS Bull*, forthcoming.
24. Vossberg, 1854, Taf. 18.
25. E.F. Jacob, *The Register of Henry of Chichele*, ii, 1937, p. 206 Canterbury and York Soc. 42. The brass is at Bobbing, Kent, M.S. I, but it was not executed in accordance with the testator's wishes.
26. PCC 24 Holgrave; the male figures and inscription of this brass of 1505 survive at East Grinstead, Sussex (M.S. I).
27. *Testamenta Eboracensia*, ii. 278; *MBS Bull*, 17 (1978), 13. The brass is at St Peter's, Leeds, M.S. I.
28. Wyrley, 1592.
29. Waller, 1975, pl. 1.
30. *Portfolio Plates*, 12.
31. Lee, 1979, nn. 2 3, 6.
32. Galbreath, p. 92; Pietra Sancta, 1638; Lee, 1979, nn. 8, 10, 13, etc; C. Oman 1978, p. 57 and figs 66–7, 79, 86, etc.
33. Illustrated in *Essex Transactions*, N.S. IX (1906), p. 34.
34. *Visitations of Essex*, 1878, Pt. I, p. 425.
35. *Archaeologia Cantiana*, XXV, lvii; see also *Visitations of Kent*, 1898, p. 167–8; *Portfolio Plates*, 410.
36. *Portfolio Plates*, 359 (Colan), 360 (Oxford).
37. *Portfolio Plates*, 386.
38. Mâle, 1908, p. 437.
39. Mâle, 1908, p. 439.
40. On the whole English antiquaries have not addressed this question, save for the penetrative article by J. Enoch Powell (Powell, 1979), who points out that crossed legs indicate forward movement, and that the horizontal effigy is conceived as a statue in a niche laid on its back: the cushion under the head thus becomes a structural necessity, not an iconographic one. The question is further considered in Bauch, 1976, pp. 64–7; Panofsky, 1964, pp. 26–7, 54–8 (with interesting pre-Christian parallels) and s'Jacobs, 1957, pp. 20, 25.

41. Badham, 'Status and symbolism', forthcoming; Duffy, 1992, esp. chs 9, 10.
42. Cited by Sir Anthony Wagner from an MS in College of Arms in *Arch J*, xix (1939), p 348–54.
43. The Brading tombs are illustrated in Pevsner, *Hampshire and the Isle of Wight* (1967), pl. 58; the Percy tomb in Crossley, 1921, p. 2.
44. Weever, 1630, p. 627.
45. Illustrated in *EEB*, fig. 217.
46. See Tummers, 1988, pp. 3–41.
47. See Walcott, 1880, p. 168. A tiny piece of wrought iron embedded in the side of the pier must be all that remains of the screens that enclosed the chapel.
48. Hammond, 1936.
49. See *EEB*, fig. 58 (St Ina); Norris, *Craft*, fig. 39 (St Ethelred); Blair, 1984 (St Beornwald) and Norris, *Craft*, fig. 7 (St Ulrich).
50. See especially Pugin, *Contrasts*, 1836.
51. Pugin expressed his ideas on brass design in the section on 'Sepulchral Memorials' in his *Apology for the Revival of Christian Architecture*, 1843, and earlier in an article in the *Orthodox Journal* of 1838 entitled 'Monumental Brass of the Fifteenth Century', where he praises brasses as 'truly Catholic monuments' and as most appropriate because they are distinctive, artistic and take up little space.
52. They also produced the very fine book (Waller, 1975) originally issued between 1842 and 1864.
53. 1849, part 1, p. 2.
54. Weaver, 1918.

Chapter 4

1. The numbers in brackets are to the will references listed in the appendix at the end of this chapter.
2. Inscription-only brasses (23 to 30); the lost small cross and inscription brass formerly at Aldeby (31); chalice and inscription brass (32); the lost effigies, inscription and four shields brass formerly at St Margaret de Westwick, Norwich (33); and the rectangular plate with kneeling effigies, children, crucifix and achievement (34).
3. Part of the brass is now returned to the church. The brass has been fully written up in *MBS Trans*, Vol. XII (1979), pp. 300–11, and a full transcript of the will is given.
4. di (dimidium) = half a yard.
5. R.H. D'Elboux, 1949, pp. 187–8, noted, 'John Forest of St Nicholas, Rochester, in 1526, though not indicating a brass, asked for a stone "iij fote of lenthe and too fote of brede the price thereof vij^{s} viij^{d}"'. (Rochester Consistory Court, vii, 273a.)
6. This interesting will, in which the testator requests his cousin's husband in London to 'make' his stone and brass, is referred to at greater length in *MBS Bull*, No. 29 (1982), p. 3.
7. Hood, 1938, p.159.
8. This quite extraordinary will with details of the brass, and some indication of its testator, will be found fully discussed and transcribed in *Norfolk Archaeology*, vol. 38, pp. 280–95.
9. A full account of this delay in Margaret Paston's husband's tomb, and also of her own brass appears in *MBS Bull*, No. 17 (1978), p. 13.
10. See *MBS Bull*, No.11 (1976), p. 9, where there are further instructions for the grave to be well kept, and 'I give to the mason to finish up the stone again decently 3*s* 4*d*'.

Chapter 5

1. Greenwood and Norris, 1976, p. 14.
2. Emmerson, 1978, p. 60.
3. Knowles, 1936, p. 38.
4. The brasses concerned are a shrouded male figure in the possession of the author, one of his wives now in the Museum of Archaeology and Ethnology in Cambridge, and a second wife which was offered for sale in 1908, current provenance unknown; and the figures of a shrouded man and wife at Biddenham, Beds., all of *c.* 1510. The template was apparently used for both semi-profile male and female figures.
5. Page-Phillips, 1969, p. 39.
6. For example Emmerson, 1978, figs 1–7; Badham, 1979, figs 19, 52, 67–69; Greenwood and Norris, 1976, pp. 26–7.
7. Haines, 1861, p. clxxxviii.
8. Druitt, 1906, pp. 12–13.
9. Macklin, 1907, p. 34.
10. Kent, 1949, p. 70.
11. Page-Phillips, 1958.
12. Greenwood, 1971, pp. 2–12.
13. Emmerson, 1978, pp. 50–78.
14. Badham, 1989, York.
15. Badham, 1989, Fens.
16. Badham, 1980, pp. 41–67.
17. Mann, 1957, p. 35.
18. Hartshorne, 1907, p. 26.
19. Emmerson, 1979.
20. Blair, 1987 (in *EEB*).
21. Illustrated by direct photograph in Norris, *Craft*, 186, and with a rubbing in Emmerson, 1978, pl. XI B.
22. Greenwood and Norris, 1976, pp. 30–1.
23. Badham and Blatchly, 1988, pp. 290–1.
24. Kent, 1949, p. 92.
25. Hutchinson and Egan, 1993 et sqq.
26. Norris and Badham (forthcoming).
27. Emmerson, 1990.

Chapter 6

1. Illustrated in Bertram, 1977, no. 14. The association was detected by Stephen Freeth in 1989.
2. Stephenson, 1900–03; Page-Phillips, 1980.
3. Wood, 1881–99, p. 140.
4. Norfolk Record Office, Rye ms 17, vol. 5, f. 109; cited in *MBS Bull* 24 (1980), p. 10.
5. *Oxford J*, Vol. I, (1899), p. 309.
6. See William Durrant, *St Dionis Backchurch*, 1872, which cites the churchwardens' accounts from PRO Exchequer, Queen's Remambrancer, 4–70, London, on p. 8: 'Item soulde ijc qtr and halfe of marbelers mettall that was upon the graves and upon ye tombs sould in lad lane at xxvjs. viijd. the c. iiili. iijs. iiijd.'
7. See a seventeenth-century MS in the University Library, Ghent, Hs. G12.925,

Grafschriftenverzameling toebehorend aan L. G. de Crombugghe-Loevelde, f.197.r. Also a sixteenth- or seventeenth- century MS in poss. R. van Belle, whose article on this brass is pending publication in Belgium.

Chapter 7

1. Nitz, 1980. Mention must also be made of Robin Emmerson's excellent MA report, a revised version of which was published as Emmerson, 1978.
2. Saunders, 1932, p. 220.
3. Saunders, 1932, p. 221.
4. Evans, 1949, pp. 139–60.
5. Stone, 1955, pp. 136–9, 148, 163–6, 178–9, 183–6, 199–202, 214–15, 218–19.
6. On changes in the interpretation of these brasses see Norris, 1987 (in *EEB*).
7. Lasko and Morgan, 1973, pp. 8, 29.
8. Kent, 1949, pp. 70–97.
9. e.g. Badham, 1979; Emmerson, 1978; Greenwood and Norris, 1976; Norris *Memorials*, 1977 and *Craft*, 1978.
10. e.g. Trivick, 1969; Bertram, 1971; Busby, 1973, especially pp. 50–77.
11. Dennison *Flemish Brasses*, 1986.
12. Binski, 1980, and 1987 (in *EEB*).
13. *Age of Chivalry*, 1987, especially pp. 171–3.
14. Nitz, 1980, pp. 33–73; see also H.K. Cameron's review in *MBS Trans*, Vol. XIII (1982), pp. 275–9.
15. Norris, *Craft*, p. 93; figs 12, 74, 75.
16. Norris, *Craft*, p. 88. For a case of indifference to quality of design see Emmerson, 1979, pp. 322–5.
17. cf. Rogers, 1987, p. 154–7.
18. Panofsky, 1964, p. 53.
19. Binski, 1987, p. 88. The effigy in the Temple Church was classified as a 'York series B' by B. and M. Gittos, in *ISSCM Bulletin* 3, 1980.
20. cf. Adhémar and Dordor, 1974, nos 364, 439, 465bis–468, 593, for French incised slabs; *Age of Chivalry*, 1987, no. 33, for a window from Brinsop, Herefs., ibid, no. 151, for Bodleian MS, Douce 231.
21. Binski, 1980, pp. 73–7. For the work of the Madonna Master see Sandler, 1983, passim.
22. cf. Sandler, 1983, p. 16. It is noteworthy that the Psalter of Robert de Lisle contains the first known depiction of a brass (ibid., pl. 4).
23. cf. Adhémar and Dordor, 1974, nos 359, 361, 404, 464, 510, 528.
24. Binski, 1987, p. 88. The brass's original central position in the church, rebuilt in the 1290s, suggests that the Septvans commemorated was closely involved in that rebuilding (Tower, 1928, p. 109).
25. cf. Norris, *Craft*, pp. 81–2. For links between Lincolnshire incised slabs and local brasses see Greenhill, 1986, pp. 51, 55, 132. Norris and Badham (forthcoming) will show links between London brasses of *c*. 1270–1360 and incised slabs.
26. Greenhill, 1986, pp. 25–6, pl. 3 (Boston 18).
27. Cameron, 1979, pl. XXXV.
28. Edleston, 1932–3, p. 60, pl. VI; Greenhill, 1986 p. 4, pl. 21 (Ashby Puerorum 1), 22–4 (Boston 7). For further links with the Smalenburgh slab see Badham and Sutton, 1981.
29. Nitz, 1985, p. 90.
30. Dennison, 'Fitzwarin Psalter', 1986, p. 56.

31. Lasko and Morgan, 1973, no. 33.
32. cf. Norris, *Memorials*, pp. 66–7.
33. *Age of Chivalry*, no. 98.
34. RCHM, *Westminster Abbey*, 1924, p. 28, plan on p. 32. Eleanor de Bohun's will, dated 9 August 1399, refers to the possibility of a transfer. The fragmentary inscription evidently described Thomas as being buried 'among the kings', indicating that the brass was not prepared at the time of his first burial.
35. RCHM, *Westminster Abbey*, pp. 30–1, pls 54–6, 187, 199; Norris, *Memorials*, pp. 51–3.
36. Eden, 1937, pp. 18–19. The figure of a Mortimer at Thaxted is comparable with the brass of Sir John de Wyngefeld, Letheringham, Suff., 1389 (*Portfolio Plates*, 1988, pl. 68).
37. Schloss Pommersfelden ms 2934 (348), f. 10, *Age of Chivalry*, no. 688.
38. *Portfolio Plates*, pl. 88.
39. Knowles, 1936, pp. 117–36.
40. Norris, *Memorials*, p. 133.
41. Greenwood and Norris, 1976, pp. 28–32.
42. cf. Badham, 1979, pp. 17–18.
43. *Age of Chivalry*, no. 613.
44. Norris, *Craft*, fig. 175; *Portfolio Plates*, pls 107, 195.
45. *Portfolio Plates*, pl. 114.
46. Norris, *Craft*, p. 83.
47. Evans, H.F.O., 1960.
48. Goodall, 1987, pp. 264–6.
49. van Belle, 1983, pp. 55–88.
50. cf. Sutton and Visser-Fuchs, 1990, pp. 10–18.
51. Tudor-Craig, 1975, pp. 289–90, pl. LXIa.
52. e.g. the Hours of James IV (Macfarlane, 1960, pp. 3–21) and Queen Mary's 'Certain Prayers' (Strong, 1983, no. 39).
53. Hodnett, 1973, no. 862, fig. 66.
54. Hodnett, 1973, no. 2514, add. fig. 18.
55. *Portfolio Plates*, pl. 238.
56. On these see Scheller, 1963.
57. Smith, 1807, col. pl. opp. p. 244. For the brasses see Norris, *Memorials*, p. 53; *Age of Chivalry*, no. 139.
58. Cameron, 1960, pp. 56–9.
59. Strong, 1983, no. 5.
60. Cameron, 1960, p. 58.
61. On Gerard Horenbout see Duverger, 1930, pp. 81–90; Winkler, 1943, pp. 54–64; Paget, 1959, pp. 396–402; Dogaer, 1987, pp. 161–8.
62. Malibu, J. Paul Getty Museum, Ludwig IX.18, f. 40; see von Euw and Plotzek, 1982, col. pl. on p. 259.
63. On their work see Esdaile, 1946, *passim*.
64. *Portfolio Plates*, pls 381, 383. Cf Norris, *Memorials*, p. 233.
65. Norris, *Memorials*, pp. 235–6.
66. Lewis, 1974, pp. 23–5, nos 23–8. On the Vaughans see Williams, 1933, pp. 2–10, 17–21, pls I–XIX; Glenn, 1934, pp. 291–301; Corbett and Norton, 1964, pp. 48–94.
67. Williams, 1933, p.6, pl. IX.

Chapter 8

5. Research at the US National Bureau of Standards, published in *Nature*, 15 June 1973, pp. 243, 422.

Chapter 9

1. Bodleian Library MSS Dep. c 225, f. 106, 108.
2. W. Suffolk Record Office, Bury St Edmunds: see *MBS Trans*, Vol. X (1964), p. 93.
3. British Library Add MSS 32478–9.
4. Gough, 1786–99.

Chapter 10

1. *Lisle Letters*, Appendix 6, Vol. I, pp. 699–700.
2. *Lisle Letters*, No. 79, 21 November 1533, Vol. I, p 620.
3. *Lisle Letters*, No. 516, 30 April 1534, Vol. III, pp. 50–1.
4. *Lisle Letters*, No. 239, 25 July 1534, Vol. II, p. 224.
5. Hutchinson and Egan, 1993 et sqq.
6. *Visitations of Devon*, pp 45–8.
7. Blake, 1915, pp. 72–9.
8. Tangye, 1984, p. 12.
9. Andrews, 1962, pp. 255–7.
10. Whetter, 1988, pp. 106, 108.
11. Granville, 1895, pp. 61–7.
12. Inquisitions post mortem of John Bassett, 1529 (PRO ref. C142/48, No. 83 for Cornwall; C142/47 No. 13 for Devon).
13. Rowse, 1941, p. 87.
14. *Lisle Letters, passim*.

Bibliography

Adhémar, J. and Dordor, G., 'Les Tombeaux de la collection Gaignières: Dessins d'archéologie du XVIIe siècle', *Gazette des Beaux-Arts*, 6e Période, LXXXIV, 1974.

The Age of Chivalry: Art in Plantagenet England 1200–1400, exhibition catalogue, Royal Academy of Arts, London, 1987.

Alcuin Club, *The Ornaments of the Ministers as shown on English Monumental Brasses*, Collections, vol. XXII, 1919.

Andrews, J.H.B., 'Chittlehampton', *Transactions of the Devonshire Association*, XCIV (1962), pp. 255–7.

Ashmole, Elias, *History and Antiquities of Berkshire*, Reading, 1736.

Badham, S., Blair, W.J. and Emmerson, R., *Specimens of Lettering from English Monumental Brasses*, Phillips and Page, 1976.

Badham, S., *Brasses from the North East,* Phillips and Page, 1979.

Badham, S., 'The Suffolk School of Brasses', *MBS.Trans*, Vol. XIII (1980), pp. 41–67.

Badham, S. and Sutton, T., 'A Fourteenth-century Flemish Composite Slab from Rippingale, Lincolnshire', *MBS Trans*, Vol. XIII (1981), pp. 152–4.

Badham, S., 'An interim study of the stones used for the slabs of English Monumental Brasses', *MBS Trans*, Vol. XIII (1985), pp. 475–83.

Badham, S. and Blatchly, J., 'The Bellfounder's Indent at Bury St Edmunds', *Proceedings of the Suffolk Institute of Archaeology and History*, Vol. XXXVI (1988), pp. 290–1.

Badham, S., 'Monumental Brasses, the Development of the York Workshops in the Fourteenth and Fifteenth Centuries', in BAA, *Medieval Art, Architecture and Archaeology in the East Riding of Yorkshire* (1989), pp. 165–85.

Badham, S., 'The Fens 1 Series: An Early Fifteenth Century Group of Monumental Brasses and Incised Slabs', *JBAA*, CXLII (1989), pp. 46–62.

Badham, S., 'Richard Gough's Papers Relating to Monumental Brasses in the Bodleian Library, Oxford', *MBS Trans*, Vol. XIV (1991), pp. 467–512.

Badham, S. and Norris, M. *Early Incised Slabs and Brasses from the London Marblers*, forthcoming, 1997.

Bauch, Kurt, *Das mittelalterliche Grabbild, figürliche Grabmäler des 11. bis 15. Jahrhunderts in Europa*, Walter de Gruyter, Berlin, 1976.

Beloe, E.M., *A Series of Photolithographs of Monumental Brasses in Norfolk*, privately printed, 1890–1.

Bertram, Jerome, *Brasses and Brass Rubbing in England*, David and Charles, 1971.

Bertram, Jerome, *Lost Brasses*, David and Charles, 1976.

Bertram, Jerome, *Rare Brass Rubbings from the Ashmolean Collection*, Ashmolean Museum, Oxford, 1977.

Bertram, Jerome, 'Of Petworth and Other Marbles', *MBS Bull*, 26 (February 1981), pp. 9–10.

Binski, Paul, 'Chartham Kent, and the Court', *MBS Trans*, Vol. XIII (1980), pp. 73–9.

Binski, Paul, 'The Stylistic Sequence of London Figure Brasses', in Coales, J. (ed.), *The Earliest English Brasses*, Monumental Brass Society, 1987, pp. 69–132.

Blair, C. *European Armour, circa 1066 to circa 1700*, Batsford, 1958.

Blair, W. John, 'English Monumental Brasses before 1350: Types, Patterns and Workshops', in Coales, J. (ed.), *The Earliest English Brasses*, Monumental Brass Society, 1987, pp. 133–75.

Blair, W.J., 'St Beornewald of Bampton', *Oxoniensia*, 49 (1984), pp. 47–55.

Blake, W.J., 'The Cornish Rebellions of 1497', *Journal of the Royal Institution of Cornwall*, XX, part i (1915), pp. 72–9.

Blomefield, Revd Francis, *An Essay towards a History of Norfolk*, 2nd and more complete edn 1805 to 1810.

Bouquet, A.C., *Church Brasses*, Batsford, 1956.

Boutell, Charles, *Monumental Brasses and Slabs*, London, George Bell, 1847.

Boutell, Charles, *Christian Monuments in England and Wales*, London, 1849.

Boutell, Charles, *The Monumental Brasses of England, a Series of Engravings on Wood*, London, George Bell, 1849.

Bracken, Jim, *The Most Noble Order of the Garter as depicted on Monumental Brasses*, privately printed, 1991.

Briggs, Nancy, 'A Bibliography of Brasses', *MBS Trans*, Vol. XI (1974), pp. 149–61.

Busby, Richard, *A Beginner's Guide to Brass Rubbing*, Mayflower, 1969.

Busby, Richard, *A Companion Guide to Brasses and Brass Rubbing*, Pelham, 1973.

Busby, Richard, *The Monumental Brass Society, A Short History 1887–1987*, MBS, 1987.

Cambridge Camden Society, *Illustrations of the Monumental Brasses of Great Britain*, 1840–46.

Camden, William, *Britannia*, London, 1586 and many subsequent edns.

Cameron, H.K., 'The Brasses of Middlesex. Part X', *Transactions of the London and Middlesex Archaeological Society*, Vol. XX, pt. 2 (1960), pp. 56–9.

Cameron, H.K., *A List of Monumental Brasses on the Continent of Europe*, MBS 1971, with appendix, 1973, reprinted 1977.

Cameron, H.K., 'The Fourteenth-century Flemish Brasses at King's Lynn', *Arch J*, CXXXVI (1979), pl. XXXV.

Cherry, J., 'The Dunstable Swan Jewel', *JBAA*, 3 ser., 32 (1969), pp. 38–53.

Coales, J. (ed.), *The Earliest English Brasses*, Monumental Brass Society, 1987.

Corbett, M. and Norton, N., *Engraving in England in the Sixteenth and Seventeenth Centuries*, Part III: *The Reign of Charles I*, Cambridge University Press, 1964.

Cotman, John, *Engravings of the most Remarkable of the Sepulchral Brasses of Norfolk and Suffolk*, issued in parts to 1819, 2nd edn, 1838/9.

Creeny, Revd W.F., *A Book of Facsimiles of Monumental Brasses on the Continent of Europe*, London & Norwich, 1884.

Creeny, W.F., *Illustrations of Incised Slabs on the Continent of Europe*, London, 1891.

Crossley, Fred, *English Church Monuments*, Batsford, 1921.

Cutts, Edward L., *A Manual for the Study of the Sepulchral Slabs and Crosses of the Middle Ages*, Parker, 1849.

d'Elboux, R.H., 'Testamentary Brasses', *Antiquaries Journal*, vol. 29 (1949), pp. 183–91.

Dennison, L., 'The Artistic Context of Fourteenth-century Flemish Brasses', *MBS Trans*, Vol. XIV (1986), pp. 1–38.

Dennison, L., 'The Fitzwarin Psalter and its Allies: a Reappraisal', in Ormrod, W.M. (ed.), *England in the Fourteenth Century: Proceedings of the 1985 Harlaxton Symposium*, Boydell, 1986, pp. 42–66.

Dogaer, G., *Flemish Miniature Painting in the 15th and 16th Centuries*, Amsterdam, B.M. Israel, 1987.

Druitt, H., *A Manual of Costume as Illustrated by Monumental Brasses*, Alexander Moring, 1906, reprinted 1970.

Dugdale, W., *The Antiquities of Warwickshire Illustrated*, London, Thomas Warren, 1656.

Duverger, J. 'Gerard Horenbault (1465?–1540) hofschilder van Margareta van Oosterrk', *Kunst*, IV, (1930), pp. 81–90.

Eden, F.S., 'Secular Pedigree Windows', *Journal of the British Society of Master Glass-Painters*, VII, no. 1 (1937), pp. 18–19.

Edleston, R.H., 'Incised Monumental Slabs – II', *61st and 62nd Annual Reports of the Peterborough Natural History, Scientific and Archaeological Society*, 1932–3, pp. 48–61.

Emmerson, R., 'Monumental Brasses: London Design *c.* 1420–85', *JBAA*, Vol. CXXXI (1978), pp. 50–78.

Emmerson, R., 'William Browne's Taste in Brasses', *MBS Trans*, Vol. XII (1979), pp. 322–5.

Emmerson, R., 'Design for Mass Production: Monumental Brasses made in London *c.* 1420–85', *Artistes, Artisans et Production Artistique au Moyen Age* (1990), pp. 133–71.

Esdaile, K.A., *English Church Monuments 1510 to 1840*, Batsford, 1946.

Evans, J., *English Art, 1307–1461*, Clarendon Press, 1949.

Evans, H. F. Owen, 'Latten Lecterns', *MBS Trans*, Vol. IX (1960), pp. 375–8.

Evelyn, John, *The Diary*, ed. Bray, Wm, London, 1818.

Franklyn, J., *Brasses*, Arco, 1970.

Galbreath, D.L., *Manuel du Blason*, rev. and ed. Jequier, J., Lausanne, Spes, 1977.

Glenn, T.A., 'Robert Vaughan of Hengwrt and Robert Vaughan the London Engraver', *Archaeologia Cambrensis*, LXXXIX (1934), pp. 291–301.

Goodall, J.A. 'Death and the Impenitent Avaricious King: A Unique Brass discovered at Frenze, Norfolk', *Apollo*, 1987, pp. 264–6.

Gough, Richard, *A History of Myddle*, Folio Society, 1983.

Gough, Richard, *The Sepulchral Monuments of Great Britain*, London, Pt I, 1786; Pt II, 1796; Intro. to Pt II, 1799 (usually bound in five volumes).

Granville, R., *The History of the Granville Family*, Exeter, 1895.

Greenhill, F.A., *The Incised Slabs of Leicestershire and Rutland*, Leicestershire Arch. and Hist. Soc., 1957.

Greenhill, F.A., *Incised Effigial Slabs*, Faber, 1976.

Greenhill, F.A., *Monumental Incised Slabs in the County of Lincoln*, Newport Pagnell, Francis Coales Charitable Foundation, 1986.

Greenwood, R., 'Haines's Cambridge School of Brasses', *MBS Trans*, Vol. XI (1971), pp. 2–12.

Greenwood, R. and Norris, M., *The Brasses of Norfolk Churches*, Norfolk Church Trust, 1976.

Griffin, Ralph, and Stephenson, Mill, *A List of Monumental Brasses remaining in the County of Kent in 1922*, Headley Bros., 1923.

[Haines, Herbert], *A Manual for the Study of Monumental Brasses*, Oxford Architectural Society, 1848.

Haines, H., *A Manual of Monumental Brasses*, J.H. and J.A.S. Parker, 1861.

Hammond, Lt., 'A Short Survey of the Western Counties' (1634), in *Camden Society Miscellany* XVI, 1936.

Hartshorne, A., 'On the Brass of Sir Hugh Hastings in Elsing Church, Norfolk', *Archaeologia*, Vol. 60 (1907), pp. 25–42.

Hodnett, E., *English Woodcuts 1480–1535*, revised edn, Oxford University Press, 1973.

Holmes, G., *The Oxford Illustrated History of Medieval Europe*, Oxford University Press, 1988.

Hood, Christobel (ed.), *The Chorography of Norfolk*, Jarrolds, Norwich, 1938, p.159.

Hunter Blair, C.H., 'Armorials on English Seals from the twelfth to the sixteenth centuries', *Archaeologia*, 89 (1943), pp. 1–26.

Hutchinson, R. and Egan, B.S. 'History Writ in Brass: the Fermer Workshop 1546–1555', in *MBS Trans*, XV, pt. 2 (1993) and following issues.

Kent, J.P.C., 'Monumental Brasses – a New Classification of Military Effigies', *JBAA*, 3 ser., Vol. XII (1949), pp. 70–97.

Knowles, J.A., *Essays in the History of the York School of Glass Painting*, SPCK, 1936.

Lack, William, Stuchfield, H. Martin and Whittemore, Philip, *The Monumental Brasses of Bedfordshire* (1992); *Berkshire* (1993); *Buckinghamshire* (1994); *Cambridgeshire* (1995): the series is to continue.

Lasko, P. and Morgan, N.J., (eds.), *Medieval Art in East Anglia 1300–1520*, Jarrolds, 1973.

Lee, B.N., *British Bookplates, a pictorial history*, David and Charles, 1979.

Leland, John, *The Itinerary*, ed. Lucy Toulmin Smith, Carbondale, 1964.

Lewis, J.M., *Welsh Monumental Brasses: A Guide*, National Museum of Wales, Cardiff, 1974.

Lind, K., *Mittelalterlicher Grabdenkmaler*, 1894.

The Lisle Letters, edited by Muriel St Clare Byrne, University of Chicago, 1981.

Macfarlane, L., 'The Book of Hours of James IV and Margaret Tudor', *Innes Review*, XI (1960), pp. 3–21.

Macklin, H.W., *Monumental Brasses*, 1st edn, Sonnenschein, 1890, many subsequent edns.

Macklin, H.W., *The Brasses of England*, Methuen, 1907.

Male, Emile, *L'Art Religieux de la fin du moyen age en France*, Paris, 1908.

Mann, J.G., 'Greenwich Armour and Sculptured Tombs', *The Connoisseur*, August 1931, pp. 88–95.

Mann, J.G., 'Armour in Essex', *Transactions of the Essex Archaeological Society*, N.S. XXII (1939), pp. 276–98.

Mann, J. G., *Monumental Brasses*, Penguin, 1957.

Manning, C.R., *A List of the Monumental Brasses remaining in England, arranged according to counties*, Rivington, 1846.

Meara, David, *Victorian Brasses*, Routledge and Kegan Paul, 1983.

Nitz, M., *Entstehung und Bedeutung der englischen Messinggrabplatten*, Munich, Nitz, 1980.

Nitz, M., 'Aristokratischer Stolz und mönchische Einfalt auf Messinggrabplatten des 14 Jahrhunderts in England', in Schuschard, J. and Klaussen, H., (eds.), *Vergänglichkeit und Denkmal: Beiträge zur Sepulkralkultur*, Bonn, 1985, pp. 81–91.

Norman, Vesey, *Arms and Armour*, Weidenfeld and Nicholson, 1964.

Norman, A.V.B. and Pottinger, D., *Warrior to Soldier 449–1660*, London, 1966.

Norris, M.W., *Brass Rubbing*, Studio Vista, 1965.

Norris, M.W. and Kellett, M., *Your Book of Brasses*, Faber, 1975.

Norris, M.W., *Monumental Brasses: The Memorials*, Phillips and Page, 1977.

Norris, M.W., *Monumental Brasses: The Craft*, Faber & Faber, 1978.

Norris, M.W., 'Views on the early knights', in Coales, J. (ed.), *The Earliest English Brasses*, Monumental Brass Society, 1987, pp. 1–7.

Oman, C., *English Engraved Silver 1150–1900*, Faber, 1978.

Page-Phillips, J., 'A Sixteenth-Century Workshop', unpublished, 1958.

Page-Phillips, J., *Macklin's Monumental Brasses*, George Allen and Unwin, 1969.

Page-Phillips, J., *Children on Brasses*, George Allen and Unwin, 1971.

Page-Phillips, J., *Palimpsests – the Backs of Monumental Brasses*, Monumental Brass Society, 1980.

Paget, H., 'Gerard and Lucas Hornebolt in England', *Burlington Magazine*, CI (1959), pp. 396–402.

Panofsky, E., *Tomb Sculpture: Its Changing Aspects from Ancient Egypt to Bernini*, Thames & Hudson, 1964.

Pevsner, N., *The Buildings of England*, Penguin, 1950 onwards (a volume for each county).

Philipot, John, 'A Book of Church Notes', ed. Councer, C.R., in *A Seventeenth-century Miscellany*, Kent Archaeological Society Records Publication Committee, 1960, pp. 68–114.

Pietra Sancta, S., *Tesserae Gentilitiae*, 1638.

The Portfolio Plates of the Monumental Brass Society, consolidated publication, Monumental Brass Society, the Boydell Press, 1988.

Powell, J.E., 'Vertical-Horizontal?', *Costume*, 13 (November 1979), pp. 1–7.

Pugin, A.W.N., *Contrasts: A Parallel between the Noble Edifices of the Fourteenth and Fifteenth Centuries, and Similar Buildings of the Present Day*, 1836.

Pugin, A.W.N., 'Monumental Brass of the Fifteenth Century', *The Orthodox Journal*, 12 May 1838.

Pugin, A.W.N., *An Apology for the Revival of Christian Architecture in England*, 1843.

Rigold, Stuart, 'Petrology as an Aid to Classification of Brasses', *MBS Trans*, Vol. X (1966), pp. 285–6.

Rogers, N.J., 'The Earliest Description of the de la Mare Brass', *MBS Trans*, Vol. XIV (1987), pp. 154–7.

Rogers, N.J., 'English Episcopal Monuments', in Coales, J. (ed.), *The Earliest English Brasses*, Monumental Brass Society, 1987, pp. 8–68.

Rowse, A.L., *Tudor Cornwall*, Jonathan Cape, 1941.

Royal Commission on Historical Monuments (England), *An Inventory of the Historical Monuments in London, I, Westminster Abbey*, HMSO, 1924.

Ryder, P.F., *The Medieval Cross-slab Grave Cover in County Durham*, Architectural & Archaeological Society of Durham & Northumberland, 1985.

St John Hope, W.H., *Stall Plates of the Knights of the Garter 1348–1485*, 1901.

St John Hope, W., *Heraldry for Craftsmen and Designers*, Pitman, 1913.

Sandler, L.F., *The Psalter of Robert de Lisle in the British Library*, Harvey Miller, 1983.

Saunders, O.E., *A History of English Art in the Middle Ages*, Clarendon Press, 1932.

Scheller, R.W., *A Survey of Medieval Model Books*, Haarlem, 1963.

s'Jacobs, H., *Idealism and Realism, a study of sepulchral symbolism*, Brill, 1957.

Smith, J.T., *Antiquities of Westminster*, London, 1807.

Stephenson, Mill, 'A List of Palimpsest Brasses', *MBS Trans*, Vol. IV (1900–3), pp. 1, 97, 141, 189, 219, 251, 293.

Stephenson, Mill, *A List of Monumental Brasses in the British Isles*, 1926, Appendix, 1938, reprinted 1964.

Stone, L., *Sculpture in Britain: The Middle Ages*, Penguin, 1955.

Stow, John, *A Survey of the Cities of London and Westminster and the Borough of Southwark*, (1st edn), 1598, many subsequent edns.

Strong, R., *Artists of the Tudor Court*, exhibition catalogue, Victoria & Albert Museum, London, 1983.

Sutton, A.F. and Visser-Fuchs, L., *The Hours of Richard III*, Alan Sutton, 1990.

Tangye, M., *Tehidy and the Bassetts*, Redruth, 1984.

Tower, R., 'The Family of Septvans', *Archaeologia Cantiana*, XL (1928), pp. 105–30.

Trivick, H. H., *The Craft and Design of Monumental Brasses*, John Baker, 1969.

Tudor-Craig, P., 'Fragment of panel painting of the Flagellation in the possession of Canterbury Cathedral and the Martyrdom of St Erasmus belonging to the Society of Antiquaries', *Antiqs J*, LIV (1975), pp. 289–90, pl. LXIa.

Tummers, Harry, 'The Medieval Effigy Tombs in Chichester Cathedral', *Church Monuments*, Vol. III (1988), pp. 3–41.

Van Belle, R., *Ikonographie en symboliek van de beschilderde grafkelders en memorietaferelen*, Sint-Andreies/Brugge: Heemkundige Kring Maurits Van Coppenolle, 1983.

Van Biervliet, Lori, 'James Weale and Monumental Brasses', *MBS Trans*, Vol. XIV (1987), p. 115–22.

Victoria & Albert Museum, *List of Rubbings of Brasses*, (2nd edn.), 1929.

The Visitations of the County of Devon, ed. by J.L. Vivian, pub. privately, Exeter (1895).

The Visitations of Essex, Harleian Society, 1878.

The Visitations of Kent 1619–21, Harleian Society, 1898.

Von Euw, A. and Plotzek, J.M., *Die Handschriften der Sammlung Ludwig*, Bd. 2, Cologne, 1982.

Vossberg, F., *Siegel des Mittelalters von Polen ... und Preußen*, 1854.

Wagner, Sir A., 'Heraldry' in Poole, A.L. (ed.), *Medieval England*, 2nd edn., Oxford, 1958.

Walcott, M.E.C., 'The Early Statutes of the Cathedral Church of the Holy Trinity, Chichester', *Archaeologia*, Vol. 45 (1880).

Waller, J.G. and L., *A Series of Monumental Brasses from the 13th to the 16th Century*, issued in parts between 1842 and 1864, reprinted Phillips and Page, 1975.

Weaver, L., *Memorials and Monuments*, 1918.

Weever, John, *Antient Funeral Monuments*, 1631.

Wells, Edward, *The Rich Man's Duty*, ed. J.H. Newman, Parker, 1840.

Whetter, J., *The History of Glasney College*, Padstow, Tabb House, 1988.

Williams, I.J., 'Early Welsh Line and Mezzotint Engravers', *Archaeologia Cambrensis*, LXXXVIII (1933), pp. 2–10, 17–21, pls I–XIX;

Winkler, F., 'Neuentdeckte Niederländer II, Gerard Horenbout', *Pantheon*, XXXI, 1943, pp. 54–64.

Wood, Anthony, *History and Antiquities of the Colleges and Halls in the University of Oxford*, 1786.

Wood, Anthony, *Fasti Oxoniensis*, 1790.

Wood, Anthony, *History of the University of Oxford*, ed. J. Gutch, 1792–6.

Wood, Anthony, *City of Oxford*, ed. A. Clark, Oxford Hist. Soc., 1881–99.

Wyrley, W., *The true use of armorie*, 1592; (STC 26062) reprinted 1853; text reprinted by Sir William Dugdale as *The antient use of arms*, 1682, attributing it to Erdeswicke, the Staffordshire antiquary.

Index

List of Subscribers

Ali, J.Z., BA (Oxon.), Bramley Fold Farm, Hawshaw, Bury, Lancashire BL8 4LG
Archer, E.P., 18 Hope Street, Lanark, Strathclyde, Scotland ML11 7NE
Arthur, Mrs J.M., Candelmas, 6C Leafield Road, Biggar, Lanarkshire ML12 6AY

Badham, Miss S.F., FSA, Dawn Cottage, Purrants Lane, Leafield, Oxfordshire OX8 5PN
Baker, Prof. J.H., FBA, St Catharine's College, Cambridge CB2 1RL
Barrick, Mrs J., BEd (Hons.), Marsworth, 9 Vicarage Gardens, Linslade, Leighton Buzzard, Bedfordshire LU7 7LL
Bayliss, J.C., BA, 31 Churchfields, Hethersett, Norwich, Norfolk NR9 3AF
Bell, A.G., BSc, 3 Grange Drive, Park Lane, Cottingham, North Humberside HU16 5RE
Bennett, S.G., 17 Sandown Avenue, Mickleover, Derbyshire DE3 5QQ
Birtles, J.F., FCIS, Stable Cottage, Williamstrip Park, Coln St Aldwyns, Cirencester, Gloucestershire GL7 5AS
Blair, C., OBE, MA, FSA, 90 Links Road, Ashtead, Surrey KT21 2HW
Bowman, J.H., MA, 17 Park Road, London W7 1EN
Bradbury, G.G., 16 Bread Street, Warminster, Wiltshire BA12 8DF
Brownridge, Dr D.S., MB, BS, MRCS, CRCP, Vern House, Old Worcester Road, Hartlebury, Kidderminster, Worcestershire DY11 7XQ
Busby, R.J., FLA, 1 Palmerston Close, Welwyn Garden City, Hertfordshire AL8 7DL
Butler-Stoney, M.C., Burwood Hall, Mileham, King's Lynn, Norfolk PE32 2RA
Byrom, C.M., BA, CBiol, MIBiol, GradICSA, 11 Sarum Court, 2 St Osmunds Road, Poole, Dorset BH14 9JN

Careless, G.C., Flat 5, 43 Cambridge Road, Aldershot, Hampshire GU11 3LF
Catling, Dr H.W., CBE, MA, DPhil, FSA, Dunford House, Langford, Lechlade, Gloucestershire GL7 3LN
Chaddock, M.J., 63 St John's Avenue, Bridlington, East Yorkshire YO16 4ND
Cherry, J., MA, FSA, 58 Lancaster Road, London N4 4PT
Clark, Mrs A., 28 Hertford Road, Digswell, Welwyn, Hertfordshire AL6 0DB
Coales, J., FSA, The Mount, Parsonage Hill, Somerton, Somerset TA11 7PF
Cockerham, P.D., MA, VetMB, MRCVS, Sunny Corner, Rame Cross, Penryn, Cornwall TR10 9DX
Cockerham, Dr R.G., BSc, PhD, FRSC, 77 Buryfield Road, Solihull, West Midlands B91 2DG
Coker, Miss B.A., BEd, 46 St Bartholomew's Road, East Ham, London E6 3AG
Cole, Sir Colin, KCB, KCVO, TD, FSA, Holly House, Burstow, Horley, Surrey RH6 9RG
Cole, S.W.T., The Villa, The Street, Stonham Aspal, Stowmarket, Suffolk IP14 6AQ

Cook, D.B., Flat 1, 26 The Grove, Isleworth, Middlesex, TW7 4JU
Council for the Care of Churches, Fielden House, 10 Little College Street, London SW1P 3SH

Dennison, Dr L.E., MA, PhD, Manor Farm, 77/79 High Street, Watchfield, Swindon, Wiltshire SN6 8TL
Desler, Miss R., Flat 3, 120 Barrowgate Road, Chiswick, London W4 4QP
Dobson, J., 311 Rayleigh Road, Thundersley, Essex SS7 3XA
Dowden, Mrs A., BA, 17 St Mark Drive, Colchester, Essex CO4 4LP
Draffin, Mrs M., BA, 3 Hornedale Avenue, Barrow-in-Furness, Cumbria LA13 9AS

Easter, C.J., BA, c/o 26 Venn Close, Stoke Fleming, Dartmouth, Devon
Edwards, J.W., 10 Meadow Way, Carlton Colville, Lowestoft, Suffolk NR33 8LF
Edwards, Mrs N.R., MA, FSA, 43 Maltese Road, Chelmsford, Essex CM1 2PB
Egan, B.S.H., 110 Clarence Road, Stony Stratford, Milton Keynes, Buckinghamshire MK11 1JG

Farman, P.D. and Hacker, P.F., 4 Hollins Crescent, Harrogate, North Yorkshire HG1 2JG
Flux, Mrs I.D., 14 Fort Street, Sandown, Isle of Wight PO36 8BA
Fox, A.E.L., BA, 8 Lexington Court, Royal Crescent Lane, Scarborough, North Yorkshire YO11 2RJ
Freeth, S.G.H., BA, 71 College Road, Epsom, Surrey KT17 4HQ

Gibbs, L.G., ISO, TD, 48 London Road, Brentwood, Essex CM14 4QG
Gittos, Mr and Mrs B.C., 4 Linden Road, Yeovil, Somerset BA20 2BH
Glogg, J.J.T., 95 Park Crescent, Erith, Kent DA8 3EA
Good, M.S., MA, LRAM, 84 Hertford Street, Cambridge CB4 3AQ

Harris, Miss A.L., MA, 14 Doonamana Road, Dun Laoghaire, County Dublin, Ireland
Harris, Rear-Admiral M.G.T., King's Lodge, Church Street, Whitchurch, Hampshire RG28 7AS
Hawes, J.E., 201 Hillcrest Road, Newhaven, East Sussex BN9 9EZ
Heseltine, P.J., 3 Earning Street, Godmanchester, Huntingdon, Cambridgeshire PE18 8JD
Hopkinson, D.S., 3 The Squirrels, Hertford, Hertfordshire SG13 7UT
Houghton, Miss J.E.M., ALA, 8 Glyn Place, East Melbury, Shaftesbury, Dorset SP7 0DP
Howell, I.P., 58 Elder Close, Badger Farm, Winchester, Hampshire SO22 4LH
Hutchinson, D.R. Barton Cottage, Church Street, Amberley, Arundel, West Sussex BN18 9NE

Jenkins, Mr and Mrs R.P., Fugitives Drift, 31A Victoria Street, Fleckney, Leicester LE8 8AZ
Jones, W.B., BA, 432 Jones Avenue, Fort Atkinson, Wisconsin 53202, USA
Jury, Mrs O.R., The Old House, Green Lane, Wootton, Northampton NN4 6LH

Kent, Dr J.P.C., BA, PhD, FSA, 16 Newmans Way, Hadley Wood, Barnet, Hertfordshire EN4 0LR

Lamp, R., Feddersenstr 15a D-22607 Hamburg, Germany
Lankester, P.J., c/o Royal Armouries, Armouries Drive, Leeds LS10 1LT

Larimore, T.J., 43 Reginald Road South, Chaddesden, Derbyshire DE21 6NG

Lawrence, P.A., Barnfield, Church Lane, East Peckham, Tonbridge, Kent TN12 5JJ

Lillistone, D.C., BA, 75 Quarry Lane, Ecclesall, Sheffield, South Yorkshire S11 9EA

Linn, Mrs E.A., Mandarin House, 33 High Street, Hurstpierpoint, West Sussex BN6 9TT

London Brass Rubbing Centre, St Martin-in-the-Fields Church, Trafalgar Square, London WC2N 4JJ

Lystad, Mrs J.T. BSc, Farley View, Crawley, Winchester, Hampshire SO21 2QD

McQueen, P.I., LLB, 55 Albany, Manor Road, Bournemouth, Dorset BH1 3EJ

Meara, Revd D.G., MA, FSA, The Rectory, 39 Fishers Field, Buckingham MK18 1SF

Mendelsson, W., 57 Leeside Crescent, London NW11 0HA

Moir-Shepherd, J.B., MA, FRCS, Goxhill Lodge, 90 Thorne Road, Doncaster, South Yorkshire DN2 5BL

Moor, J.L., LLB (Hons.), BA (Hons.), Candlemas Cottage, 4 Stretton Road, Much Wenlock, Shropshire TF13 6AP

Moore, Dr and Mrs R.M., 8 Mirning Crescent, Aranda, Australian Capital Territory 2614, Australia

Pack, Revd Fr J.B., Nazareth House, Durnford Street, Stonehouse, Plymouth, Devon PL1 3QR

Page-Phillips, Mrs B., BA, Claysgarth, New Street, Somerton, Somerset TA11 7NU

Paige-Hagg, M.A., BTech, MSc, 37 Saxon Way, Old Windsor, Berkshire SL4 2PU

Pettman, I.S., FRSA, 21 Cleaver Square, Kennington, London SE11 4DW

Powell, D.C.I., LLB, 7 Elliott Terrace, The Hoe, Plymouth, Devon PL1 2PL

Powell, Rt Hon. J.E., MBE, 33 South Eaton Place, London SW1W 9EN

Read, I.M., 1 Castleside, Sheriff Hutton, York, Yorkshire YO6 1RF

Reader, P., 1 Scott Drive, Lexden, Colchester, Essex CO3 4JD

Reast, Mrs C.E., BA, Crosby House, High Street, Chipping Campden, Gloucestershire GL55 6AL

Rogers, N.J., MA, MLitt, Sidney Sussex Cottage, Cambridge CB2 3HU

Salmon, Dr J.R., 11 Old Park Ridings, London N21 2EX

Saul, Dr N.E., MA, DPhil, FSA, FRHistS, Gresham House, Egham Hill, Egham, Surrey TW20 0EX

Scott, P., LLB, 31 Naples Drive, Westlands, Newcastle-under-Lyme, Staffordshire ST5 2QD

Seeliger-Zeiss, Dr A., Inschriften-Kommission der Heidelberger Akademie der Wissenschaften, Karstr. 4, D-69117 Heidelberg, Germany

Seibold, Mrs P.M., BMus, MEd, 921 Knox, Birmingham, Michigan 48009, USA

Simpson, Miss E.M., Sunnylands, 30 Eastfield Road, Pickering, North Yorkshire YO18 7HU

Smith, Mr and Mrs L.A., East Cliff Cottage, East Cliff Parade, Herne Bay, Kent CT6 5HU

Smith, R.D., 21 Reginald Avenue, Cuxton, Rochester, Kent ME2 1DZ

Smith, Revd W.J.T., 7 Trelawn, Church Road, Boreham, Chelmsford, Essex CM3 3EF

Spencer, Mrs M.E., 24 Trinity Road, St Johns, Narborough, Leicester LE9 5BU

Starr, C.R., MIPM, FRGS, ARHistS, 63 Abbey Gardens, London W6 8QR

Stuchfield, H.M., Lowe Hill House, Stratford St Mary, Suffolk CO7 6JX

Surman, K.R., BSc (Econ.), 13 Green Crescent, Flackwell Heath, High Wycombe, Buckinghamshire HP10 9JQ

Taylor, A.A.H., BSc, 31 Bennett House, Headlam Road, London SW4 8HE

Taylor, Revd S.G., BA, 2 Manor Road, Little Shelford, Cambridgeshire CB2 5HF

Tighe, W.J., MA, PhD, c/o Department of History, Muhlenberg College, Allentown, Pennsylvania 18104, USA

Titterton, J.E., BSc (Eng.), ACGI, CEng, MIEE, 7 Cecil Aldin Drive, Tilehurst, Reading, Berkshire RG3 6YP

Wheaton, F.D.P., 3 Ashwood Gardens, Hayes, Middlesex UB3 4LT

Whittemore, P.J., 5 Brendon Villas, Highfield Road, Winchmore Hill, London N21 3HP

Willatts, Miss R.M., MA, Barlows Cottage, 2 Barlows Lane, Wilbarston, Market Harborough, Leicestershire LE16 8QB

Wright, Ms J.M., 7 Wood Glen Road, Scarborough, Ontario M1N 2V6, Canada

Zweigler, N., Demollstr. 17, D-80638 München, Germany